The Quiet Betrayal

THE QUIET BETRAYAL

by

SIDNEY L. DE LOVE

with an introduction by

RALPH G. NEWMAN

NORMANDIE HOUSE · PUBLISHER

Chicago, Illinois, 1960

Copyright *1960 By Sidney L. DeLove*

Dedicated to

"WE, THE PEOPLE"

AND OUR NOBLEST SHRINE,

Independence Hall, Philadelphia, Pennsylvania

JULY 4, 1776

Contents

Introduction

"WE'VE TALKED OF THE REAL MEANING OF INDEPEND-
ENCE HALL *at school," wrote a teen-aged girl to a bank president. "I have a brother in seventh grade and we've discussed
little else at home . . . whether or not I win (the essay contest)
. . . I want you to know that I feel I have been a winner just to
have worked on my theme. It started so many of us thinking about
many things that we grow up taking for granted . . . no matter
what my vocation, I shall dedicate it and myself in every way
that I can, to show how proud I am to be an American . . . With
God's help and men like you to inspire youth, I want to help
make my America better, too. I accept the challenge that you
offered when you started so many of us thinking what Independence Hall really means."*

*The young writer came from a privileged home and she was
addressing Sidney L. DeLove, president of one of our leading
Federal savings institutions in the country. But the contest which
she eagerly had entered had nothing to do with Mr. DeLove's
business activities—it was a personal activity rooted deeply in his
heart and to which he is continuingly dedicated.*

*This letter is not unusual for Mr. DeLove because he has re-
ceived over 2,000 like letters from parents, teachers and students
in the last four years of this contest.*

But—the reason for writing this book can be said to be unusual.

And—The author is an unusual man.

"The Quiet Betrayal" is a discerning, courageous and stirring presentation of sound convictions of a truly dedicated man. It is in part an indictment of his neighbors, friends and fellow citizens. It was never intended to be pleasant reading nor entertaining. On the contrary, its sole purpose is to disturb and provoke reason and emotion, and to start serious thinking and appraisal of the inevitable disaster facing us as he sees it. For his efforts and expense, the author does not seek nor want remuneration nor personal gain of any kind. In his own words: "This book was written because I feel under serious moral obligation to present this evidence to my fellow citizens for their consideration and action."

"The Quiet Betrayal" speaks for itself, but I feel that I can be of service to the reader if I briefly introduce the author. Sidney L. DeLove is a man who loves his country actively.

He was not born here, but he came here as a boy of 10 from France. A member of a distinguished and wealthy family which was virtually wiped out during World War I, Mr. DeLove had tasted and known oppression and terror as an orphan in Europe. From the moment of his arrival in the United States, he began to understand and appreciate the meaning of our American heritage of freedom. He did not waste the opportunities offered him in our blessed land. He worked his way through school, distinguished himself as a student and won scholarships and honors in extracurricular activities. Upon graduation from law school he began the practice. World War II interrupted his law career and Mr. DeLove volunteered for active duty in 1938. Before this tour, he had been active in R.O.T.C. and C.M.T.C. and commissioned an Infantry Lieutenant in the United States Army in 1936. In World War II, he held high posts in Military Intelligence here and in Europe. Upon his discharge in 1948 he decided not to re-enter the practice of law, but instead assumed the presidency of a leading financial institution which position he holds today.

Even as a high school student and throughout his college years and later on with his family, Mr. DeLove spent his vacations

x

visiting national parks and historical shrines. He visited Phila-
delphia and explored Independence Hall for the first time in 1929.
The birthplace of our Republic came to epitomize for him every-
thing that America was conceived of, the quintessence of the
meaning of the American dream. He understood and realized that
one cannot love his country without knowing its history, its pur-
pose, its ideals and principles, the events and the men who shaped
them. Throughout his whole life this consummate devotion to his
adopted land permeated his thinking and activities.

It seemed natural that in 1954 when his institution needed new
quarters that the building should reflect the significance of our
American dream. The building he built is a magnificent and fit-
ting resemblance of our hallowed shrine in Philadelphia. It is
known today as the Independence Hall of Chicago. Simultaneously
he founded the Independence Hall Association comprised of mem-
bers from all walks of life. The only qualification to become a
member is that you are a loyal, active and responsible American
citizen. There are no dues nor any contributions paid by members.
The purpose of this non-profit organization is to educate, inspire
and promulgate patriotism sustained by a reverential devotion and
love for our country. Independence Hall is now one of Chicago's
treasure houses of American history. It is a museum of Americana
containing priceless state papers, rare manuscripts, art, bronzes
and a most extensive United States currency collection. Also one
of the finest American firearm collections in the country tracing
the history of our nation. These are all on display and open to the
public.

The activities of the Independence Hall Association are varied
and extensive. Some of its projects are distribution of patriotic
literature, sponsorship of radio programs known as the "Know
Your History" hour and "Chicago Speaks," broadcasting celebra-
tions and programs on our national holidays, maintaining the In-
dependence Hall library containing exclusively volumes on Amer-
ican history, biography and geography, sponsoring lectures and
patriotic movies, and, lastly, the sponsorship of its nationally-

acclaimed essay contest among the elementary schools in the area of Independence Hall. As the 7th and 8th grade students' prize for writing a winning essay on such subjects as "What The Flag Means to Me" and "What Independence Hall Means to Me," over 100 winners and chaperones are sent annually on an 8-day, all-expenses-paid trip to these national shrines—Valley Forge, Gettysburg, Philadelphia, Washington, Richmond, Williamsburg, Monticello, Alaska, etc.

Mr. DeLove believes that you cannot love your country too much, and if you do love America you are obligated to do something about it to keep it so it does not perish from the face of the earth, and that you cannot do anything about it unless you understand it, its philosophy, its history and its great personalities whose lives went into the building of America. This belief is at the core of this edifice and all of its activities.

Mr. DeLove has become very apprehensive about the quality of education offered to our youth both at home and in our schools in the area of citizenship training. He sees loss of our heritage through ignorance or faulty understanding resulting in complacency and apathy, hence his efforts to keep the American dream alive and growing for these young people.

"The Quiet Betrayal" is a frank statement of an outspoken patriot who doesn't know the meaning of the word "equivocation." You may not agree with him entirely. You may feel that he is too harsh or maybe too lenient on some groups of our society. Whatever your reaction, this book will force you to think of the significance of our American blessings. This is the plea of a sincere man who loves his country and is deeply concerned about its future. Everyone interested in the welfare and destiny of our nation and in preserving humanity's greatest experiment in self-government should read this book.

RALPH G. NEWMAN

Prologue

WHEN I SELECTED THE TITLE FOR THIS VOLUME, *there were several suggestions that* The Quiet Betrayal *expressed an overly negative thought. It was felt that a positive title, one that would indicate not only a crisis but a solution, might better represent the purpose of this book. I don't think so.*

Essentially, The Quiet Betrayal *has to do with just that—a quiet betrayal. It points out that we Americans are betraying our country, ourselves, and our children. Now, it is certainly true that this crucial situation can be corrected. Loyal, responsible Americanism is all that is needed, and I have taken great care to stress this simple truth. But the main task of the book is to lay hand on the betrayal itself, to bring it out into the open where everyone can get a good, clear look at it.*

It is my conviction that if and when we recognize the self-wrought betrayal underway in America—that it is caused by the erosion of our national character, and that it is levelled at our own personal freedoms and liberties—common sense will dictate a moral and spiritual return to the fundamental concepts of 1776. While anyone familiar with the facts can single out the breaks in the wall of our national tradition and sound the tocsin, it remains for you and your countrymen to grapple positively with the problem. So that while there is definitely a POSITIVE side to this story, what ensues depends entirely upon each reader and the meaning he attaches to it.

You will find no new interpretations of the American story presented in this book, nor any so-called "modernized" political concepts. The purpose of this work is to apply irrefutable lessons of history to documented facts of present-day moral aimlessness and political apathy. The increasing distortion of basic values, marked especially by spiritual indifference and material reverence is todays greatest danger. We cannot survive as a free nation if we do not now take steps to strengthen our individual character; our responsibilities as a free people are too great.

True, we have been building skyscrapers, splitting the atom, conquering space, but at the same time, we have ceased to build men—we have ceased to build Americans.

Centuries ago, man invented an instrument of great power, greater than the harnessed nuclear energy that we stand so in awe of today. That power has come down to us an an individual respsonsbility, with each American's freedom hanging in the balance. That power is government. *It can be wielded by individual citizens for their common good, or it can be surrendered to the State for ultimate human enslavement. History has proved over and over again that self-government is the only safe repository of freedom; whenever and wherever people have relinquished this power to the State, a nation has fallen. It is in this manner—refusing to rule—that we are betraying ourselves and our children today.*

The American dream is a culmination of five-thousand years of reaching out for full and free expression of human aspirations in a free society. It was this dream which drew the spiritually thwarted and politically oppressed to our shores, not a rash promise of gold in the streets. These people placed security of their liberty far above any paternalistic protection of their property under tyanny. And it is this dream, not material progress, which must remain our most noble bequest to mankind.

Character as such is not inherited. Ideals and principles are not inherited. These must be transmitted through teaching and

xiv

by direct example. We have become lax in our performance of both of these obligations. We have forgotten that citizenship: the preparation for, and practice of, and preservation of our republic is everyone's main business. There can be no avoiding of this issue. Shall we remain true to the principle that man is created with God-given rights and God-charged responsibilities upon which this nation was founded and by which it has grown? Or shall we accept the pagan philosophy of an all-powerful State whose citizens have no individual significance, who are mere chattels of the State?

The time has come for us to reacquaint ourselves with our own tradition and way of life. The meanings of citizenship and patriotism must once again find its way into our lives and into our educational system. We adults have set aside our birthright, our American heritage, in adjusting to the pressing tempo of 20th-century life. Our schools have forced Americanism out of the classroom to make way for temporary trivialities. They no longer turn out the high caliber of citizen which America requires.

There are many signs which point to this disastrous national decay, and I have tried as objectively as possible to place some of them under the spotlight of truth. The result may be disturbing, perhaps even frightening, but it cannot be denied or disregarded. We have too much at stake.

This small volume can lay claim to none of the usual aspirations of authorship, and I sincerely apologize for whatever literary shortcomings the reader may encounter along the way. It was written for only one reason: Anyone having knowledge of a betrayal *is under serious moral obligation to warn those who are being betrayed. This I felt compelled to do and have done to the best of my ability.*

SIDNEY L. DE LOVE

Chicago, February 22, 1960

XV

PART ONE

An American Crisis

Men came, and men tried
To build freedom—and men died;
And more came, and all knowing
That freedom's breeze was here blowing.
The tide flooding, the tide flowing,
The colonies planted, the states growing,
Liberty founded on sacred themes—
A nation builded and forward going,
A nation bursting out at the seams!
The tide is flowing, deep and wide;
The tide is in—and we are the tide!
And this is the meaning of all they did;
This is the sacred purpose hid
In all the trouble and pain and tears
And the slow travail of the bitter years;
This is the meaning, this is the goal—
Liberty for the human soul![1]

CHAPTER 1

THE CRIME

A Violation of Character

❦❦

Yes, we did produce a near perfect Republic. But will they keep it, or will they, in the enjoyment of plenty, lose the memory of freedom? Material abundance without character is the surest way to destruction.   THOMAS JEFFERSON

❦❦

AND SO AMERICA CAME TO BE, a nation with courage, daring and determination steeled in the marrow of her people's bones. Here, on just five per cent of the earth's sprawling surface, took place the greatest moral, political and ideological revolution in the history of civilization. Here, for the first time, each individual human being was crowned a sovereign and recognized an equal of his neighbor. For the first time, no individual nor any group of individuals nor the Government could take away, limit or interfere with the inalienable rights of man. A government was founded which adhered to ethical and moral values. The State was created by individuals acting together for the mutual interest of all; the State was given its power by the people, to serve each individual in securing his God-given rights by guaranteeing his personal liberties as a free man. Here in America, originated a new order wherein power was derived from God, vested in the individual, and through the consent of the individual conferred upon the State. The individual was protected against the arbitrary exercise of government force, free to voice his own opinions, free to worship, read, and assemble, free to achieve the ultimate in personal growth through his own

3

labor, initiative and resourcefulness. His human dignity and the sanctity of his soul became a part of the American concept of government.

Once and for all, our founding fathers abolished the ancient fallacy that government has rights which might or might not be granted to the individual, depending on the benevolence of those in power. Our forefathers declared that all rights belong to individual persons, and that the right of government to exercise limited power is a gift of the individual. This declaration by the founders of our nation nullified the erroneous assumption that man exists for the government—a chattel of the State—and lifted him to a position of responsibility and nobility. After five thousand years of varying degrees of enslavement, the individual at last emerged as the most important segment of society.

Our founding fathers having tasted the bitter oppression of despotic Government and sought to insure for all time that no segment of Government could in time acquire dominion over the others. To this end they retained for the citizen the prime source of authority; sovereignty for the State, and to the Federal Government the delegated specific powers. They introduced the check-and-balance system. They dispersed powers, distributed authority and decentralized decisions within the governmental structure. The real source and strength of our American Democracy is *the individual citizen.*

None but the United States can offer so priceless a heritage to her sons. No land but that of Liberty could have inspired a great statesman to cry out, "My God! how little do my countrymen know what precious blessings they are in possession of and which no other people on earth enjoy. But will they keep it, or will they, in the enjoyment of plenty, lose the memory of freedom?" Material abundance without character is the surest way to destruction.

Those words were wrenched from the heart of Thomas Jefferson. They were spoken not in disparagement of his countrymen but in praise of America. Yet Jefferson did, in effect, issue a timeless warning to the people: Take care, lest through

4

ignorance and lack of appreciation you trade your blessings for oblivion.

Had the author of our immortal Declaration of Independence been able to compare the citizens of today with his contemporaries, he might rather have phrased his warning, ". . . how little do my *descendants* know . . ." For *there* is the crux of impending disaster—an American crisis more imminent than war itself.

How little we seem to know or care about the precious blessings we have inherited. How indifferent we have become to our sacred trust of preserving that inheritance for ourselves and our posterity. Have we forgotten so soon that our lofty position and our abundant material possessions are only possible because of this legacy? History has clearly shown that whenever moral value and basic principles are sacrificed for utilitarian conveniences the result is self-wrought enslavement and a loss of far more than mere material comfort. The greatest physical luxuries—the biggest cars, the fanciest homes, the finest television sets,—are worthless without an appreciative understanding of the way of life that made them possible. And when such things are acquired only through a compromise of character and responsibility they cannot last . . . because on these terms the very way of life that made them possible cannot last. Freedom, liberty, self-government, these are our most precious possessions. If these blessings are carelessly allowed to slip away, whatever material gains we have secured will quickly disappear under the tyranny of the authoritarian state which must follow. Self-government demands strong, dedicated character. The sovereignty of the individual over the state is a measure of his character; it is a day-to-day challenge which cannot be taken for granted, be delegated or approached in an apathetic manner. When the character of a nation weakens, when—as in America today—the people constantly look to the government as a magic cure-all and a miraculous money machine, the power of government must inevitably change hands. The state becomes ruler and the individual becomes its chattel.

5

We need only look at the symbol of the American character to weigh ourselves against the self-governing citizens of yesterday and measure the citizens of tomorrow. The time to do this is now, before it is too late, before we betray the sacred trust which stands today as the only hope of the world. Let us take a good long look at Uncle Sam, the familiar symbol of the American character and spirit, the mirror of the American mind. Uncle Sam stands as the personification of a U. S. that requires no punctuation marks—the all-inclusive U.S. that was created when free men chose to unite. Uncle Sam is, in fact, you and I, We The People of the United States of America.

No crisis in the past was too great for Uncle Sam to overcome. In war and in peace he defended the honor and wealth of America. Whenever the alternative was failure, he met with success; wherever defeat threatened he emerged victorious.

When this champion of free men was young, he sat at table with men like Tom Jefferson and Ben Franklin and he ate well. Today he is fed a conglomeration of bureaucratic broth, and sugar-coated security. The strong constitution for which he became world-renowned is now but tissue where it once was tendon; *Uncle Sam is a very sick man.* Today his condition is such that he can no longer attend to his job properly; much of his wealth has already been allocated elsewhere and the very possessions of his private ownership have become vulnerable to confiscation!

If symptoms are the presage of fatality, then witness the shadow of death that now hovers above the *character* of you and me. Witness the Uncle Sam who once moved with eager stride from Plymouth to the sandy coast of California. When the ethical and spiritual qualities of human character do not keep pace with material advancement, decay is bound to result. One can sit idly in the lap of luxury just so long, and then the softness of false contentment will creep into his limbs and sap their strength.

The less they are used, the softer they become.

The less they are used, the more paralyzed they become.

As for Uncle Sam, he no longer can stand on his own two

6

feet. He has ceased to move. He is ready for the wheel chair that the State is building for him—he is willing to let the Government push him around. But who will give the direction? Uncle Sam in the wheel chair, or the government behind it pushing?

His eyes, which once possessed the clear vision of an eagle, have become near-sighted. He can see nothing far-reaching.

He hears quite well with one ear. But he is stone deaf in the other.

Observe the "red" area on his left side, symptom of a dissease called Communism. The infection has already penetrated so deeply and spread so far that most of his right side is numb. This ailment, Uncle Sam seems to have decided, can be peaceably lived with. It's painless, thus far.

His voice has taken on a kind of snide cynicism. It isn't the voice he used when he stood face to face with a king who had vowed to kill him, nor that voice which told this king: "A prince whose character is thus marked by every act which may define a tyrant, is unfit to be the ruler of a free people."

Today he speaks to bureaucrats and power-seekers with a soft begging voice and attitude "please" and an insipid, whispering "thank you."

A cancer of complacency has crept into Uncle Sam's bones —while enterprising quacks, who thrive on his helplessness, prescribe tranquilizers and sleeping pills. Just take it easy, he is told, relax, give your independence, individuality, and obligation of self-government a rest— the Government will take care of everything.

Our Uncle Sam is dying from loss of a special type of blood, rare and vital. It is the type that flowed through the veins of Patrick Henry and Nathan Hale, the kind that pumped the hearts of men like George Washington and Abraham Lincoln. Our freedom requires that we search deep within our hearts, for there this blood will be found. Our personal liberty demands that each of us donate unstintingly to the great transfusion that is needed if Uncle Sam is to survive.

Perhaps that is asking too much. To demand that every

7

individual give of his own substance is a serious thing. Yet there were men who gave their lives for this very cause.

But how worthy this cause? How important? If the moral precepts and steadfast character that transformed a wilderness into a wonderland merit preservation, then the cause is worthy. If Lincoln was right when he said, "Our defense is in the preservation of the spirit which prizes liberty as the heritage of all men, in all lands, everywhere. Destroy this spirit, and you have planted the seeds of despotism around your own door." If this be true, then the cause is worthy. If by saving the life of Uncle Sam we can save our own lives then freedom's demand is indeed a worthy cause!

Consider for a moment the intrepid career of Uncle Sam, that you may determine for yourself whether this life we hold in our hands is worth saving. At the offset he was known simply as Independence, born of Liberty in the summer of 1776 at the State House in Philadelphia. There he struggled, suffered, and grew up. Young Sam felt the full weight of British boots slash across his tender face during the first seven years of his life — and he matched death breath for breath. He lay sprawled on the rich soil of America, too young to do more than cry out his own name. This small son of Liberty watched, as brave men died that he might live, and he grew strong as their blood mingled with his. Young Sam watched—and he vowed never to forget.

Then, in 1778, just a week before his twelfth birthday, Sam became an uncle. Through the adoption of our federal Constitution, and the divine providence of God, he became an integral part of each American's way of life, a fountainhead of spiritual and material progress.

How quickly and how straight he grew in those formative years! Lean, determined, self-reliant, he inhaled the air of this new Republic and exhaled a sigh of irrepressible enthusiasm. His faith in the future of America was unlimited, and it was based squarely on a deep-seated belief in the individual's integrity and common sense as a responsible citizen.

By the end of the 18th Century Uncle Sam had acquired a

8

world-wide reputation as a hard-working, rugged individualist, restless by nature, with a fine sense of humor and a generous heart. He believed, as Mr. Franklin had told him, that early to bed and early to rise, makes a man healthy, wealthy and wise. And thus did he live—a symbol of the new concept that placed the individual above the state and before the open flood-gates of opportunity.

A visitor from Britain remarked in 1796 that ". . . the spirit of servility to those above them so prevalent in European manners, is wholly unknown to Americans; and they pass their lives without any regard for the smiles or frowns of men in power." The characteristics of a nation destined to surpass all others had already taken shape; a spirit of independence had already replaced colonial servility. Four million individual Americans lived without fear "of men in power" because they were those men. And they knew it.

This same year, 1796, President Washington took Uncle Sam aside and in his official *Farewell Address* advised him: "The name of American, which belongs to you in your national capacity, must always exalt the just pride of patriotism more than any appellation derived from local discriminations." Uncle Sam accepted this advice and pledged his life to patriotic devotion to the United States. America was no longer a vision, it was a young nation bursting with energy, proud to exist, eager to test its newly won freedom.

Uncle Sam was healthy and wholesome in those days! Though he was far from being wealthy by material standards, through the blessings of nature his riches were manifold. His backyard was a boundless frontier, washed by a silver web of rivers and streams, adorned by lofty mountains and rolling acres of moist black earth. He possessed the highest waterfalls, the deepest canyons, the thickest forests. His woods were rife with game, his lakes with fish. Uncle Sam was one-tenth urbanite and nine-tenths farmer. He lived in a log cabin that he built himself, and raised Indian corn and rye on land that he'd cleared by hand. He ate with the simplicity of taste and hearty appetite that honest labor gives to a man: Brown 'rye

9

and Injun' bread, corn-pone or hoe-cake, hominy with salt pork or codfish, washed down with rum, cider or steaming coffee. Uncle Sam went to bed tired at night, slept in sound, child-like slumber, and awoke with an uncontained joy in his heart.

He loved his country.

Death removed one of his most selfless compatriots in the winter of 1799, and Uncle Sam journeyed to Mount Vernon to pay tribute to the father of his country. Still but a youth, he stood over the bier of George Washington, wept, and whispered to posterity, "First in war, first in peace, first in the hearts of his countrymen." Even in death, the Father of Our Country added to the spiritual growth of American character. For Uncle Sam learned that the deeds of an honorable man can never fade from the memory of those who loved him. He learned that a lifetime of devoted service is a precious thing. He learned in the finality of this occasion how true the American concepts of individual worth and human dignity are.

During the years which followed, preceding the War of 1812, there was little change in the American character. Uncle Sam was too busy to acquire vices, too grateful to shirk his responsibilities to God and government, too independent to become lazy, too proud and patriotic and practical to let others do his thinking for him. There was still a wilderness to be tamed, towns and cities to be built. There were still the political and economic systems which, like rough diamonds, needed polish and refinement. Uncle Sam worked round the clock, established schools, churches, markets, missions, hospitals, newspapers. He amended the Constitution, negotiated the Louisiana Purchase, and established West Point Military Academy on his twenty-sixth birthday. He even found time to fall in with Johnny Appleseed, and their subsequent Odyssey yielded fruit-bearing trees across 100,000 square miles of American soil. He was, as the saying goes, *turning out just fine*.

Uncle Sam lived close to nature and developed a deep faith in the fundamentals of life. He believed in the land. He believed in the people and in their Maker. He believed

10

strongly in the private acquisition of material wealth, but only as a means to enrich his American heritage, never as an end in itself.

For years he fought the elements to protect these things in which he believed. Then abruptly, in 1812, he learned that it can also become necessary to fight men for the same reason. Uncle Sam, who treasured his right to free enterprise, found British ships blockading foreign and American ports. He, whose entire system of government was based on the inalienable right of man to individual liberty and freedom from state tyranny, witnessed foreign impressment of American seamen. Not much of a diplomat in those days, Uncle Sam simply told John Bull to *stop*. And when John refused, Uncle Sam set out in "Old Ironsides" to accomplish by war what he could not with words.

Whether this second conflict with England could have been avoided, or whether it should have been directed against Napoleon (who by President Madison's own admission had captured more American vessels since 1807 than the British), is a matter of discussion for historians. But that Uncle Sam fought valiantly to safeguard his rightful heritage no man can deny.

He was young and green, undisciplined in military strategy; nevertheless victory was not long in coming. Fourteen months after America declared war, Uncle Sam stood on the bridge of his half-sunk flagship *Lawrence*, battle-weary but proudly erect, to accept the laconic and unmistakeably American report of Captain Oliver Perry:

"We have met the enemy and they are ours." And little more than another fourteen months was to pass before Perry's battle report became applicable to the war as a whole.

At the conclusion of the war, Uncle Sam once more resumed his role of citizen-pioneer. For the half-century to follow his every move was dominated by two exigencies: individual progress, and the anathema of slavery. The former crystalized itself in an ever-expanding frontier; in inventions of every description from the safety pin to the fire engine; in

11

thousands of miles of railroad track, in scores of colleges and universities; in an abundance of famous authors, industrialists, artists, athletes, statesmen and entrepreneurs. As it had been in 1776, and has been ever since, *progress* was the *key note* of American character.

The issue of slavery, which began to boil in 1777 when Vermont became the first state in the union to abolish it, ended with the intrastate Armageddon that requires no further delineation here. The manner in which it affected Uncle Sam, however, is both significant and enlightening. Upon close inspection—at any given moment in the history of slavery—one can discern its ulcerous growth within the sensitive core of his conscience. Uncle Sam could not live with it and feel undefiled.

An emancipation petition was submitted to Congress as early as 1790 by the Quaker "Society of Friends." A year later Virginia's George Mason, one of America's greatest patriots, warned Uncle Sam that slavery was like a slow poison that would corrupt future legislators with habits of despotism. The signs of impending holocaust multiplied. In 1807, Congress passed an act prohibiting African slave trade. In 1820, Elihu Emree founded his powerful monthly agitator, the *Emancipator*.

On the day that marked Uncle Sam's fiftieth birthday, July 4th, 1826, his family doctor, Thomas Jefferson, and another who had assisted at his birth, John Adams, both died, leaving him with a group of physicians who differed in their diagnosis.

The ulcer of slavery had already done its work, and he now realized that he was on his way to an inevitable nervous breakdown. But this crisis was caused by internal tension, not by internal decay. And therein lies the fundamental difference between the American crisis of 1861 and the American crisis of today. Behind Uncle Sam's collapse was an irreconcilable personality split, a frustrating barrage of pro and anti-slavery societies, insurrections, the Kansas-Nebraska Bill, Fugitive Slave Law, Dred Scot Decision, and the like.

Uncle Sam took his case to two specialists, Abraham Lincoln for the North and Jefferson Davis for the South. One

12

said cut out the ulcer. The other said let it alone and it won't cause any more trouble. The decision was up to Uncle Sam. "Doctor" Davis argued that slavery itself was not the cause of the patient's condition, but rather the yankee-induced irritants that had caused the ulcer to fester. "Doctor" Lincoln put a big hand on the patient's shoulder and said, Sam, "Slavery is founded on the selfishness of man's nature—opposition to it in his love of justice. These principles are in eternal antagonism, and when brought into collision so fiercely as slavery brings them, shocks and throes and convulsions must ceaselessly follow."

The patient could either flee from responsibility, or face the issue with foresight and integrity. He was free to choose a life with or without slavery. There was little hesitation. *Operate,* said Uncle Sam.

What followed was one of the most harrowing operations ever performed by human hands. Uncle Sam was on the table for four years, and countless incisions were made before the ordeal was over. These wounds, that were made by honest men, left red, raw scars across his body—some of them are still not completely healed. But the inherent devotion and sincere loyalty of a people managed somehow to pull him through. When it was all over, he found a nation that was broken yet whole, divided in its mourning but united under one Constitution. And though he felt much older that day than his *fourscore and seven years,* Uncle Sam rose slowly to his feet and began the long journey home. He was once more at peace with himself; before long he would smile again.

And now began one of the most phenomenal periods of growth in the nation's history. American Democracy had been won, tested, and found to be a most effective system of government. The theory of government by, for and of the people was now an established practice. The ideas of individual freedom, sovereignty, and personal liberties were almost three generations old, and had had ample time to become assimilated.

Suddenly, or so it seemed, Uncle Sam was no longer an

13

ordinary individual, not at all the "common man" extolled by lesser democracies. Suddenly, there was no mountain he could not climb, no tree he could not fell. There was no profession at which he could not succeed, no problem he could not lick. If he wanted to, he could become president! If he felt like it, he could make a million dollars!

He had discovered only this: his Heritage.

There is nothing better than a free man, unless it is a better free man. There is no greater incentive than equality of opportunity, except perhaps equality of opportunity once tasted. There is no fuller happiness than the striving for a goal, save one achieved and another one in sight. There is nothing sadder than a thankless American citizen.

Here then was the best of free men who had tasted of equal opportunity all his life, who had achieved ten thousand goals and had ten thousand more in sight, who had been bequeathed the gifts of all who went before him. Here was the American matured—Uncle Sam.

He shoved back the wild frontier for necessary elbow-room until by 1890 the Superintendent of the Census was obliged to report:

"Up to and including 1880 the country had a frontier of settlement, but at present the unsettled area has been so broken into by isolated bodies of settlement that there can hardly be said to be a frontier line."

But that didn't stop Uncle Sam. The spirit that helped blaze trails across a continent turned to other challenges. Uncle Sam became obsessed with the unlimited potential of his own unshackled hands, and he set them to revolutionizing everything within their reach. At once, American housewives had sewing machines, vacuum cleaners, ice machines, clocks, egg beaters and scores of other appliances. Some of today's most famous universities came into being. The world became familiar with private American dynasties as Rockefeller organized Standard Oil, Westinghouse invented air brakes, and Heinz pioneered the canned-goods industry. Suddenly America had a Brooklyn Bridge, a Grand Central

14

Station, a United States Weather Bureau. Henry Ford introduced mass production to the business man and cheap cars to the consumer. Labor acquired the union and the eight-hour day.

Uncle Sam proved that the American economic system was capable of almost unlimited productive capacity. It grew out of the new nation's constitutional right to private property. From this individual right to keep the fruit of one's own labor, evolved the simple, natural concepts of free enterprise, supply and demand, risk and reward, initiative and opportunity, competition in quality, quantity, and price. In the American market place there was but one guiding principle' The best goods and services for the least amount of money for as many people as possible.

Free enterprise was a challenge to Uncle Sam. He reached out to harness electricity, fire and water-power. The rest of the world watched with disbelief as American rail mileage reached an all-time peak of 253,000 miles, as towering steel structures erupted from the world's new industrial Mecca, where luxuries were becoming no less common than the necessities of life. By the 1920s, life expectancy in the United States had lengthened by ten years. Illiteracy had dropped to a new low. One out of every four Americans owned his own automobile. Out of the climate of individual freedom came higher personal incomes than even Uncle Sam had dreamed possible. In short, he had it made!

Or so it seemed to him.

"He had it made."—What parasitic treachery lurks within that modern American cliche! With the throbbing of one heartbeat does a lifetime have it made? Does one who is building *betterment* ever really have it made? With indepedence and freedom as his material, Uncle Sam was building something more than packing plants and tractors and baseball bats; he was building a land of Liberty wherein government was the servant of the people and the all-important individual was the sovereign ruler of the State—a land of Liberty, never made but always in the making. Uncle Sam forgot that free-

15

dom and independence are not "gifts" but rights which must be continually earned through responsible self-government.

A fundamental and far-reaching change crept into the spirit of Uncle Sam during that first wave of modern American prosperity, a change begun in our own lifetime and more dominant today than ever before. He turned his back on the very tradition he had carved out of the wilderness. He spurned the advice he had been given as a young man by the great men who had fathered and nourished his existence. He began to reject time-honored absolutes as old-fashioned ideas, truth as something tentative and pliable, values as pragmatic and valid only as they became immediately useful. For the first time in his life, Uncle Sam mistook passive certitude for the "eternal vigilance" his forebearers had cautioned him to observe. The American character began to compromise individual rights and duties for a more authoritarian state. Liberty's mighty son became lazy, believing now that the machine had been made, man's proper place was in an armchair. He began to look around for "easy" money and lower standards. He found a new slogan in "buy now, pay later." He decided that state compulsion rather than private incentive would gain the best performance from free man, and that bigger government meant the same thing as better government.

And then the roof caved in. Uncle Sam woke up one chilly October morning in 1929 to learn that thirty million dollars had been lost due to the collapse of the stock market. Depression danced out from behind a speculative mania that saw one billion new securities floated that year. And President Hoover's earlier announcement that "in no nation are the fruits of accomplishment more secure," was followed by the grim truth: "As a nation, we *must* prevent hunger and cold to those of our people who are in honest difficulties."

Uncle Sam could not believe his eyes. He, who had proved the worth of his free-enterprise system in a dozen previous depressions, who just a decade earlier, in "a war to end all wars," had once more shown the world his mettle, now cow-

16

ered in fear. There was no strong American character to guide the country through this crisis. The "crash" had smashed his courage and shattered his self-confidence. Just when character, spirit, and deep belief were vitally needed, Uncle Sam threw off principles and the high trust of his heritage in his confusion and despair. Thirteen million hungry Americans walked the streets in search of employment. Uncle Sam walked the streets. *He wanted to work again.* In the old days he would have strapped his belongings to the back of his horse and moved West. He would have shoved the frontier back a little further, cleared himself a patch of rich new land, and been back in business. But now he walked the streets and didn't know what to do. The frontier was gone. The dignity of individualism was lost. Independence had given way to depression. The spirit of 1776 which had laid progress and prosperity at the feet of American society no longer permeated the atmosphere of America. Uncle Sam was truly dazed. He knew the wants and needs of the individual. But now the individual was no longer of importance, or so he was told. Now, he was to direct his energy toward the nation, the country—the State. He was asked, what cruel monster was this State, that in a single day destroyed achievements of a lifetime? And he wondered, while he walked the streets. The State did not cause the crash. In fact, lack of State regulation made much of it possible.

Uncle Sam decided that the individual American did not know what was best for this giant called the State. He decided that the State alone knew what was best for the individual in times of crises. And then he sold his soul to the State for a piece of bread and bowl of soup!

For the first time in his life, Uncle Sam went back on the promise he had made to every great American, famous or nameless, who ever lived.

He gave up.

He made a "deal" to serve the government which his Fathers had created to serve him and, in rationalizing this tragic flight from responsibility, he claimed it was only temporary.

17

Thus, did Uncle Sam's spirit, the American character, continue to change. He traded his individual sovereignty for "welfare" from a federal authority. He bartered his own mother, Liberty, for a synthetic "security."

But for all of the concessions he made in return for prosperity—concessions of freedom that still threaten individual liberty today—it took an international war to put Uncle Sam back on his economic feet, not the federal government. Once more he was called upon to deliver his country from the slashing talons of a foreign power. And once more the spark of his youth rekindled the flame of American glory. Uncle Sam entered World War II and the people felt his presence and they praised his name. Once again he took on the substance of a nation and inspired greatness.

Just after the start of World War II, a famous portrait of Uncle Sam by Dean Cornwell was reproduced in many of the nation's magazines. Beneath the portrait was printed one of the last eulogies, perhaps the final epitaph, of America's Uncle Sam:

Modern methods, modern efficiency—but the same old flaming spirit of 1776. What else could give men the *vitality* to produce tanks, guns, planes, armaments in such enormous quantities? What else could enable the railroads of America to handle millions of troops with such precision and smoothness . . . to haul *twice* the tonnage of war materials pre-war experts estimated them capable of? That spirit, as much as mechanical excellence and natural resources, is America's tower of strength. Its 'secret weapon.'

Ah yes! The flaming spirit of 1776. Once more that marvellous quality lifted America's heart. The land of liberty was at war and Uncle Sam was fightin' mad. How well we knew him then. He towered high above his 165 million nephews, a symbol of human courage with his legs spread wide and his star-spangled top hat shoved back defiantly. His familiar cravat hung loose in 1941. His strong hands were clenched for action, his chest heaved with the spirit of his birth, and his rolled-up sleeves revealed the might and muscle of America.

18

Once again this noble son of our Founding Fathers caused the American soul to seeth with the spirit of freedom.

But that was ninteen years ago. Have you noticed Uncle Sam — lately?

Those who know him, who have seen his scars and shaken his hand in admiration and respect, know also that on September 2, 1945, after 1,351 days of bitter war and twenty million lost lives, that precious spirit was left once more to die. Under the magic spell of victory, it was cast off along with our empty ration books and the blue stars that hung in our windows. We returned to the ease and comfort of civilian indifference. Uncle Sam tied his tie, rolled down his sleeves and relinquished the major part of his right and responsibility of self-government. He bought a new hat decorated with dollar signs instead of stars, slipped into a grey flannel suit, and became a "playboy."

He dissipated quickly, of course. Uncle Sam was born and raised in a warm climate of honesty, thrift and self-reliance; he could muster little resistance against the freezing environment of guile, cupidity, deceit and complacency. His new role as lavish entertainer and big spender of other people's money kept his "social" calendar filled. And the "social" events he attended on the floor of Congress called for an ever-increasing amount of "social" drinking from the public fount—until he ultimately developed a craving for it. He did not have time to discern the difference between being sociable and socialistic. Friends, relatives, and people he had never seen before in his life, hounded him incessantly, rich and poor alike, and he gave and gave again—never questioning where the money came from. With a business suit on, he also attracted many federal "salesmen" with new "deals" to offer him. They were there to confront him no matter which way he turned. Uncle Sam found no peace in his new role, but the government was always ready to do his paper work for him. His "friends" took care of all the details. All he had to do was take it easy, enjoy life, question nothing, do as the government advised, and spend enough money to keep all of his smiling bureaucrats

19

happy. At least, that's what he was told and shamefully he swallowed this poisonous broth.

But no one bothered to tell Uncle Sam what must inevitably follow. It began with just an occasional headache or upset stomach, nothing really alarming. Now and then a true friend gave him an aspirin or two to pep him up. But then the headaches and upset stomachs began to occur more frequently. Uncle Sam grew weaker, thinner—and the government grew stronger and fatter. He stayed in bed most of the time to save his strength. At one point he might have recovered just by having his stomach pumped, but there was no one around to call the doctor. Now, it's going to take more than a stomach pump. It is going to take a transfusion of strong, loyal American blood.

If our country is to survive as a free nation, if the individual is to win out over the State, the moral character of each and every American must be taken into account. The signs of decay must be clearly observed, and the decay cut out. If America is to survive, we must save the life of Uncle Sam and renew within him once again the spirit of the past, the lifeblood of our precious heritage. That we might fail to meet this challenge is the crisis of our time.

CHAPTER 2

THE ACCUSED

Our Birthright for a Mess of Pottage

❊❊

All that is necessary for the triumph of evil is that good men do nothing.   EDMUND BURKE

❊❊

IT SHOULD BE CLEARLY UNDERSTOOD by every citizen that the crisis now confronting the United States is unmatched by any other in the history of our country. We have encountered national emergencies many times in the past, but on each of these occasions the issue was set before us in plain terms. Retaliative measures for survival were almost reflexive. If the dilemma was war—we fought. If it was political corruption— we cleaned house. But this time we are faced with a crisis that has neither a conveniently definitive label, nor a precedent plan for survival. It is not the kind of trouble one can outlaw with a constitutional amendment, or overcome by bullets and bombs or political purges.

We can do nothing until we accept this fact: We, the People, are faced with nation-wide moral erosion of individual character. That is the charge, abstract in appearance but as concrete as Madison Avenue, the unvarnished truth of an American crisis more repugnant than famine or flood. Indeed, the issue is one of *decay*—as real as green mold on stale bread— and it is exclusively ours with which to contend.

The federal government, no matter how extensively it attempts to "plan" our welfare, "plan" our economy, our edu-

21

cation, and our private lives, will do nothing more than speed us on toward disaster. When a national crisis evolves out of state intervention and centralization, it will not be solved by a greater degree of state intervention and centralization. The ultimate conclusion of government planning was never more forcibly brought home than in the following remark taken together with its historical ramifications:

"And, my countrymen, you already know that, after all, I have some fairly important plans in my mind, vast and splendid plans for my people."

The remark concluded a speech delivered in Berlin, December 1941, by Adolph Hitler.

Like the deceived people of Germany, we Americans have come to believe that the growing bureaucratic monster in Washington has "important plans in mind" for us. We have somehow brainwashed ourselves into thinking that the federal government has "vast and splendid plans" which can guarantee each of us cradle-to-grave security without depriving us of our rights and liberties and making us ultimately slaves of the state.

Power can be shared, but the ultimate *souce* of power cannot be, it must remain sovereign. Once the source of government power begins to fluctuate between the individual and the State the end does not come until one has become completely subservient to the other. Government, by its very nature, demands an absolute authority. If one were to concoct from the entire political knowledge of mankind, a potpourri of influential ideas as divorced from one another as the Ten Commandments are from Machiavelli's *Prince,* or as the Declaration of Independence is from the Communist Manifesto, there would emerge this most significant of universal questions:

Should human welfare depend upon the responsible individual or on a responsible State?

Man's search for an answer has led him to establish and discard all manner of governments, religions and social systems; participate in untold wars and revolutions; and experience numerous combinations of freedom and slavery. Never in

22

the history of human experiences has there been world-wide acceptance of one or the other of the tremendous propositions contained in those dozen words.

And never before the birth of our nation had such an inviolable allegiance been pledged to one of them!

We had our choice: the "State" or the "Individual"— and we staked our lives on a consummate faith in the worth of the individual. We made him the responsible segment of our Republic, the prime source of authority, and this noble concept of man became the fountainhead of our American character. America became a kingdom of kings wherein the citizen is the real sovereign. The only sovereign.

With each early refinement of this new concept there emerged a new facet of our political disposition; America's concept of the individual became at once the cause and effect of her growth. Our system of private enterprise is a manifestation of this concept. It has contributed as much to our national character as it has to our economy. Similarly, when a handful of sage statesmen developed the pattern of our three-part system of government, they both drew upon and added to this revolutionary attitude toward the individual. And in this way the United States consequently raised human welfare to a hitherto non-existent level, while concomitantly the national character of free, responsible individuals grew to maturity.

With our entire way of life founded on this American concept of the individual, it is not difficult to understand why the moral decay of American character increases in direct proportion to the shifting of responsibilities from the citizen to the state. Indifference and apathy corrupt the very ideal of America as a society under God made workable by individuals who are responsible for this society's welfare, and whose national characteristics stem directly from this high trust of self-government.

It was individual irresponsibility that prompted Juvenal to write of Rome 2,000 years ago, "Now that no one buys our votes, the public has long since cast off its cares; the people

23

that once bestowed commands, consulships, legions and all else, now meddles no more and longs eagerly for just two things, bread and circuses."

Juvenal recognized what the people themselves failed to see. He witnessed the signs of internal decay in a people who were willing to trade their political sovereignty for food and entertainment. The same kind of internal decay caused many other nations to go the way of Rome. As history has shown, tyranny is easy to maintain because it is founded on violence and terror. A republic is difficult to maintain because it is founded on freedom and liberty which must be watched over and defended by the people. This important distinction was grimly pointed out to us more than one hundred years ago when the English historian Thomas Macauley warned:

"Either some Caesar or Napoleon will seize the reins of government with strong hands or your republic will be as fearfully plundered and laid waste by barbarians in the 20th Century . . . engenederd within your own country by your own institutions."

How prophetic was Maculey's charge? Is our country being plundered and laid waste from within by her own people? Are we destroying America?

These are questions that, once raised, cannot go unanswered. We have but one recourse, and that is to confront the person who can supply the answers, the self-governing individual—ourself.

Compare the twentieth Century American to his predecessor of 1776. By and large, he is characterized by swift flight from respsonsibility, looking more and more for government "bread and circuses." The society of sovereign individuals is today a society of passive conformists. This colossal economic waste and character-destroying cancer is laying the foundation for inevitable servitude. Government paternalism, welfare state or socialism, is the front entrance to Communism, totalitarianism or Fascism. It is certainly not Americanism. It is diametrically opposed to our concept of a free society.

As Benjamin Franklin and other vigilant patriots feared, we

24

have allowed our material abundance to breed moral dissipation. "Ill fares the land to every foe a prey where wealth accumulates and men decay."

Every error in action starts with a fallacious philosophy. Every nation that has fallen fell because its principles were corrupted by individuals who tried to compromise them.

We cannot remain a great nation by giving ourselves up as individuals to selfishness, physical comforts and cheap amusements. We cannot hold on to our precious heritage through ingratitude to the men, women, the deeds and the shrines that comprise this special legacy. Material advance demands a corresponding moral advance. Every disaster of mankind resulted from compromising ideals.

And yet we continue to live by the new materialistic standards that have developed during the past half-century. We have forgotten that a people cannot build a better society with temporary deceit. The deceit is not temporary. It eats into the flesh of a nation as surely as a deadly disease and it spreads as rapidly as the most frightening of plagues. It becomes a permanent part of society. When expediency is substituted for character in daily living, freedom in the minds of men is soon lost.

We must realize and accept the fact that every individual American is responsible for the national character. The degree to which we meet our responsibilities does, in fact, directly determine the condition of that character. Fulfillment of responsibility to God and country sustains it in good health. Allocation of responsibility to any power other than the individual citizen, or simply ignorance of its existence, does irrevocable harm to it. Character is not something we can leave or take. The difference between a strong and weak national character is not unlike the difference between a foundation of rock and a foundation of sand. And because the foundation of our republic is character, it is equally true that the difference between responsibility and irresponsibility is similar to that between freedom and slavery.

On the back of every dollar bill the reverse side of the

25

Great Seal of the United States is reproduced. There is an inscription which reads, *"Annuit Coeptis, Novus Ordo Seclorum* MDCCLXXVI."—"God has favored our undertaking, A New Order of the Ages—1776." It is worth noting that our founders did not merely refer to a political system or to a form of government. The Great Seal states that the American Revolution established a new order—a new way of life which grew from a concept of personal freedom and responsibility that extends into all phases of American life— economic, religious—all forms of social intercourse.

And therein lies the supreme importance of strong, personal character. In America, the individual is not only accountable for his own government, but he has also a moral and social responsibility toward his fellowman. Today, our character decadence is manifest in our attitude toward our own government and in our day-to-day living as well. The contemporary social and moral environment of America should be at a higher level than ever before. We have advantages our ancestors never dreamed possible. We have the most comprehensive educational system in the world, and communication media that reach into every corner of the nation. And yet, in a routine day: 37 people are murdered; 272 others are feloniously assaulted: Another 57 are criminally assaulted; 1,095 married couples initiate divorce proceedings; 801 cars are stolen; 475 larcenies and 1,620 burglaries occur; 172 people are robbed; 4,700,000 alcoholic citizens over-indulge; $295,000 worth of *base* literature is purchased; and 1,452 youngsters are haled into court for a wide assortment of juvenile crimes.

These are wretched enigmas of American character. They comprise just a fraction of the immorality that casts a shadow of disgrace and dereliction over our sense of duty.

True, only a minority of Americans are criminals, but the moral responsibility of free men does not begin or end at a line drawn by law. We Americans are the special human fulcrum by which the American standard of behavior is raised and lowered. To deny this fact, we would have to deny six thousand years of proof that social corrosion is the destructive outgrowth

26

of individual indifference. Destruction is but indifference given time. The entire fabric of organization within American society is nothing more than a multiple of the individual citizen and an instrument of his will. If we fail to suppress evil with our power to do good, what earthly force can perform this duty for us?

It is sobering but true that we must stand responsible for the folly and crimes of others, insofar and as long as we remain free to set the standard of national character. Thereupon rests the burden of all our blessings.

While statistics of crime and wantoness are made by a small minority, these few people are nevertheless products of the environment which we, the majority, have created. We cannot stand aloof from this fact. When every day, over a thousand adolescents commit crimes we cannot stand piously on the side and claim blamelessness. As the drought must accept blame.for the famine, adult citizens must recognize their responsibility for the phenomenal rise of juvenile delinquency over the past years. It may be said that we have a right to choose oblivion for ourselves—to drink away our self-respect, to lower the dignity of marriage, to personally nullify the Ten Commandments---but we have no right to deprive our children of their heritage through our own indifference.

J. Edgar Hoover, Director of our FBI, has pointed out repeatedly that the misconduct of young people is little more than the projection of our national character. "Juvenile delinquency," he has testified, "is a product of adult neglect. Without exception, acts of omission or commission by adult citizens underlie every young offender's misdeeds."

Again: "Whenever adults are indifferent to the needs of youngsters, delinquency rates will be high. Lacking the wholesome guidance which is essential to the development of good character and moral values, the child is literally set adrift to seek his own path to responsible citizenship."

And again' "While a number of factors underlie the delinquency problem confronting us, none is of greater importance than parental neglect. Far too many mothers and fathers

27

display no real interest in their children's problems, associates or activities. Consciously or unconsciously neglectful parents look upon the moral education of their children as a responsibility of the schools and the clergy."

This testimony by Mr. Hoover, the best informed expert on juvenile delinquency in the country, is irrefutable evidence of character decay. As every other sign which points to this same conclusion, whether civic, social, or moral, it comes down to a shifting of responsibility from the individual to a group or government.

The signs of decay are evident in the transcripts of testimony pertaining to Communism in education which consumed approximately one thousand pages.

They were evident at West Point Military Academy in 1951, when ninety cadets had to be dismissed for breaking their word of honor by cheating.

They are evident in every American home and building that has been disassociated with the American flag because displaying it is "old-fashioned" or too "provincial."

The signs of decay can be seen in every large business organization that has established explicit policy prohibiting executives from taking active part in political affairs. Through this foolish guise of good business procedure, intelligent businessmen who should know better help to undermine our republic by denying basic civil rights to thousands of able citizens.

The evidence of moral deterioration is a matter of public knowledge regarding labor union racketeering and political regimentation of many thousands of the labor force.

It is equally within public view wherever the "bribe" or the "pay-off" has been devolped into a respected art. Even the Internal Revenue Bureau has recognized this moral aimlessness in its rules and regulations governings income-tax deductions for business gifts!

In the fact of these signs, and hundreds of others just as evident, can we honestly claim that we are unaware of the dangerous change in American character, or that no change has occurred? Have we not thrown off many of our individual

28

responsibilities out of mere laziness and unconcern and permitted our material abundance to breed moral decay?

What of our role as self-governing citizens? One of the major grievances in the Declaration of Independence, the priceless document which established our right to self-government, was that the British government had ". . . erected a multitude of new offices, and sent hither swarms of officers to harass our people, and eat out their substance."

We could almost make the same charge today against the confiscatory system of taxation levied on the private citizen who is forced to support a monstrous, wasteful bureaucracy in Washington, D.C. Taxation was one of the major issues in 1776 because our Founders believed that every man is entitled to keep the fruits of his own labor. They believed citizens should contribute to the support of the Government, but surely they would not have allowed the government, *as is the case today,* power to tax *ninety-one* per cent of a man's personal income, and levy *fifty-two* per cent on corporate profits.

We profess our belief in the right to private property as protected by a government of, by, and for the people; and acknowledge our obligation to support the government. But it is also our responsibility to make certain that the government is not supporting us. If the government is allowed to wield arbitrary power of taxation, there must result a definite infringement upon the individual's right to private property. It must require a dangerous relaxation of each man's obligation to self-rule. Few Americans would frankly agree to arbitrary power of taxation by the federal government. And yet, in effect, that is exactly what we have done.

One of the clauses of our federal Constitution states that "No capitation or other direct tax shall be laid, unless in proportion to the census or enumeration herein before directed to be taken." It means simply that Congress can levy a direct tax only in proportion to the numbers of people within the different states, that if one American has to pay everybody has to pay, and that it must be the same for persons in every state. This clause underlies the fact that the United

29

States has always recognized fair taxation as a necessary evil, that the people must pay the cost of securing their rights. But government is a system, not a human being, and we are responsible for its upkeep, not its financial flights of fancy. This responsibility stems from our more fundamental obligation to *limit* the power of government. Prior to 1913, whenever the above clause had been abused to tax citizens unfairly, judicial action was taken and the government was put in its place. In 1894, for instance, Congress passed an income-tax law which they had no right to make, and a year later the Supreme Court found it unconstitutional. Only three decades earlier, Carl Marx had publicly announced that the power to tax was "the power to destroy," and he advocated a steeply graduated income tax as an instrument for a socialist revolution in America. But America wasn't buying any of his socialism in 1894.

However, with the adoption of the Sixteenth Amendment in 1913, we gave the federal government "the power to destroy" just as Marx had hoped we would. The Sixteenth Amendment revises the time-honored safeguard of the "power of the purse" thusly:

"The Congress shall have power to lay and collect taxes on income, from whatever source derived, without apportionment among the several states, and without regard to any census or enumeration."

In other words, we made it constitutionally legal for Congress to tax all kinds of incomes arbitrarily, and at any rate so legislated. We made it possible for the Government to rescind our right to private property.

This was done in the name of expediency. Principles are always compromised under other names than tyranny or betrayal. At the time we had reduced duties on 958 articles—so the government needed more money; there were heavy floods in the West and South—so the government needed more money; there was talk of war, trouble with Mexico—so the government needed more money. It was claimed that there was no time to sit down and think about the consequences . . . there never is, when basic principles are about to be sacrificed.

That was forty-five years ago. We have since felt the consequences on every pay-day and at the end of every tax year. We have learned that government has no set cost. Government will spend as much as it can collect and still demand more. And we, the People, who pay for this gargantuan farce, do not have the character and courage needed to re-claim our right to limit the power of government. There is another Amendment, the ninth, which says, "The enumeration in the Constitution of certain rights shall not be construed to deny or disparage others retained by the people."

That would mean, for example, that our right to direct Congress to lay and collect taxes to pay the debts and provide for the common defense and general welfare of the United States, should not be construed to deny or disparage, for example, our right to private property. And this right is further clarified by the Constitution which explicitly states that no person shall "be deprived of . . . property, without due process of law; nor shall private property be taken for public use, without just compensation."

Bureaucrats may argue that the government needs more and more of our private incomes because of its ever-increasing centralization and the hundreds of financial obligations it has today that it never had before. But the issue is not one of money. It is not just the personal income that we turn over to the government that signifies a decay of national character, it is the rights and duties and individual responsibilities that we turn over—of which confiscatory taxation is but one inevitable result.

This large-scale movement toward federal centralization is nothing less than a manifestation of civic indifference on the part of citizens. Perhaps modernization has made it easy for government to demand and get more of our private wealth, but at the bottom of the problem is the fact that we have willfully bartered our individuality and self-reliance for a false "security," for economic "protection" and free government

31

handouts. The government upkeep for which we are responsible is a paltry sum compared to the atrocious waste and even unconstitutional spending which has resulted from our political apathy.

To cite one example, as recent as twenty years ago the size of the public domain amounted to about 365,000,000 acres. None of this land had been *sold* to the government. Nevertheless, despite these millions of acres of land, within the past twenty years the government has purchased about 22,000,000 acres from private interests boosting the total value of government owned property to an unbelievable $264,000,000,000.

Where did the federal government get the money to buy this land?

In a typical fiscal year, approximately half of the governments income comes from private income, another fourth from private corporations, and the remaining fourth from various excise, employment, estate, and gift taxes, customs and miscellaneous receipts.

The answer then, is that the federal government bought 22,000,000 acres of property from private citizens and paid for it with money taken from private citizens.

And that, in a nutshell, is the essence of all transactions involving government enterprise. It can do one of two things. It can either take money out of your left hand, subtract its "expenses," and put what remains in your right hand; or it can take money out of either one of your hands, subtract its expenses, and give the remainder to someone else.

Many Americans seem to feel that they have better things to do than spend their time investigating the expenditures of government. But it is this sort of complacent resignation that allows government "bigness" to flourish and grow. Much of our income tax goes for the cost, not of government, but of government *power* and the performance of responsibilities that belong to that *power*. In effect, we are not only shifting our sovereignty from the individual to the state, but we are paying the government to take it off our hands!

We are spending billions for defense, more than half of

government income. Most of it is used to combat Communism and Communist agression, to develop nuclear weapons, and to investigate subversive activities. But how much are we spending in defense of Uncle Sam to save the American character, without which our nation will plunge into an abyss 2,000 years deep—the same abyss into which Rome fell. Who will deny that a strong, loyal American character is a better defense against foreign ideologies than armament or Congressional committees?

Fifty years ago a man named Vladimir Ulianov, who called himself Lenin, established Bolshevism with seventeen supporters. Forty years ago he conquered Russia with 40,000 supporters. Today, although he is dead, there are 900 million people living under the ideology of Communism which he preached! Is this stampeding intellectual disease something at which we can fire intercontinental missiles? In light of Communism's fantastic growth, must we not accept the fact that more is needed than a list of subversive people and organizations if we are to meet its mounting strength effectively?

While the government is spending billions of dollars to defend against Communism, our greatest weapon stands idle and it doesn't cost a dime—the powerful, positive weapon of *Truth*. There is only one way to defeat an idea and that is with a better idea; there is only one way to fight Communism and that is with *Americanism*. When Dr. Frederick Schwarz, one of the world's foremost experts on Communism, appeared before the United States Committee on Un-American Activities, he was asked by committeeman Weil: "What must be done if we are to survive?"

"We must," replied Dr. Schwarz, "build a strong base of freedom-loving people articulate in their faith, in their love of country, in their love of God, in their love of home, and in their love of law, and we must rally the spiritual forces in the heart of man and recruit dedicated personnel to raise barriers against Communism in every area of the world."

"The fundamental foundation of opposition to Communism

33

is an informed public opinion and a dedicated public character. On these alone the necessary legislative, administrative, judicial, military, and economic and education programs may be built."

Thus, once again we are brought back to the need of strong character, to the individual person and his importance in the the world scheme. We must recognize that above and beyond governmental action and spending, in the long run it will be you and I who will defeat, or succumb to, the false ideology of Communism. We cannot transfer responsibility to the federal government; we cannot, instead of fighting Comunism with personal Americanism, pay the government to fight our battle for us.

This also applies to all of our responsibilities as self-governing individuals. Bureaus are political parasites, not American citizens. A bureau cannot replace you or your sovereignty. Still, aside from the expense of national defense, the government's income is distributed roughly in this fashion: approximately seven million dollars are spent as interest for the public debt, about two percent of its total income goes for general government expenses and the rest is divided up among a number of bureaus. The premise governing the creation of bureaus is quite simple. Anytime we, the people, tire of a particular duty or responsibility—or if the government feels that it can do a better job of it—a bureau is formed to take care of the matter. Through taxation increases, we pay the bureau an amount of money, and in return it wields our governing power for us.

It is a premise which not only governs the creation of bureaucracy; it also governs the creation of statism and meaningless citizenship.

At present, the bureaucratic Frankenstein which we have created dips into almost every facet of our lives, including these general categories: welfare, social security, housing, education, research, agriculture, foreign aid, natural resources, transportation, communication, finance, commerce, industry, labor, and veteran's programs. Add to these a "catch-all" which might be called miscellaneous. A listing of all the de-

34

partments and divisions which fall under these general headings would require a book in itself.

Our attitude seems to be: Why should we bother with economic and social problems if the government is willing to? And bureaucrats themselves are quick to ask: Who knows more about these problems, government experts or the general public? Or more specifically, who is more familiar with agricultural problems, the government or the people? The answer is, of course, the *farmer*. In the past several years, for instance, six different government bureaus lent $35,000,000 to encourage increased poultry production. And a seventh bureau is spending $12,000,000 to buy surplus eggs in order to remove them from an over-supplied market!

In addition, by allowing government agencies to do our business for us, billions of dollars have been invested in surplus farm products, and millions of dollars have been invested in warehouses to store them.

This is called price stabilization.

However, at the same time huge irrigation projects are bringing thousands of acres of desert land into more cultivation, at a cost as high as $1,000 per acre.

What this may be called, defies the imagination.

Government is a notoriously inept businessman. But mismanagement of funds is not the most important issue. Such foolish bureaucratic spending is merely another external sign of our country's internal decay, a sign of something much more hazardous to our way of life. The farm program is just one small part of a crucial movement toward unlimited centralization of government power. Indeed, we must not confuse the cause with the consequence, or spending with the authorization to spend. We have given the government power to regulate vast areas of our economy. We have attempted to create wealth by taking it from one person and giving it to another. We have allowed the ICA to spawn a monster with more than 8,000 heads, and turn the fine idea of foreign aid into the laughing stock of our country. We smile when we read in the paper that our government has sent airplanes to

35

countries which have yet to master the ox-cart; or when Marshall Plan tractors rust away for years on foreign docks because they are sent at a rate faster than backward countries can absorb them.

The American of today kneels before the great god government with gifts of money, and he rejoices like an infant at feeding time then the government returns a fraction of this hard-earned money. Why? Because it is labeled "benefit" or "subsistence" or "security" or "insurance" or "social project" or "welfare" or any of a dozen other illusions by which statism will eventually abolish our powers of self-government.

Our nation was born in an atmosphere of war, and the war was fought by our forebears because they were sick and tired of having someone else "plan" their economic and political environment. We grew strong because our ancestors won individual freedom to carve out their own security, obtain their own benefits with their own hands, tools, and capital, and institute their own social program of welfare. And now we are shifting those same rights back to a central authority.

The signs of this character decay are all around us. The results are still pending. But there is one documented record of the effects of our crime against character that should arouse the common sense of every American citizen. The testimony of hundreds of American G.I.s who had lived in the prison camps of Korea bears witness to our extreme patriotic neglect. Major William E. Mayer, an Army psychiatrist who spent four years studying military brainwashing, has described the testimony of prisoners who returned. The following excerpts are from conclusions he based on detailed questioning of nearly 1,000 United States soldiers who were captured in Korea and underwent Communist brainwashing:

Q. What do you consider the basic defect revealed by the success of this Communist program on so many Americans? What's missing? What's wrong?

A. The basic defects lie in three areas:
First, in the area of character development and the development

36

within young people of an internalized system of discipline . . .

Q. What about the soldiers' knowledge of the U.S. Constitution, its guarantee of personal freedoms, and the American system in general? Did the American prisoners seem to know and understand such things?

A. Many of them didn't. Almost to a man the returnees lamented their lack of actual information, knowledge, about our democratic system . . .

Q. Do you find that soldiers seem to have less respect than you would expect for what we call patriotism?

A. Yes, I do.

Q. What seemed to be their attitude toward patriotism?

A. I think a great many people feel that references to patriotism and love of country are somewhat embarrassing, unsophisticated, or foolish flag-waving. I think this is to a very considerable degree the result of well-meaning liberals, so called, as well as others whose intentions are clearly destructive, to create the attitude that we should abandon love of country and patriotic ideals . . .

Q. Do you think what we call good old-fashioned patriotism might have bolstered some of these soldiers in their resistance during capitivity?

A. I do, although this was not an idea that I entered the study with. It was an idea that so many returnees expressed in one way or another that it was an inescapable conclusion.[1]

Here is another inescapable conclusion. Had we not abandoned our love of country and patriotic ideals long before our young men went to war, no enemy on earth could have devised an effective "brainwashing" to ensnare them. What "brainwashing" could have swayed the allegiance of men like Nathan Hale and Samuel Adams?

No matter how centralized authority may become, there will never be a Bureau of Patriotism, nor a Bureau of Self-respect, Human Dignity, or Moral Law.

Much has been said of the demoralizing effect of an unnecessarily huge and unwieldy bureaucracy. Its encroachment on areas traditionally reserved for the free exercise of the free will of a free people are unfortunately far too numerous. Yet it would be folly to deny that much of the will of the people as expressed at the polls and through their duly elected representatives can be implemented only by the creation of bureaus to carry out the provisions of legislative acts. From the day Washington appointed a cabinet to advise him in his executive functions, a bureaucracy was created. What causes deep concern to those who would hold fast to their freedom from an all-devouring paternalism is the extension of government by agencies into areas where only public lethargy and unconcern permit them to operate.

The only way in which we, the people, can stem this tide of power usurpation is for us to shake off our lazy "Let George do it" attitude and address ourselves to an active and earnest participation in the matter of self rule. If we have abdicated our sovereign powers, we must reassume them by rising out of our slothful indifference and by letting our voices be heard so loudly and so clearly that those who seek only to fatten themselves at the public trough will tremble and waddle away to long-deserved oblivion.

Bureaucracy fattens on its own regenerative powers. More begets more. And the more we delude ourselves into believing that we can ever get something for nothing, the more our bureaucratic buddhas will smile complacently and gather yet more of our sovereign power into their engulfing arms.

To compromise ideas and methods is Democracy, but to compromise principles is nothing short of destruction. The omens of this destruction are everywhere in sight. Can we deny our guilt? Could any man of American conscience?

CHAPTER 3

THE APPEAL

Citizens, Govern Yourself

✿✿

If you would be revenged of your enemy, govern yourself.

BENJAMIN FRANKLIN

✿✿

IN THE PRECEDING CHAPTER it was shown that America is in dire peril due to the internal decay caused by individual irresponsibility. In writing of such crucial facts, one can force a hesitant pen to accept the unpleasant demands of objectivity, yet it is wholly impossible to fling harsh accusations at one's countrymen without later adding a word about the necessity for doing so. It seems necessary to avow that discreet ambiguities or delicate euphemisms will not save our Republic, that there is no longer time for subtle hints about the impending disaster. There is a need for action, not meditation. It is true that what has elsewhere been described as the "dust of indifference gathered on a golden page of history," has here been stripped of its rhetorical charm and openly called decay, like green mold on stale bread. It is true that the guilt which has elsewhere been attributed to parties and programs and problems and patterns has here been assigned to people—to yourself and myself.

Yet the documentation of these sober facts is offered to corroborate an appeal, not a condemnation. And this appeal, this unvarnished plea, aspires to lower no man's eyes, but rather to open as many as possible. It aspires to fulfill an unbounded faith in every American's inherent capacity for self-government.

Many years ago, at a dinner commemorating his feats against Tripoli, one of our early naval heroes was called upon to propose a toast. With great sincerity he expressed this memorable thought: "Our Country! May she always be in the right, but our country, right or wrong!"

It would be convenient to apply that glowing sentiment to America's people; to salve the sting of truth by proclaiming in gladsome terms, "The people, right or wrong!" But no man has the right to alter God's law in such a fashion. We have no more right to express this sentiment than to proclaim, "The people, free or enslaved!"

* * *

There is a question that has not been asked for a long, long time. For what does America stand? It seems that we are much more interested in analyzing what the Soviet Union stands for. The word *Communism* appears in newsprint in the United States millions of times each day. Our elected representatives give frequent and impassioned speeches about it. The heads of American and Russian government pay neighborly calls on each other. Our scholars write books which vehemently condemn the opposing ideology. Our clergymen attack Communism from the pulpit and our entertainers satirize it on the stage. Undoubtedly, the average American has considerable knowledge of what that word is all about, which is as it should be.

But—Mr. President, members of Congress, distinguished editors, authors, reverend ministers, priests and rabbis, free and prosperous citizens: anti-Communists each and all—who among you will define AMERICANISM as clearly and as fluently as you do Communism?

What of our own "ism"? How often is it found in an American newspaper, or ennobled by an American speaker? To what radio station does one turn the dial for an "up to the minute" news broadcast about Americanism? We have turned Communism into a household word—but at what dinner table in America will you find Americans discussing Americanism? Can it be that our greatness was founded on a list of negative beliefs. Or has it resulted from combining a free-dom-loving people with a particular Declaration of Independ-ence, a special Constitution, and a specific Bill of Rights?

Do we say it all, when we speak of democracy, or when we speak of free enterprise, or individual liberty, or human dig-nity—or are all of these beliefs, and more, part of a broader concept which can only be called *Americanism?* And if this is true, is there not somewhere within our fifty states one friend of Liberty among us who will rise before his countrymen, and give to Americanism, the same sort of positive significance that Lenin gave to Communism?

There are other questions that we must ask ourselves, and that we ourselves must answer. How can we permit the same American dictionary that describes Communism as "a theory that all individual ownership should be abolished," to define Americanism as a "peculiarity of pronunciation"? How can we possibly afford to entertain, with this kind of self-mockery, those who would enslave the world?

Instead of Communists, why are the Russians not known as anti-Americanists at this moment in history? Why, instead of *anti-Communists*, are we not known as Americanists? Why have these two words rarely, if ever, appeared in print with similar connotations?

Have we nothing to offer?

In the world today there are literally millions of intelligent human beings who are dedicated to the task of turning our children into slaves of Communism! This is not an opinion, or a guess; it is a cold fact. Millions of intelligent Americans must see to it that the Communists fail. In attempting to bring the American crisis to the fore, thus far little has been said on behalf of our youngsters. This was no oversight, however. The tremendous responsibility of educating our school children, of endowing them with a clear understanding of their Amer-ican heritage, is much too overwhelming to treat parsimoni-ously. This area of citizenship education constitutes a glaring omission within our public school system, a misfeasance—dis-

41

graceful and inexcusable—that can be traced directly to the decay of American character.

With the shadow of world Communism now extended into all parts of the globe, American youth are entitled to a definitive course in Americanism. Had such a course, the cultivation of birthright, been given to the past several generations of Americans, we would not now be faced with a head-long rush toward totalitarianism. We dare not withhold this training from the citizens of tomorrow. The flame of Liberty's torch has burned too low.

Americanism is not new. As a subject for young children, it has traditionally been composed of American history, taught thoroughly and meaningfully to develop the qualities of citizenship and patriotism they will need to govern themselves in adult life. Americanism belongs in every American classroom as a course that will introduce our sons and daughters to their special heritage. It is as fundamental and necessary as the proverbial "three R's."

A program of Americanism exists nowhere in American schools today.

That bears repeating: In the United States our system of education does not contain a single course in Americanism. Mark this comparison! In the Soviet empire, Communism *IS* their system of education.

While Russia's system of indoctrination and brainwashing is to be condemned at once, the utter indifference of private American citizens toward our educational defiiciencies in Americanism is just as culpable. Add to this educational shortcoming an even greater enemy—our own adult ignorance of genuine Americanism— and it becomes clear that every educator and every parent must recognize that until such a course is taken into our public school curriculum, there is little hope for the survival of the United States as a free nation.*

*The need for a program of Americanism in our schools is so essential, and opposition by "one-worldites," "international reformists," and "socialist" elements to such a program so astoundingly intense, that PART II of this book is wholly concerned with the destiny of American youth. Our generation has made the American dream insecure for our children. They must redeem what we elders have failed to preserve. The least we can do is prepare them for the task.

42

It can be said that two groups of citizens—the youth and the adults—will decide whether or not we shall succeed in re-establishing the system of government and way of life devised by the founders of the American Republic. Our young people must be specifically educated to take their place in America's representative system, and to pass their heritage on to future generations. This "must" will never be realized, however until adults reclaim the rights and duties they have relegated to "committees" and "departments" at almost every level of government. Adults must first take a stand, and with confidence once more proclaim that the supreme law is the weal of people. And they must admit to themselves that the weal of people rests on one paramount system of behavior: Citizenship.

Let's be very candid, very honest with ourselves. Citizenship —that is to say, the care and maintenance of individual liberty—has lain dormant for so long that the idea behind it may appear startling even to those of us who profess to embrace it. The idea is simply this:

Freedom is not free.

Freedom is a product of responsible individuals and is secured only through wise self-government. Today, there are persons who would quickly voice their disagreement with such an idea, many who believe that freedom is a gift of God. This latter idea is more pleasant; something dependent upon one's own responsibility toward it, is seldom as appealing as "something for nothing." It is a simple matter to claim that freedom is a right rather than a responsibility. It is easy to disregard the obvious difference between our God-given right to freedom and freedom itself. And yet we know better. We know that such things as freedom, wealth and virtue are not Providential bequests, but goals for which we must strive. We know that every American baby is not born with a bank account, but with in *inalienable right* to try to acquire one. We know that the first ten amendments to the Constitution are a Bill of Rights, not a Bill of "Goods." There is a growing tendency to regard it as such.

43

Citizenship is an individual job; it is the personal, practical work which stems from our personal rights. It is so important that its only alternative is enslavement. Nevertheless, it is hardly necessary to point out the status of citizenship in contemporary America. We have watched the pendulum of government power swing from the individual to the state. We have witnessed politics turn into personality contests. We have even allowed ourselves to be re-named. Americans are no longer citizens, they are "consumers." The American is no longer judged by his achievements as a man, he is judged by the amount of material wealth he has been able to acquire. A sort of hysterical aura of materialistic sophistication has spread across the United States. Money seems to veil the face of America twenty-four hours a day, hiding her great beauty, preventing her from seeing where she is going, or why. The death rattle of a nation is drowned out by the jangle of cash registers. Few people have time for citizenship anymore. Few people really remember what it is all about.

Ask an atomic-age American about the latest trends in automobiles and he will give you a half-hour dissertation on design. Ask him what the current "cost-of-living scale" is and he will tell you within a fraction of the penny. But ask him what the current disposition of citizenship is and he will more than likely shrug his shoulders, smile indulgently, and reply, "Okay, I'll bite; what's the punch-line?"

And shamefully enough, we must admit that this facetious reply would be all too apropos. Citizenship is a tragic joke—, complete with a punch-line: The country with the greatest civil gospel ever preached has somehow spawned a society of civic agnostics!

When will we face up to this issue? When will we quit rationalizing and theorizing, and sidestepping the problem with the usual surface treatments? When will we really go at this materialistic rejection of citizenship and see if something cannot be done? Somewhere along the line we acquired the notion that self-government is not essential. Today, we have decided that it is impossible. Yet, in our hearts, we know that this attitude is wrong. Every great leader we have ever had expressly stated the important role of individual citizens in a republic.

Benjamin Franklin said it in two words: "Govern yourself."

John Marshall, the great champion of constitutional law, put it in the most lucid terms possible: "The government of the Union is emphatically and truly a government of the people. In form and in substance it emanates from them. Its powers are granted by them and are to be exercised directly on them and for their benefit."

Still we refuse to believe that in our roles as citizens we are capable of anything constructive. We reject the advice of great men like Marshall and accept instead the hopeless rationalization that we are defenseless creatures who "can't fight city hall." Is there any quicker way of losing interest in something than by deciding that it cannot be done, or that any attempt at it will be a waste of time? This is precisely the attitude we have developed toward self-government. As soon as we surrendered to the idea that it was impossible, we began to lose interest in citizenship. We broke faith with America.

When a person loses interest in something, in this case citizenship, he ceases to acquire knowledge about it. He ceases to participate in it. He denounces his loyalty toward it. Eventually he becomes so divorced from it that it is completely meaningless for him. Ironically, most of us sincerely maintain that we think citizenship is important. It is difficult to conceive of any American who would not endorse this claim. But, important, why? Important, for whom? In what way? To what extent? When we attempt to back up our easily made claim, we begin to realize how hollow it is.

According to modern standards, and new "pragmatic" values, citizenship is outmoded. We have what is today considered an air-tight argument against it: It's boring. It's funereal. It's vague, thankless, futile. This is so because citizenship cannot be bought or sold, it is not union-made, it contains no offices or bureaus with titles or ranks. It offer no salaries or fringe benefits. It isn't even deductible. We simply have no time or room for it in our complex, specialized and autonomous social system.

No, we have never actually applied those evasive qualifications to the practice of citizenship, but only because we have never bothered to compare it with the new "values" and material standards that we *do* feel are important. This "something-for-nothing" philosophy, however, has become our chief means of measuring worth and there is little doubt that it underlies our negation of civic responsibility. We have changed a lot since the days when citizenship was worth more than a dollar contribution "to the party of your choice."

We have lost that American *Indefinable*.

America no longer casts her magic spell.

She doesn't reach into hearts.

She doesn't inspire.

She doesn't sing anymore. When we turned our backs on her she lost her voice. Yes, America used to sing a song for her people; for the dairy farmer up in Wisconsin and the stock broker in New York; for the housewife down in New Mexico and the mechanic in Arkansas; for all of us, the rich, the poor, the weak, the strong; she reached into our hearts and put something special there. She sang to people of every class, color and creed her proud song of precious rights, of human dignity and equal opportunity. She sang to men of varying talents her beautiful song of the common ground shared by the greatest and the least of them as citizens of her sovereign republic. She sang the law of the land.

The people of America were just like people everywhere in the world except for that proud little tune that stirred in their hearts. But that was all it took. The spirit of America singing came whispering through all the fields where the corn was high, and all the fields where the corn had failed. It dodged among all the skyscrapers of all the big cities, and it hummed among the jam-packed tenements on all the wrong sides of all the railroad tracks. And it gave the people something—call it strength of character—that made them feel ten feet tall, that made the rest of the world gasp with awe and

46

turn green with envy. We prized our citizenship, and guarded it jealously. A glimpse at Old Glory would instantly spark patriotic devotion and love for our land in the young and old.

Somehow, we've lost it . . . the magic knack of being an American.

Now we need it, now as never before we, who turned our backs on America to give the Twentieth century a run for its money, need that precious *Indefinable*. But can we regain it? Can we even slow down enough to put citizenship back in its true perspective? There is only one honest answer: *We can try*. We can surely try! America has a crisis on her hands. Her whole wonderful way of life is at stake. If we can prevent the Fall of America by giving the attributes of free people free rein? Then it's surely worth a try.

Perhaps if we turn around and face America, look directly at her, take an interest in her—perhaps we'll hear her song again. Maybe America will once again reach into our hearts, as she did in the past, and put something special there. A grain of liberty, a tiny draught of her lyrical air—something American—that can square a man's shoulders and lift his eyes to distant hills and horizons. Something American, that will inspire each one of us to speak out and be heard, to rise and take part, in this fearful time of our lives. Perhaps America will sing her song, and we Americans will once again declare our independence, this time from a pseudo-philanthropic government that gives us money instead of justice and protection. We Americans will once again labor eagerly for what we want, and experience the pride of accomplishment and feel a security that no amount of centralized social insurance can supply. We shall owe no debt of gratitude to bureaucrats; but each of us will take up his responsibilities and rule. And then the government will do something it hasn't done for many, many years. The government will obey.

Good citizenship is not only a duty, it is a high trust and a rewarding privilege. And those Americans who accept it as a fundamental part of their personal scheme of life will find a great advantage in their favor; for the fathers of our country were men of keen vision. In the early years, when the song of America was in every man's heart, they had the foresight to set it down on paper, or at least as much of it as was possible to set down on paper. (Part of America's song will never appear in print, because part of it was sung in a language that no man can translate. Part of her song is earth and rock and oxygen. Another part is a raw-boned farm kid who became a mechanic, worked sixteen hours a day, and eventually turned the plain name of Ford into something legendary. Another part was a boy named Lincoln, great not because he was born in a log cabin, but because he got out of it—because he rose above poverty, ignorance, lack of ambition, shiftlessness of character, contentment with mean and low aims—and became a man immortal. Another part was buried in a tomb at Arlington . . .) Yes, part of America's song is etched in nature and part of it is scrawled on the back of a piece of time—but the greatest refrain of all was written down and passed along with our heritage.

These are the lyrics of Liberty: The Declaration of Independence, The Constitution, The Bill of Rights. Here are the magic, immortal words that can transform a possible slave into a private prince; that can turn a nobody into the biggest somebody in the world. Within these philosophical masterpieces lies the greatness of our past and the hope of our future, the rules and regulations of human happiness. They rest there like a vein of raw gold waiting for the people of this nation, each man together with his family, to turn them into riches, to read and study them, to understand and cherish them, to live by them. When that day comes it will mark the beginning of our return to true freedom and true greatness.

Every blessing that we enjoy today—every home in America, every job, all of the places that exist for our needs and comforts, the places where we go to buy our food, to get well, to laugh to forget, to kneel and worship, every necessity and every luxury—can be traced back to the inspired document which begins with these historic words:

When in the course of human events it becomes necessary for one

48

people to dissolve the political bands which have connected them with another, and to assume among the powers of the earth the separate and equal station to which the laws of nature and of nature's God entitle them, a decent respect to the opinions of mankind requires that they should declare the causes which impel them to the separation.

Thus did Thomas Jefferson begin his invaluable message to you and me, the Declaration of Independence which was read and adopted July Fourth, 1776, by the Representatives of the United States of America in General Congress Assembled. What do these opening words mean? They mean something almost unbelievable. They mean that in the space of a few moments a handful of mortals created a nation where just moments before no nation had existed. Those few words mark a pause in the course of human events, during which time a few British colonies ceased to exist, and in their place was born the most fabulous country the world has ever known.

Men created a nation by mutual consent and declared that human beings are born, live, and die free. It was a nation created by them and for them, not they for the nation. The shaping of America was not an accident. This new republic was *designed* to become great, for the men of '76 were not just declaring their independence from the British Crown; they were declaring their, and our, independence from all forms of despotism and tyranny.

Here is the rock upon which America was built:

We hold these truths to be self-evident: that all men are created equal; that they are endowed by their creator with certain inalienable rights; that among these are life, liberty, and persuit of happiness; that to secure these rights, governments are instituted among men, deriving their just powers from the consent of the governed; that whenever any form of government becomes destructive of these ends, it is the right of the people to alter or abolish it, and to institute new government, laying its foundation on such principles, and organizing its powers in such form, as to them shall seem most likely to effect their safety and happiness.

Here is a living statement of rights and principles, which

49

had been in man ... in his heart and mind ... for centuries, but which had never before appeared in a system of government. Here are the timeless truths for which each generation of Americans has been held responsible right down to the present. And now it is our turn. We are the sole heirs to the truths and to the responsibility that goes with them. The responsibility involved here is a personal, individual and daily thing, a matter of character. External hazards have nothing to do with it. Hazards like Wilhelm, Hitler and Khrushchev are sporadic emergencies that become our responsibility whenever they arise. But the hazard of Government, the ever-present task of preserving our human rights and political principles, this is the eternal duty of Americans, the challenge that turned subjects into citizens.

The Declaration of Independence was a revolutionary document. It was revolutionary because it abolished one form of government and created an entirely new order, a new view of mankind, a new concept of human goals. The Declaration restored the chain of power that God Himself had established: first God; second, the people; and third, government. The Declaration recognized the inherent totalitarianism of government based on any other hierarchy of power, be it monarchy or Communism, and declared that the people derive their power from God alone, that government is responsible to the people and the people subject only to the laws they make through it.

The American Revolution was like no other before or since. It did not shift the ruling power from a king or dictator to the state, or from the state to an absolute ruler. It had nothing in common with the French Revolution which was based on a Declaration of Rights proclaiming: "the origin of all sovereignty resides essentially in the nation." Our Declaration maintained, rather, that nations are created by men and therefore all sovereignty rests in the individual, not in the nation he creates. The Founding Fathers knew that the state as sovereign can deprive men of their rights at will. They had trusted the long accepted claims of authoritarian government

50

to act in the name of "the common good," and they had felt the despotic effect of such claims. They decided that the new American republic would be governed as far as possible by the private initiative of free individuals. They affirmed that liberty and equality must never be leased to man-made institutions, and that without them life has no human dignity. They declared that war with liberty and equality is better than peace without these precious rights.

Freedom, liberty, equality—these rare flowers of wisdom and fellowship have passed through millions of American hands, unscathed, intact, ready to pass through millions more in the years ahead. God gave every man the right to these blessings. But the blessings themselves are moved by the hand of man; they are sacred duties passed from father to son. We were each born with the inalienable right to life, liberty, and the pursuit of happiness—but so were the 500,000,000 slaves in Red China. The rare flower of freedom that we now hold in our hands grew out of our Delaration of Independence, and it represents the sweat and blood and vigilance expended during the past 184 years by our ancestors. It is ours now, to hold, that we might inhale its fine, intoxicating aroma; but only for a moment, a lifetime, before we pass it on to the patient hand of posterity. This is the tremendous responsbility that has come down to us with our heritage. This is what Tom Jefferson intended us to understand when he wrote of the equality of each man and his God-given right to life, liberty and the pursuit of happiness.

God created no kings or courtiers, no kaisers or fuehrers. But He knew that among men there will always be some who attempt to oppress others. He created each man with certain rights to use against all forms of violence, and against one form in particular—government. Indeed, violence, or force, is the principle on which all governments necessarily operate. But, though man finds it necessary to restrain government through the use of his fundamental rights, he also finds that government is the only means by which he can secure his rights! This universal paradox of human nature was the stag-

51

gering problem which confronted the Founders of America. It was this paradox that inspired them to devise a "government of the people," whereby each man's individual rights remained more powerful than the principle of force by which he consented to be governed. The limitations of the unique principle of force which these first citizens consented to were later promulgated as our Constitution. The extent of power inherent in each individual's rights was added as a Bill of Rights. And this unprecedented approach to government, this whole complex business designed to keep the fragile flower of freedom passing safely from hand to hand, became known to the world as the Republic of the United States of America.

This was the vision of Jefferson and his brilliant countrymen as they listed the repeated injuries and usurpations suffered under King George III. It was this vision of individual human beings, of themselves and of you and me, as the most important entities on the planet Earth, that gave us a glimpse of the genius, the breathtaking drama, the timeless significance, contained in our Declaration of Independence. It was this splendid vision of a great sovereign republic, membered by free and independent citizens, that will forever moisten the eye of the patriot who reads about it—and which once moved a people to openly declare:

. . . That these united colonies are, and of right ought to be free and independent states; that they are absolved from all allegiance to the British crown, and that all political connection between them and the state of Great Britain is, and ought to be, totally disolved, and that as free and independent states, they have full power to levy war, conclude peace, contract alliances, establish commerce, and do all other acts and things which independent states may of right do.

To this declaration was added a final, ringing phrase, the disclosure of a "secret weapon" by which a handful of brave people hoped to withstand the wrath of England's mighty empire:

And for the support of this declaration, with a firm reliance on the protection of divine providence we mutually pledge to each other our lives, our fortunes, and our sacred honor.

Thus did America sing her song, while Thomas Jefferson set this first great stanza to paper. How right Lincoln was when he wrote eighty years later, "All honor to Jefferson—the man who, in concrete pressure of a struggle for national independence by a single people, had the coolness, forecast, and capacity to introduce into a merely revolutionary document, an abstract truth, applicable to all men and all times, and so to embalm it there, that today, and in all coming days it shall be a rebuke and a stumbling-block to the very harbingers of reappearing tyranny and oppression."

The republic that the Declaration of Independence made possible in 1776, was made a reality shortly thereafter by the Constitution of the United States. This great document resulted from the wisdom amassed through all previous attempts of men to combine freedom with government. Fifty-five state delegates—among them James Madison who is rightfully called "the Father of Our Constitution"—composed the most superb, written foundation of government known to man.

If there is a secret of success embodied in our Constitution, if there is one key phrase that makes the whole idea workable, it is to be found at the very beginning of the Preamble: "We, the People . . ."

Before a single word of law had been written, the authors named the only authority and source of power for all that was to follow. Instead of setting up a living dictator, the people dictated a living document and declared it to be the supreme law of the land. They delegated a limited amount of their power to a Federal Government, and kept the rest. And, just to make sure, they disseminated this limited power among three separate branches, the executive, legislative, and judicial. To be doubly sure, they instituted a system whereby any two of these branches could check the power of the third.

In other words, the strongest single governing power legally wielded in Washington today, is a double-checked third of a fraction of the power which resides in the people!

53

The only possible way in which the federal government can acquire more power than "We, the People," gave it, is by usurping more power from us. To do this requires either decadence on the part of the people, or a reaching beyond constitutional limits by the government. Once the government violates the law of the land there is only one power great enough to curb its advance toward despotism. That power is the people. Plainly enough, the people are responsible for the federal government. What happens when this responsibility is ignored has already been seen. According to the Hoover report, to cite one more instance, we have allowed much of our power to shift toward the political power plant in Washington. The committee found inefficiency and waste to the tune of billions of tax-payers' dollars, rampant bureaucracy, infringement of American liberties, and widespread competition by government with private enterprise.

The framers of our Constitution would certainly gasp with horror if they were alive to witness the "unwritten" amendments that the federal government has added to their republican thesis. Members of Congress, said Benjamin Franklin, "are of the People, and return again to mix with the People, having no more durable pre-eminence than the different grains of sand in an hourglass. Such an assembly cannot easily become dangerous to Liberty. They are the servants of the People, sent together to do the People's business, and promote the public welfare." But it surely never occured to Franklin that the people might let these servants become masters. In 1787, public servants were committed to the people, not to welfare legislation. Farm subsidies, unemployment compensation to five million people, public housing projects were not being offered in wholesale fashion. The public servants were not spending 12 to 15 billion dollars more than their annual revenue. There were no billion-dollar programs to lull the people into political lethargy. To an extent Franklin would never have conceived possible, centralization and bureaucracy have reached a point where a distinguished panel of economists recently offered this cure for inflation: take five million cars

54

and plow them under like we did pigs during the post-depression days! They were dead serious.

The question arises: how, under a Constitution which has served us so adequately for so many years, can the federal government suddenly riddle it with loop-holes and weaken it with absurd interpretations? The answer is fundamental to our freedom. We have lost sight of what it is that our Constitution constitutes. It constitutes a means —an unsurpassed means— through which people proceed to govern themselves. The officials in Washington exist simply because they make self-government a little more convenient—simply because 180 million of us cannot all squeeze into the white house at the same time.

Their power is picayune compared to ours because it issues from ours. There is not one elected or appointed official at any level of government anywhere in the United States who would dare disobey our command. But we have been so busy lately, listening to commands that are disguised as promises or benefits, we haven't bothered to give any of our own for quite some time. We no longer back up the Constitution with our hire-and-fire power of the ballot, or our tremendous power of public opinion. We do not utilize our Bill of Rights and we do not comply with our Bill of Duties. Every inalienable right has a corresponding duty, if for no other reason than the responsibility of citizens to exercise their rights.

Americanism is based on fundamental rights superior to any federal authority, superior, in fact, to our own self-governing power. These rights are recognized in our Constitution as inalienable: free speech; a free press; freedom to worship unmolested; freedom to assemble; the right to dissent; the right to petition against grievances; the right to trial by one's peers; and the right of sovereignty as a people of a republican form of government which can exercise only such powers as are delegated to it by the people.

Our first duty as citizens is to maintain our rights and use them to sustain our form of government and way of life.

We are duty-bound to work and fight for the right of each

55

individual to worship God in his own way, and to recognize and venerate the moral values that underscore our natural rights.

It is our civic duty to guard, and rise in defense of, our own and our neighbors' rights. We must answer with outspoken criticism, every attempt by a local or federal government to infringe upon our rights. And we must allow any countryman to say what he thinks is right via any medium of communication, even though his views may contradict our own.

As citizens of a country in which freedom of the press is vital to good government, we must rise against any unconstitutional measures of censorship, and at the same time respect our self-imposed restrictions of decency and morality. With the right of a free press goes one of the most important responsibilities of citizenship, *that of being well informed.* No man can govern himself properly unless he is fully aware of the current political issues; unless he knows what his representatives are up to at home and abroad, and whether their policies are good or bad.

This intelligent exercise of citizenship is not a simple thing to carry out in practice. The principles of government laid down at our country's founding are as valid today as they ever were. But their perpetuation in a nation which has undergone radical changes in composition since its birth requires perceptive recognition of what has taken place.

What began as a relatively simple agrarian community has grown into one of extreme complexity. Where once those who tilled the soil were ten times as numerous as those who dealt in commerce and trade, today this ratio has far more than reversed itself. The industrial revolution tore apart the fabric of the society known to our forefathers.

The very achievement of our great industrial development necessarily brought about numerous adjustments in the social order and in our economic pattern. The rights of management and labor, which previously had required comparatively little delineation, became matters of primary concern. Laws for the regulation of the new industrial colossus had little precedent

56

on which to draw. So they often took forms which the founding fathers could hardly have anticipated. And yet, almost incomprehensibly, the Constitution was found to contain all the principles by which our social order can guide its way. Clearly there are timeless values in the principles on which our nation is based and in the Bill of Rights which guarantees a full life and a free one, now and in the future.

Today, every citizen must decide for himself whether he wants to live in a welfare state or a republic based on free enterprise in a private and competitive economy. Each citizen must decide which political candidates will best represent the system of government established by our forebears, and then do everything within his civic power to see that they are elected. He must ferret out at the election poll, every professional bureaucrat and would-be-autocrat seeking election or re-election.

It is a fallacy born of defeatism to assert pessimistically that the individual citizen is impotent to make his will felt in the complex political structure of today's society. One need only recall the crushing blow delivered.

A solitary newspaper editor, battling against one of the most powerfully entrenched city machines in our political history, singly aroused a dormant public by his relentless and unceasing exposure of corruption that the seemingly impregnable combination of evil forces came down in ruin. Justice was swift and terrible when a handful of aroused citizens decided to make its voice heard.

The almost unbelievable collapse of apparently impregnable political dynasties in countless communities gives testimony to the truth that we, the people, still rule the land—if we choose to exercise our power. It does not always require a politically expert crusader to bring an end to government misrule. It was a ground swell of public revulsion that toppled Jim Curley and Boss Crump from their arrogant and cynical citadels. And Teapot Dome proved to a somewhat skeptical people that not even public servants in our highest government places are immune to searching inquiry and deserved condemnation for betraying a sacred trust inherent in each and every public office.

In every community there are voices to be heard, calling out against those who misuse the people's power and betray their trust. If, too often, these intrepid champions of clean and honest government go unheard, it is we the people who have failed in not heeding their warnings or by denying them our support.

Every American has the sacred duty to remind himself periodically of the price that was paid for his freedom, of the traditional way of life that has preserved his freedom, and of his own important role in perpetuating that way of life.

Each of us ought to remember the closing words of Benjamin Franklin after the signing of the Constitution. On that memorable afternoon one of the great Citizens of America rose slowly to his feet, and pointed to a gilded half-sun carved on the high back of George Washington's chair.

"I have," said Franklin, "often and often in the course of this session, and the vicissitudes of my hopes and fears as to its issue, looked at that . . . without being able to tell whether it was rising or settling; but now at length I have the happiness to know that it is a rising and not a setting sun."

There is only one way by which we can keep that sun from setting, and that is an active understanding of what made it rise.

CHAPTER 4

THE DECISION

A Rebirth of Patriotism

❀❀❀

*Love of country is not an image of sentimental imagination.
It is as real, it is as vibrant, it is as sacred, as life itself.*

HON. SOL BLOOM

❀❀❀

AMERICA IS NEITHER A BEGINNING NOR AN END. She is a dedication to betterment, the promise of past deeds, the heritage of posterity. America is purpose, a never-endingg ideal. Americans may depart, but America remains constant—This hallmark of freedom is our legacy and responsibility—yours and mine.

The brilliant French political writer, Alexis de Tocqueville, visited America and wrote at great length about the people he came to know so well. Among other things, he said:

"I sought for the greatness and genius of America in her commodious harbors and her ample rivers, and it was not there; in her fertile fields and boundless prairies, and it was not there. Not until I went to the churches of America and heard her pulpits aflame with righteousness did I understand the secret of her genius and power. America is great because she is good, and if America ceases to be good, America will cease to be great."

The secret of our genius and power is simple goodness. Can we hold the good of material advance in our stream-lined age and avoid the bad? If the American dream is to remain our goal, we must lift our communal, spiritual and intellectual lives above the level of our material abundance. This task be-

59

longs solely to the people. Unless the individual citizen accepts the responsbilities of freedom, he will lose his heritage and its blessings for himself and his children.

This, then, is truly "D-Day" in the life of every American who believes in the principles of our way of life.

Once again our mighty Union is met on a great battlefield to test whether or not a "nation so conceived and so dedicated, can long endure"—and to decide, in this latter half of the 20th century, whether or not a "government of the people by the people, for the people, shall . . . perish from the earth." What will it be? Shall we take up the duties of individual sovereignty, or shall we continue to stand idly by and watch the lofty pillars of this republic come crashing down upon us?

On the face of things, it would seem that the answer is perfectly obvious; it would seem that America will surely reclaim her national character rather than chance the consequences of statism. Unfortunately, the obvious and the actual are not always the same. As history has so often proved, men are inclined to "rearrange" realities when they become overly troublesome or inconvenient. The dying words of republics are: "It can't happen here!" This is so because there is an innate human tendency to measure peril within the limited confines of one's own experience. Motivation controls behavior, be it good or bad, and the strongest motives we possess invariably lie within the realm of first-hand experience. The fear of starving to death, for example, may serve in some measure as a motive for eating, but the familiar experience of periodic hunger is the chief reason why we sit down to the table. In the same way, it is possible that a fear of authoritarian regimentation, or some similar drastic form of governmental "starvation" unknown to a free people, is too remote as a motivational force to meet the challenge at hand.

What then are we to conclude? Do we lack the basic experience or emotional stimulus necessary to recover the ground we have lost? Much is expected of us in this time of crisis. The preservation of our heritage demands that we alter the very atmosphere of modern America. We are obliged to par-

60

ticipate in the government of an almost recondite world power. We are to re-assert our right to equality under God and the law, reform the national character, curtail the centralization of our federal "Frankenstein." We are expected to exert a very *real* amount of effort to retrace our steps and right every wrong. Might not the motive of selfishness, or laziness, cancel out the motive of fear of despotism, and leave us resigned to our national inertia—leave us indifferent to our very indifference? As we veer closer and closer to self-destruction, the danger lies in the fact that it most assuredly might!

But Americans need never act out of fear of self-destruction or hatred of tyranny alone. We have a far better motive—the only motive within our nation's common experience that is strong enough to overcome love of self—and that is love of country. Survival, *life itself*, is one of the most powerful forces within man, and yet the history of America is filled with moving accounts of men who laid down their lives for their country. These acts of supreme heroism were inspired by deep love of America. Mindful of this, we cannot help but realize the importance of patriotism as an incentive for our fight against internal decay and external ideology.

Love and hate are the most powerful forces in the world. Communism is based on hatred, such intense hatred that it has become a monstrous power in the world. But it is not our nature to hate. America's power is derived from love, love of liberty, equality, personal freedom. It is this great passion, a good stronger than the most evil of hatreds, that must inspire us to zealously and unselfishly defend our heritage—that must motivate you and me to stand up and face the American crisis. Anything less will fall disastrously short of the mark.

No book, this nor any other, can fan the fire of American devotion unless the spark of love is already in your heart. No matter how many facts or statistics are cited, they are of no value and have no meaning other than that which you give to them. Pages of print are not the answer. They were not the answer on that fateful night of April the eighteenth when Will Dawes and Paul Revere sped toward Lexington to warn that the British were marching on Concord. Will Dawes did not stop to hand out copies of the Coercive Acts. Paul Revere did not stop to name each man in Pitcairn's regiment. They warned the people of an American crisis, and thereafter everything was up to the people.

The problem is not as complex or devious as it may seem. It is, in fact, a problem that can be met with a simple *yes* or *no*. There was nothing that called for a cold, theoretical analysis in the reaction to Paul Revere's legendary ride. The minutemen of Massachusetts had two choices: they could stay home and do nothing, or they could answer the call to arms. Our position is just as clear. We can assume the virtues and actions of a patriot, or we can continue on our haphazard flight from responsibility. *Yes*, it was *patriotism*, not fear of the British, that turned those early Americans into a selfless army of "embattled farmers." And it is patriotism not fear, not facts or figures, that will motivate a return to the traditional American way.

Let's not beat around the bush: patriotism is dormant in America. In the past it was one of America's most sterling qualities. Today it is scorned. Semantics has played cruel havoc with the meaning of American patriotism. In some quarters it has been appropriated as a by-word by persons who are actually opposed to its original meaning, just as the Communists have attempted to re-define democracy and appropriate it as a name for their system of enslavement. Others are under the impression that patriotism is identical with nationalism. This belief is wrong, even in the non-corrupted sense of these two words. When nationalism meant a consciousness of, and pride in, the individual character and spirit of a people as it was felt by the people themselves, it was still only a part of patriotism. (To reveal the incongruity of this belief as it now stands, we need only note that that a single dictionary finds it possible to include among its definitions of *nationalism*, two completely antithetical views of the word, namely: "zealous patriotism" and "a socialistic movement advocating the nationalizingg of industries." The word has

62

been so abused that we end up with the implication that a zealous patriot is one who advocates socialism!)

Still others—ranging from those who look to the United Nations for a solution to all of our problems through a "super" government, to the self-appointed apostles of "one-worldism"—have twisted patriotism to suit their requirements, absurdly denouncing it as narrow isolationism. This fallacious smearing is exposed, of course, by every American grave on foreign soil, from the Anzio beach to the hills of Korea.

Perhaps the worst misconception of all, and the most wide-spread, is entertained by those who look upon patriotism as "old-fashioned" or "foolish flag-waving." This idea is partly the outcome of our new mundane character, and partly due to the debunking pseudo-concepts of patriotism bantered about today. In general, we either ignore patriotism or regard it as part of the past.

And yet, to save our nation from internal destruction we must be motivated by this same love of country that is now held meaningless. It seems, therefore, that if we are to initiate a rebirth of patriotism, the place to start is with a clarification of the word itself.

Carl Van Doren, historian and Pulitizer-Prize biographer of Benjamin Franklin's life, once wrote: "Patriotism aims at uniting people in a few essential thoughts and feelings. Personally they may think and feel as differently as they happen to. They need to do this for the sake of their general strength. But unless they agree on points of national history and policy, attitude and faith, their nation will sooner or later fall apart."

Professor Van Doren's is as good a definition as one is likely to find. Patriotism is made up of thoughts and feelings that unite people. The thoughts have to do with points of national history and policy. The feelings derive from mutual attitudes and faith.

We can thank William Tyler Page for collecting these thoughts and feelings (as the "briefest possible summary of American political faith, and yet ... founded upon the fundamental things most distinctive in American history and tradi-

63

tions") in his brilliantly comprehensive, "The American's Creed." This document is a perfect composite of fundamental patriotic literature. With words borrowed from Washington, Madison, Jefferson, Webster and Lincoln, and with whole phrases taken from the Declaration of Independence and from the Constitution, the author composed the first paragraph with the essential thoughts, and the second paragraph with the essential feelings, that unite Americans:

THE AMERICAN'S CREED

I believe in the United States of America as a government of the people, by the people, for the people, whose just powers are derived from the consent of the governed; a democracy in a Republic; a sovereign Nation of many sovereign States; a perfect Union one and inseparable, established upon those principles of freedom, equality, justice and humanity for which American patriots sacrificed their lives and fortunes.

I therefore believe it is my duty to my country to love it, to support its Constitution, to obey its laws, to respect its flag, and to defend it against all enemies.

These are the basic thoughts and feelings that formed a bond of fellowship among individual Americans, and transformed a people into one, indivisible nation. These, the great highlights of America's history, comprise a nucleus of mutual understanding and common endeavor that has cemented our devotion to a common cause and perpetuated our American way of life. America is today a country of specialists, each man's mind and time required by the field he has chosen. The physician, engineer, lawyer, chemist, advertising man; each speaks the language of his own profession, each is absorbed within the ever-narrowing bounds of a highly concentrated area of life. As specialization has increased so phenomenally over the past decades, Americans have found themselves with less and less in common. Even the history of America has grown and become diverse to an extent which has altered our ground of common interest. That is why the American Creed, the creed of patriots, is so vitally important today. These essential thoughts and feelings that inspire love of country remain part of the heritage of every American no matter what his profession may be or how specialized his knowledge may become. Patriotism—to be gained only through knowledge and understanding of the great men and events of our history—is the soul of our nation.

For well over a century Americans, individually and as a nation, lived by the American Creed. It is only recently that our nation has begun to "fall apart," as Professor Van Doren warned. How do we differ from Americans of the past so drastically that our leaders are politicians rather than patriots? So fundamentally, that patriotism has become the rare exception rather than the rule? What has been added to, or subtracted from, American thought and feeling to effect such an utter change? What was so special about the majority of those early Americans?

This is not the first time such questions have been asked.

At one time or another during the early stages of the American experiment, every major country in the world was trying to figure out what made Americans *American*. Throughout the last century this nation was busily achieving goals that other countries had been unsuccessfully seeking for literally thousands of years. Droves of foreign visitors arrived on our shores to investigate this new form of republican democracy and to learn, if possible, what made it such a remarkable success.

They arrived at a number of conclusions, some true and some quite distorted, but almost every observer agreed that the inimitable element of young America was a certain trait that its inhabitants shared, a unique outlook completely foreign to that of Europeans: an almost parental pride in, and love of, the American way of life. None of them described this love as a quality reserved for the heroic or famous, or as a special atmosphere conjured up for military parades and convention halls. They observed a nation of inherently patriotic people.

From this multitude of visitors let us choose six— a Scotsman, a Frenchman, a Pole, an Englishman, a German, and a

65

Russian— and examine their candid impressions of the American patriot. (What more reliable guide do we have as we face the future, than the evidence in the history of our past?)

Alexander Mackay, a Scotsman who made an intensive study of the Western world in the first part of the nineteenth century ran across a very basic difference between American patriotism and any other patriotism. In 1849 he wrote:

"The success of the American experiment depended, as it still depends, upon the character of the people."

And he offered this reason:

"Intimately connected with the pride of country which generally distinguished the Americans is the feeling which they cherish toward their institutions. Indeed, when the national feeling of an American is alluded to, something very different is implied from that which is generally understood by the term. In Europe. ... the love of country resolves itself into a reverence for locality irrespective of all other considerations. Thus the love which a Swiss bears to his country is attached to the soil constituting Switzerland, without reference to the social or political institutions which may develop themselves in the cantons. .... But the American exhibits little or none of the local attachments which distinguish the European. His feelings are more centered upon his institutions than his mere country. He looks upon himself more in the light of a republican than in that of a native of a particular territory. His affections have more to do with the social and political system with which he is connected than with the soil which he inhabits... give the American his institutions, and he cares but little where you place him. In some parts of the Union the local feeling may be comparatively strong, such as in New England; but it is astonishing how readily even there an American makes up his mind to try his fortune elsewhere, particularly if he contemplates removal merely to another part of the Union, no matter how remote, or how different in climate and other circumstances from what he has been accustomed to, provided the flag of his country waves over it, and republican institutions accompany him in his wanderings".

66

Why did the American of yesterday treasure so his Flag and his institutions? Michel-Guellaume de Crevecoeur, who spent many years in America before returning to his native France, explains why with touching simplicity in his third and most famous "Letter From an American Farmer":

"Let me select one as an epitome of the rest," wrote Crevecoeur of his contemporaries in America, "he is hired, he goes to work . . . he finds himself with his equal . . . his wages are high, his bed is not like that bed of sorrow on which he used to lie . . . He begins to feel the effects of a sort of resurrection; hitherto he had not lived, but simply vegetated; he now feels himself a man, because he is treated as such; the laws of his own country had overlooked him in his insignificancy; the laws of this cover him with their mantle. Judge what an alternation there must arise in mind and thoughts of this man; he begins to forget his former servitude and dependence; his heart involuntarily swells and glows; this first swell inspires him with those new thoughts which constitute an American . . . he begins to form some little scheme, the first, alas, he ever formed in his life . . . He is encouraged; he has gained friends; he is advised and directed; he feels bold; he purchases some land . . . What an epoch in this man's life! He is become a freeholder, from perhaps a German boor—he is now an American—and for the first time in his life counts for something; for hitherto he had been a cypher. I only repeat what I have heard many say, and no wonder their hearts should glow, and be agitated with a multitude of feelings not easy to describe."

Thus was *patriotism* born in the hearts of our forebears, conceived by love for a country that gave them a chance to make something of themselves. So firmly did it become a part of the American character that eight decades later, in 1857, the Polish Count Adam Gurowski found that "it is almost impossible to imagine an American becoming . . . subservient forever to social caste." A patriot himself, having participated in the 1830 episode of Poland's unending revolution against Russian intervention and tyranny, Count Gurowski observed:

"With sacred jealousy the American people watch over

the national honor, over its relations with other States, over national independence. Being in possession of the highest goods, no sacrifice can be too great for their defense and preservation. No invasion from whatever quarter, no conquest, no overthrow of the existing order, could ever be successfully carried out. Not the presumed Anglo-Saxon blood, but the genuine American feeling, pouring out from constitutive principles as from a fountainhead, is the repelling force. Patriotic, exalted devotion is not an effort, but a natural lineament of character, a simple but inherent element of national life."

Nor had the devotion waned because of the temporary disunion of America in the 1860s. In the *American Commonwealth* (1888), renowned as a classic study of the American mind, Englishman James Bryce noted, "There is in the United States abundance of patriotism, that is to say, of a passion for the greatness and happiness of the Republic, and a readiness to make sacrifices for it."

". . . Now the American people are united at moments of national concern from two causes. One is that absence of class divisions and jealousies which has been already described. The people are homogeneous; a feeling which stirs them stirs alike rich and poor, farmers and traders, Eastern men and Western men—one may now add, Southern men also. Their patriotism has ceased to be defiant, and is conceived as the duty of promoting the greatness and happiness of their country, a greatness which, as it does not look to war or aggression, does not redound specially, as it might in Europe, to the glory or benefits of the ruling caste or the military profession, but to that of all the citizens."

Nor did the industrial revolution "spoil" the American people's patriotism. At the turn of the century, materialism was still viewed in its proper perspective. Work was not merely a means to acquire material wealth but an end in itself. The opportunity to labor honestly and to use and develop one's own personal gifts and abilities was cherished by Americans. Their minds were not focused on "something for nothing" and "retirement" but on achievement and human

68

dignity through individual accomplishment. In interpreting this characteristic of Americans to the Germans (and to Americans), Hugo Munsterberg wrote of "American contempt for unearned wealth."

"The true American," he said, "despises anyone who gets money without working for it. Money is not the thing which is considered, but the manner of getting it. This is what the American cares for, and he prizes the gold he gets primarily as an indication of his ability.

. . . Whether he has much or little, he keeps patiently at work; and, as no scholar or artist, would ever think of saying that he had done enough work, and would from now on become a scientific or literary rentier and live on his reputation, so no American, as long as he keeps his health, thinks of giving up his regular business . . . The economic life means to the American a realizing of efforts which are in themselves precious. It is not the means to an end, but is its own end.

Even visitors from the USSR found something about the Americans which, though grudgingly, they had to admire. Ilya Ilf and Eugene Petrov informed their comrades, "Should an American say in the course of a conversation, or even incidentally, 'I'll do that,' it is not necessary to remind him of anything at all in the future. Everything will be done. The ability to keep his word, to keep it firmly, accurately, to burst, but keep his word—that is the most important thing which our Soviet business people must learn from American business people." And, they confessed, "In all probability the American is a good patriot."

All of the above quotations[1] point to the same conclusion. In America, plain honest dedication—the fervor and loyalty of patriots—has always had a prime place in the individual's scheme of values.

The memory of these famous patriots, the founders of our country, our military heroes, our great statesmen shall forever burn in our hearts. But let us not forget that there were other patriots; that patriots are not of some rare species. Patrick Henry would not have delivered his immortal speech if that

69

convention hall in Richmond had been empty. Colonel Prescott would not have given the order, "Don't fire until you see the whites of their eyes," if he had been the only man atop Bunker Hill.

There was only one author of the Declaration of Independence, but fifty-six men faced the hangman's noose to sign it. Each one of these men was a patriot, a great patriot worthy of our highest respect, and yet there was nothing extraordinary about them. They had only one thing in common: a passionate love of country. They came from various walks of life. Some were brilliant, others had no formal education at all. Some were wealthy, others were poor. They came from twelve different directions, natives and immigrants, young and old. Like us, they were faced with a crisis. They were willing to make the sacrifices necessary. They were not merely asked to face their their civic responsibilities; they were asked to risk their lives, reputations and fortunes.

Who were those fifty-six signers? What do we owe them?

Three of them gained such monumental fame, we need only mention their names: Thomas Jefferson, John Adams, and Benjamin Franklin. *But there were others.*

There was a man named John Hart—"Honest John," they called him—who left his farm and grist mills to represent New Jersey. John Hart was sixty-five years old, and he became a traitor in the eyes of King George III. Hessian troops raided his farm at the very time his wife lay dying in her bed. John Hart was forced to flee like a hunted animal, keeping to the woods and sleeping in caves. He returned, his health broken, to find his wife dead and his children gone. He died —two years after the signing.

Richard Stockton, a judge, was another delegate from New Jersey. By signing the Declaration he too committed an act of high treason against the crown. He and his family moved in with some friends in order to avoid the redcoats, but a Tory informed on them. Judge Stockton was seized during the night, beaten, and dragged off to prison. After his release he returned to a gutted home, penniless, and was reduced to

70

dependence upon charity. The signers devotedly believed in a Creator who wants man free and not enslaved.

Every signer   young lawyers, military men, an ex-shoe-maker, an ex-bond servant, doctors, scholars, merchants, farmers   knew that his signature on the Declaration could turn it into his own personal death warrant.

Sam Adams and John Hancock both had a reward of 500 pounds on their heads by proclamation of the king. But Sam Adams (whose financial status caused his friends to chip in and buy him a new suit to wear to Philadelphia) was a hot-headed patriot who longed for independence and freedom. His friend, Hancock, not only defied the price on his head, but contributed $100,000 of his own money to the American cause, and left his fiancee waiting in Massachusetts while he presided at the convention.

Members of the Continental Congress who met in 1776 were not patriots simply because they signed the Declaration of Independence. They were patriots because they came from a people whose love of liberty could not be thwarted by a dictator who claimed power as a "divine right."

At the time of the signing an eight-year-old boy named Frederick Wolcott, who lived in a small Connecticut village called Litchfield, was busy in his backyard making bullets out of melted scrap lead. He was assisted by his mother and his eleven-year-old sister Mary Ann, who turned out more than 10,000 bullets. The father of this small clan, Brigadier General Oliver Wolcott, was in Philadelphia signing the Declaration. Who is to say that forty-nine year old Oliver was a greater patriot than eight year old Frederick?

We are inclined to think of the signers as men whose lives began and ended in the few seconds time it took to affix their signatures to that priceless piece of paper. Our fascination is drawn to the dignity of the event, to the grand triumph of the moment. But if each of us would take time to know these patriots as men and comprehend the debt of gratitude we owe them; to understand that they were Americans with private lives to lead just as we, professions to ply just as we, families

71

to raise just as we; and then consider the sacrifice they made for our country—we would at once realize what a rebirth of patriotism could mean to twentieth century America.

What is to keep us from becoming once again a nation of patriots? Are we too old? Seven of the signers were over sixty. Are we too young? Eighteen of the signers were still in their thirties. Edward Rutledge, who was later captured by the British, and whose South Carolina home was plundered by the enemy, was twenty-six when he signed.

Are we too busy making money? Each signer was willing to risk his fortune. The great Jefferson spent the last years of his life struggling against bankruptcy because the struggle for independence had left him no time for his personal affairs!

Are we afraid to be called flag wavers? The signers were called *traitors*. It is said that fifty year old John Morton, who died eight months after he signed, was the victim of a broken heart caused by loyalist friends and relatives who cruelly ostracized him for his political beliefs.

Have we too many other responsibilities? Braxton, Ellery and Sherman had eighteen, sixteen and fifteen children respectively to provide for. Only two of the signers were bachelors. The rest had a total of two hundred seventy-five sons and daughters.

Is it that love of country might be a bother? Might a rebirth of patriotism be too much trouble?

Francis Lewis signed the Declaration for New York. He was a sixty-two year old merchant from Long Island who could have lived out his life in great comfort. His home was burned down. His wife was carried off, imprisoned, and treated so brutally that she died within two years.

After signing (declaring *our* independence as well as his own) an importer named Philip Livingston was forced to live the life of a wanted man. He never saw his home again.

Abraham Clark was "bothered" with this decision: Two of his sons were prisoners of war. He could effect their release by renouncing the American cause. He signed.

The homes of New York's William Floyd and Lewis Morris

72

were plundered by the enemy. Both men and their families were "troubled" by a life of exile for the next seven years.

Patriot Robert Morris was one of the wealthiest men in America, and as an orphan had known what the lack of money could mean. Yet at times he almost single-handedly financed the American Revolution, raising funds, often borrowing thousands of dollars with his personal credit or word of honor as the only collateral. He lost one hundred fifty of the ships in his merchant fleet during the war which he helped to win —and ended up in jail because he could not meet his debts.

The list of heroic feats could be extended to include every man whose name appears on the Declaration of Independence. What moved them to perform such selfless deeds? Perhaps John Morton, a humble Pennsylvanian who entered manhood as an apprentice surveyor in his step-father's trade, spoke for all of the signers when, as he lay dying, he uttered these last words:

". . . tell them that they will live to see the hour when they shall acknowledge it to have been the most glorious service that I ever rendered to my country."

Today, patriotism requires of us, as it required of our Fathers, devotion and dedication to the task of maintaining individual freedom within a voluntary society and a free market economy. It requires that which has served as a common motive for patriots of every generation: love of the American way of life, and love of the men who shared the burdens and suffering and deaths that went into its making.

And what does the patriot get in return for his love? What special reward has America for him?

The patriot is recompensed a hundred-fold! In return for his allegiance and concern America gives him her soul-stirring history and a hope for his future. She gives him a feeling of pride at the sight of her Star-Spangled Banner. The sound of her anthem quickens his heart. Her tombs and war memorials put a tear of appreciation in his eye. America gives him knowledge and understanding of the priceless legacy he has inherited. She guides and encourages his pursuit of happiness.

73

The patriot reveres Old Glory because it is the symbol of his land. He knows what it meant when the American Flag was unfurled at the head of the Continental Army for the first time. He perceives the awesome significance of General Washington's interpretation of the flag. "We take the stars from heaven," said George Washington, "the red from our mother country separating it by white stripes, thus showing that we have separated from her, and the white stripes shall go down to posterity representing liberty."

Yes, the patriot has many rewards because he knows the value of his American heritage. And the greatest of these rewards is his United States citizenship—his right to keep the fruits of his labor, his right to self-government, his right to forge ahead. Patriotism inspires integrity and responsbility in him by fusing them with pride in his own individuality and his own country.

Shall we then, in this hour of crisis, open our hearts and our minds and allow American patriotism to be reborn? Shall we find the moral strength to assume our duties as citizens of a constitutional republic?

The decision is yours.

PART TWO

An American Manifesto

Introduction

THE CHAPTERS THAT FOLLOW *propose a key to the solution of the American crisis. Perhaps it is not the best or the only answer to the problems of our ailing nation but it is the most obvious and urgent of them. This proposal pretends to no deep or occult wisdom; it is based entirely on common sense and factual documentation. It is comprised of an educational program represented by the term,* Americanism—*here meant to include all that a young American and future citizen should know about his country. The word* Americanism *is used because it is specific and all inclusive, and because its very infrequency of use has spared it from the tyranny of semantics. Other, significant terms* (democracy, *for example) have lately taken on such a wide variety of meanings they no longer possess clear-cut definitions.*

To suggest an educational program, no matter what it might be called, is to invite trouble, or at least extemporary objections. In this case, cosmopolites are bound to consider Americanism as sounding suspiciously "anti-world." And internationalists will undoubtedly condemn it as being too vainglorious. To the former objection one can only reply (a little wearily perhaps) that today it is a geographic, economic, and political impossibility to be "anti-world"—and rightly so. We are barely able to bring ourselves to be anti-Communist in our dread of precipitating another war. As for the latter charge, what better medium is there for the establishment of genuine international understanding than an understanding of Americanism, our national purpose, and a knowledge of the valuable message America has for the peoples of the world? Internationalists are more than welcome to invent a name for Americanism, if in so doing it will enable them to accept the program that Americanism implies.

77

Others may be counted on to charge that Americanism calls for political indoctrination. In a sense, Americanism does and is intended to require indoctrination, or as it was once called, inspiration. *But certainly it does not imply political* party *indoctrination As long as human beings continue to teach, to administrate, to author textbooks, to philosophize, devise curricula, go to meetings, vote and otherwise communicate their opinions education will contain a degree of indoctrination. That is why Painter observed in his* History of Education *that, "Among no two nations of antiquity have the theory and practice of education been the same. It has varied with the different social, political, and religious conditions of the people and the physical characteristics of the country." And that is why Dr. Henry Barnard once said, "The national education is at once a cause and an effect of the national character." If a teacher who suggests that our way of life is preferable to that of Communism is "guilty" of political indoctrination, then in that sense Americanism does imply political indoctrination.*

It is nonsense to speak of "academic freedom" in relation to ten- and twelve-year-olds. Just as in their community, religious, and home life, children must also be given the benefit of guidance, discipline, qualification and direction in their citizenship schooling.

Doctrine—the doctrine of American education—not indoctrination, is the concomitant responsibility that weighs most heavily on the shoulders of the American public. Today, more than at any other time in the history of our country, American youth require an education that will prepare them for responsible citizenship, and an education that will enable them to engage victoriously in a ideological war between proponents of freedom and exponents of slavery.

This need is not being met by our schools. Traditional Americanism has been thrown out of the classroom. Moreover, it has been replaced by harmful, experimental, transient theroies.

It may not be surprising but it is appalling to have surveys indicate that less than one percent of our citizens have read the Constitution or the Declaration, or even own a copy of either; that only thirty percent of all high-school graduates entering college have studied or read the Constitution; that over seventy percent of all the universities do not teach the Constitution. In light of such abysmal facts, it is little wonder that General Omar N. Bradley recently stated:

"When I recall the political ignorance of our young troops at the start of World War II I am moved to charge that our education has failed to teach the value of the great spiritual possession to which we are born. In Europe wherever we were stationed the people were puzzled by Americans who were so indifferent to the political origins and nature of our country."

The plight of citizenship in public-school education predicates the solution here proposed in two ways. First of all, aspects of education that now make it difficult to provide boys and girls with a program of Americanism must be named, examined and dealt with. Secondly, traditional ingredients of history, civics, and government that will best provide a program of Americanism must be reclaimed, refurbished, and reinstated. Most parents want their childen to be taught fundamental Americanism, but few parents realize why Americanism is not being taught. Therefore, the reason for this is documented in full detail. These matters are treated within their specific applications, although to do this it is necessary to examine the entire background of modern education. There will be found no general condemnation of American education itself in the following chapters. Education has played a far too important role in the growth of our nation; one cannot but marvel at its giant proportions and over-all accomplishments.

And what shall be said of our teachers? Presently, and for several generations past, our schools have failed to produce loyal, responsible, patriotic citizens. Where does the blame lie? The contention here is that it lies with every member of the United States electorate. Probably the "Thinkers" in the high reaches of the educational hierachy for the past half-century are more to blame than anyone else. At the same time, it is even more likely that the American teacher is less to blame than you and I.

CHAPTER 5

THE CHANGE

From Concrete to Quicksand

〰〰〰〰〰〰〰〰〰〰〰〰〰〰〰〰〰〰〰〰〰〰〰〰〰〰〰〰

Reds produce Communists, our schools seldom Americans. We had better begin again educating our children in Americanism. One does not inherit patriotism. It must be taught and aroused.   MSGR. T. JAMES MCNAMARA

〰〰〰〰〰〰〰〰〰〰〰〰〰〰〰〰〰〰〰〰〰〰〰〰〰〰〰〰

ONE OF THE BEST REASONS for training our children to be good American citizens, and for being good American citizens ourselves, is simply that we very much like being citizens of this particular country and living its democratic way of life. Despite our indifferent attitude, there is not one among us who would consider giving up—actually renouncing his American citizenship. Yet, in failing to teach citizenship to our children we are, in effect, arbitrarily renouncing their ctizenship for them. We do not seem to recognize clearly the relationship among the things we like about America, the institutions that make them possible, and the active citizenship required to keep these institutions alive.

To become specific, television is one of the material "things" we like about America. Most people in the world do not, cannot, own a TV set. Most of us (a small fraction of the world's huge population) either own one or could if we choose.

Why?

A number of fundamental "behind-the-scenes" rights and principles embodied in our heritage have made it possible to add a television set to the typical American home. We should know, and our children should be taught, that we may sit down and watch a particular program on our own tele-

80

vision screens because (directly or indirectly) of certain rights involved in our American citizenship: the right of free speech and press and the corresponding right of freedom to look and listen, the right to assemble, to petition for grievances, to privacy in our homes, to own private property, to work in callings and localities of our choice, to bargain with our employers and employees, to go into business, compete and make a profit, to bargain for goods and services in a free market to contract about our affairs, the right to the service of government as a protector and referee, and to freedom from arbitrary government regulation and control. All of these rights are prerequisite to our television enjoyment and they form the answer to the above-posed, "why". It isn't the "hidden persuaders" of advertising that spread luxuries across the lap of America, it is the hidden liberties of our heritage.

That is why it has been wisely said by many foreign observers that the things which we Americans like best about America are the things we most confidently take for granted. Collectively, all of these countless important and trivial "things" —from chewing gum to the Manhattan skyline, from television to our American citizenship —comprise the American heritage; and whether we realize it or not, this heritage is the most valuable possession we shall ever own.

All of our "things" trace back to this same source. Free public education, like television, is another of these "things" which has grown out of our national inheritance. But of far greater significance, public education is also the *trustee* of America's heritage. The very fact that it has grown from a "little red school house" into a vast and complex system is due to our realizing that the survival of the American republic depends upon an educated citizenry. But we are failing to live up to this realization. Today, the actual educating of citizens is a "thing" taken as much for granted as our television sets. We grant each other that it is one of the basic goals of public education. We grant each other that it must be a requirement of every school to teach our youth basic Americanism and we have even promulgated laws to this

81

effect through our state legislatures. Many public aspirants in their vote seeking utterances, pledge improvement, but as the campaign ends their promise abruptly ends

But citizenship does not result merely from compulsory laws that admit it into the school curriculum. Good citizenship is not something which can be taken for granted.

Its development is in some ways analogous to that of the religious training of youth. A child may be born into a family of Catholic, Jewish or Protestant faith, for example, but the child is really not a Protestant, Jew or Catholic until he learns, understands and accepts the tenets of the particular belief upon which his faith is founded. The same thing is true in the case of citizenship. A child may be born of American parents, on American soil, but he is not really an American until he learns to love his country and accept the principles and way of life for which it stands. The religious training of our children begins at the pre-school level and it is continually broadened and enriched throughout their lives. Similarly, if a child is to become a citizen worthy of his American heritage, his growth as a citizen must keep pace with the depth and expanse of his spiritual education.

To every sincere Protestant, Catholic or Jewish parent and teacher, the religious training of youth is of supreme importance. As sincere *Americans*, these parents and teachers should also find the citizenship education of youth of utmost importance. Religious freedom itself is one of the many "things" in our heritage that we too often take for granted. No God-fearing parent would raise his child to be an atheist! No liberty-loving American should dare jeopardize the liberty of his own child! And yet, when we do not equip our youth with the knowledge and love necessary to sustain liberty, as citizens they become the equivalent of atheists.

This is not something which *may* happen; it is something that *is* happening. Since the turn of the century, America's system of public education has failed to produce the kind of citizen needed to preserve our unique heritage. Since the rise of world Communism it has failed to take the urgent, counter-

82

acting measures demanded Both of these failures stem from an absence of adequate Americanism in American schools. As will be shown, the teaching which formerly related to citizenship development has been replaced by an experimental science of social determinants a problem-solution approach concentrated on present-day social currents and under-currents. American history has been the victim of these new courses in how to win friends and influence people. It has been relegated to a place of insignificance and inferiority. American history is no longer used to inspire patriotism and loyalty in youth, but as an object of "critical disillusionment." Today the emphasis is on what is wrong with America, and much of her goodness and greatness is sacrificed to this la-mentable purpose. Moreover, in contrast to the spreading doc-trine of international Communism, something which is vaguely designated "citizenship for a new world order" has supplanted Americanism in the classroom.

These "modern" changes do not assist the teacher in build-ing citizens, they seriously handicap the teacher. They are damaging changes that distort the very concept of American ican citizenship.

Unless we adults wish to betray our own children, our schools must go back to the fundamentals of Americanism. Our young people must acquire *basic* knowledge of their coun-try. Citizenship does not result merely from participation in "student governments" or group discussions about "current events" or perusal of national periodicals to see "history in the making." These features are fine, but they are superficial in comparison to the real, dynamic material of citizenship training. To appreciate freedom our children must know what it is, where it came from, where it fits into the scheme of American values, how it may be preserved . . . or lost. They must know the "what" and the "how" and the "where" and the "why" of their God-given rights, their governmental re-sponsibilities, their role in the social, economic and political areas of local and national life, their membership in the uni-versal brotherhood of man.

For fundamental material such as this, there is but one source of knowledge: the factual and dramatic pageant of men, movements, scenes and events that make up the history of America. Our national story, when well told, is a precise statement of truth underlined by ethical and moral idealism. It is a valid record of deed and achievement (notwithstanding the blunders, failures and sorrows) that must stir the heart and imagination of every listener. American history is not only a great and indispensible teacher of patriotism, but a backlog of experience containing vital and valuable lessons for the future.

It is true that our history has grown long and will no longer fit within the covers of a single book. Textbooks must be condensed. Old episodes must be abbreviated to make room for new ones. Obviously, we cannot teach our youth the entire detailed account of America's past, and we must therefore select the most important and inspirational highlights through which they may best become acquainted with their country.

This fund of knowledge should comprise the fundamental ingredients of our common heritage. The history that we teach our children should be the essential, forthright story that has a meaning and a message for every American, young or old, male or female. It must be a strong nucleus of the truths we share, the principles that unite us; the high cause that has made us one, indivisible nation.

Today we are living in an age of specialization within specialization. Law, business, medicine, engineering, the sciences, the trades, the crafts, all have become extremely refined and technical. The mechanic may specialize not only in automobiles, but he may concentrate his skills on a particular part of a particular make of automobile. Or, even within the already highly specialized profession of medicine, the pediatrician may have little more than his M.D. in common with the geriatrician. The channels of human effort are growing narrower every day and we are consequently coming to be more and more "out of touch" with our countrymen. The nation is in urgent need of a *common denominator*, a common

84

tradition, a body of mutual knowledge that will truly make citizenship a union of citizens.

American history is that common denominator. In heroism, drama or moral idealism, our history is unsurpassed. It is the bond of understanding which can fill millions of hearts with the same patriotic emotion upon seeing "Old Glory" unfurled or hearing the familiar strains of our National Anthem. Every American should know the story of Independence Hall, birthplace of our nation; each of us should recognize with deep feeling such hallmarks of our past as Valley Forge, "Give me Liberty or give me Death," Concord, Lexington, "I have not yet begun to Fight," Gettysburg, the Emancipation Proclamation, the great moments of war and peace, the heroes of history, the places of sacred ground, the epic events, the profound and inspiring utterances of Americans as they have risen to immortal occasions. These are the great moments that have spilled honor and glory on the pages of our national history. These are the inner meanings of Americanism from which our young people may gain loyalty, devotion and the libertarian characteristics of dutiful citizenship. These and like episodes stir the imagination, imbue our determination to be faithful to the truth, and inspire patriotism and love of God and country.

We speak in fear of Communist infiltration in this country, of the possibility of Red indoctrination in our schools, but we fail to realize that warped idealists could preach their "isms" until blue in the face and there would be no harm done *unless this preaching replaced our true historical statement, our own clear sermon of America's Creed.* There is an old saying: "What does it profit the devil to whisper into one ear if God speaks into the other?" Might we not say also as a people who have faith in their way of life: "What does it profit the Marxist to whisper into one ear of youth if Thomas Jefferson speaks into the other?"

The real danger of Communism should open our eyes to the crucial fact that we can no longer shrug off our responsibility toward youth with, "What they don't know won't hurt

85

them." Today, it is what they don't know that *will* hurt the rising generation of Americans. It is certainly necessary to be on guard against Communist brainwashing and subversion, but even more dangerous is the "brainwashing" and "subversion" *that is bred in the breakdown our own national character* — the materialism, the political apathy, the moral aimlessness, the conscienceless secularism. All of these destructive traits assist in undermining our American principles and traditional ideals. Our own deteriorating American character is doing more than any foreign ideology could ever do to turn our children's minds against patriotism, loyalty, individuality, competitiveness, free enterprise, private property, self-government, and the honor and respect due to the men who made America the greatest nation in the world. Our guilt lies not only in turning young minds *against* the Creed of America through bad example, *but also in failing to turn young minds toward it in our schools.*

A recent survey taken by the Independence Hall Association[1] covering a total of 1,418 elementary and secondary schools, revealed a shocking apathy on the part of public school administrators toward the decline of Americanism in our educational system. The replies to this survey indicated that American history has lost its place in the curriculum to dozens of "social science" courses. All of the schools queried use American history textbooks which have been proved to contain errors, prejudices, and a degree of "slanted" or "debunking" material. The 1,418 schools failed to list a single common goal for the study of American history. And the overall attitude of school superintendents unquestionably denoted a complete lack of awareness of inferior citizenship training in their schools.

Although too few educators and laymen seem aware of the fact, in recent years there have been entire books written on the decline of Americanism in our schools—books that are documented with hard facts. To mention just a few of these forthright volumes, Augustin G. Rudd's *Bending the Twig*; the two hundred and ninety page sixteenth report by the Cali-

86

fornia State Senate Committee on Education; *The Turning of the Tides* by the late Hon. Paul W. Shafer and —John Howland Snow; Mary L. Allen's *Education or Indoctrination;* and Dr. E. Merrill Root's *Brainwashing in the High Schools.*

This last-named book is an outstanding critical analysis of eleven popular American History textbooks. The "brainwashing" Dr. Root refers to has nothing to do with the Communists; it is the result of our own indifference, lack of appreciation, and shameful misconceptions about America's history. The author examines the textbooks almost page by page to prove time and again that they contain debunking, half-truths, inconsistencies, and distorted opinions. Many of these books are used as basic texts in our public schools according to the IHA survey findings. And the IHA report is corroborated by the author himself: "To me," says Dr. Root, "even worse than the textbooks themselves, is the refusal of many principals, many teachers, many schools, and many Boards of Education, to see what I clearly demonstrate and to admit that brainwashing exists and that it is bad. They will not admit one item of their folly, out of the hundreds that I prove!"[2]

Our schools want what is best for our children just as much as the sincere critics of education do. There is no doubt about that. Americanism, or the lack of Americanism, is not a matter of "choosing up sides" as though political partisanship were involved. On the contrary, it is a matter that should bind Americans together in search of a common solution. It is an unpleasant subject, to be sure, but Americans have never yet consented to play an ostrich role and bury their heads in the sand to avoid a national crisis.

Every error in action has its source in a falacious philosophy, and the current tendency to approach the study of history totally void of inspiration is no exception. Citizenship education once rested on a foundation that was built with the *concrete* of absolute truths and fixed human values, immortalized by our founding fathers in such documents as the Declaration of Independence, the Constitution, and Bill of Rights.

Today, citizenship education is gradually sinking into a foundation built on *quicksand,* a pragmatic philosophy of materialism which has distorted Truth and Value. No matter how bright our youth may be, no matter how dedicated our teachers are, the youngsters of America have two strikes against them before they set foot into the history classroom because we have corrupted the very basis of our national attitude. There is an explanation, a very complex one, that can be designated by a deceptively simple word: *change.*

It is staunchly, and validly, maintained today that modern man must adjust to a world in constant flux. This is nothing new; change has always been part of the yield of time. Moses advocated change . . . as did Thomas Jefferson and Karl Marx . . . as do President Eisenhower and Nikita Kruschchev.

Should we be in favor of change, or should we oppose it? The foregoing combination of names should point up the absurdity of such a question. Change itself is neither good nor bad, it can claim no intrinsic value. The important thing to remember is that change is always relative to what was before and what will be after. This distinction is of extreme significance to present-day Americans. Adaptation to a changing environment has become so familiar in modern times that many of us have come to accept it blindly, without investigation, without the least conviction of its relative worth. In so doing we have sacrificed many traditional values and truths in the name of expediency and praticality.

It is true that these are times of amazing scientific wizardry, times in which man must keep abreast. Progress, human as well as technological, always entails change, and in this respect it is an essential factor of twentieth-century civilization. But it is disastrous to reason, after the fashion of Voltaire's Pangloss, that "change is necessary, therefore it is all for the best." Too many of us have shrugged off the vicissitudes of our age with a cynical lack of discrimination. Too many of us have "adjusted" to a world on the move, almost hypnotically, as though under some silencing spell of fatalism.

This does not lead to human growth or spiritual progress.

88

It leads to wholesale decadence and inevitable disaster. There has never been an exception to this law.

Consequently, the changes in our way of life have caused a complex and ramifying contortion of American character. In superficially "keeping abreast of the times" we have overthrown traditional verities, and have replaced them with a new set of moral, social, and political values often based on whim and self-benefit. Individualism has lost out to conformity (this being a change which was "necessary" and therefore "all for the best"). Integrity is in danger of losing out to chicanery, citizenship comes *after* businesship, quality *after* quantity, patriotism *after* worldism, prayer *after* profit; labor leadership has surrendered to bossism, human dignity to materialistic obsequiousness, independence to government largesse.

Changes of such wide-flung proportions did not occur overnight. Obviously they are not merely a result of the world's current space races. And these changes have not been so gradual that one cannot recognize them as distinct developments and trace them to their source. To a great extent, the public school system has served as a fountainhead for this evolution of American thought and deed. And as this evolution has gained momentum, American thought, in turn, functions paradoxically as an even greater mainspring of the "new" education from whence it came. The end result is a vicious circle whose barbed circumference extends further and further as this so-called wheel of "progress" revolves.

These changes in the thought and temper of the American people, and in many important aspects of citizenship education, amount to a betrayal, not only of ourselves but of our own sons and daughters. The truly tragic element of this national betrayal, however, is the manner in which the great majority of us have assimilated this new character. We have grown so accustomed to the constant occurence of *change* that the resulting decay is accepted as complacently as the daily routines of life.

Like men in all professions, like the fellow next-door, educators and teachers have grown accustomed to the trends

89

away from solid Americanism This is certainly an understandable situation, if not an agreeable one, in light of the same attitude reflected in millions of their countrymen. We cannot expect the educator to resist indiscriminate change to a greater extent than do business executives or lay-members of school committees and boards and associations across the land

The American character is eyerybody's business, and when it shows signs of endangering the future of our children, it is time for every individual to take stock of himself and his schools. In this age of specialization we Americans are prone to look upon "modern education" in the same dangerous way that we look upon "modern government." It is frequently considered too big, too "professional," too complicated for the average layman to fathom Libraries are filled with thousands of scholarly volumes devoted to educational psychology, methodology, epistemology, and other tongue-twisting educational studies. Who are we to question the professional experts?

The answer to this question is not very fancy - but it is plainly American. We own public education. The learners belong to us. The teachers are in our employ. The schools and materials are our property. The goals are set by our commission. We have not only the right but the solemn obligation to question public education. While it is true that many fine and specialized theses are beyond our critical judgment, it is equally true that much of what is called "the philosophy of modern education" amounts to basic ideas which are either right or wrong, true or false—and these are decisions which belong to the American people. Much of this "modern philosophy"—once stripped of its sophistic language and viewed as so many fundamental thoughts—reveals a source of current practice to which no *owner* of U. S. education would willfully give his approval.

It is time that we determine how the effect of these ideas has changed our character, and how it may ultimately destroy America. Without attempting to cover all of the countless factors that have gone into the making of modern education, let us briefly investigate the major changes which are destroying Americanism in our schools.

An indication of their direction was brought out quite clearly in the *Dodd Report* to the Reese Committee on Foundations.[3] This special committee of the House of Representatives disclosed that during the years 1933-1936, "a change in education had taken place from an impetus outside of the local community, and that the 'revolution' had occurred without violence and with the full consent of an overwhelming majority of the electorate." This "revolution" included these general changes:

Directing education in the United States toward an international viewpoint and discrediting the traditions to which it formerly had been dedicated.

Training individuals and servicing agencies to render advice to the Executive branch of the Federal Government.

Decreasing the dependency of education upon the resources of the local community (through huge grants by foundations) and freeing it from many of the natural safeguards inherent in this American tradition.

Changing both school and college curricula to the point where they sometimes denied the principles underlying the American way of life.

Financing experiments designed to determine the most effective means by which education could be pressed into service of a political nature.

The quiet "revolution" documented in the *Dodd Report* indicates even broader and more fundamental changes than those cited above. It insinuates a reshaping of the American mind, a passive shifting of American attitude. It suggests, on the part of the American people, a *quiet betrayal*.

To comprehend the total significance of this damaging "revolution" it is necessary to go back even further than the years 1933-1936. In the latter half of the nineteenth century a

91

shadow of doubt and discomfort was cast over the world by the discoveries of Charles Darwin. His theories of evolution and of man as merely a "logical animal" were supposed by some scholars to have proved that there was no God, that the Bible was obsolete, and that man himself was a helpless, soul-lacking creature at the mercy of his environment. The Darwinian view of man influenced many new and half-baked philosophies, most notable among them being the materialistic dialectic of Karl Marx.

As Admiral Moreell pointed out, "this nineteenth-century concept of man and the universe was not congenial to the idea of human liberty. The political idea of liberty or limited government springs from the religious idea of the character of man. So, when men came to be regarded as mere particles of matter, fragments of the natural landscape, the idea of limited government made little sense."[4]

America was influenced by this scientific view of human society. Despite the inconsistency between the new and the traditional idea of man, a philosophy less notorious but more harmful to America than that of Marx was devised by an American scholar named Charles Sanders Peirce. Regarding the American citizen as nothing more than a "logical animal" Peirce saw no reason why we should adhere to any basic truth unless it seemed "practical" to do so! He saw no reason why the great values of the American Creed should be handed down from generation to generation complete and unchanged, because he felt that expediency of the moment is the only worthwhile test of any value or system of values. Peirce seemed bent on transforming *living* into a cold, scientific method. Few Americans considered his philosophy seriously, but he was to have a lasting influence on many American "intellectuals" who should have known better. He was certainly not very adept at sugar-coating his materialistic ideas. He was an atheist and ridiculed those who were not. Men will believe in God, said Charles Peirce, ". . . so long as they cannot put two and two together." (!) Even though most Americans believed then, as they do today, that the Bible is

92

the Word of God, Peirce mockingly dismissed it, remarking, "Some mystics imagine that they have such a method in a private inspiration from on high." Those of our ancestors who revered the American traditions were also objects of his sarcasm: "If it is their highest impulse to be intellectual slaves, then slaves they ought to remain."[5] These Godless and un-American views were belied four-score earlier by no less a man than the Father of Our Country, who cautioned in his Farewell Address, "Reason and experience both forbid us to expect that national morality can prevail in exclusion of religious principles."

Charles Peirce is an obscure figure in American history, but the damaging influence of his thinking has far exceeded the space alloted him in the pages of our history. He was the first spokesman of a false, materialistic philosophy which, at this very moment, underlies public education in the United States.

Twenty years after Peirce introduced his new, "scientific" approach to America, William James called a revised version of it "Pragmatism" and began to teach it to his students. Shortly after an address given by James at the University of California in 1898, his "Pragmatism" became a popular "movement" in American education.

The philosophy of William James proved to be an excellent approach to scientific inquiry, but as a philosophy of education it proved disastrous. The reason is very simple. Human beings, not even six or seven year old human beings, can be put in test-tubes and analyzed as though they were insects. Philosophy is not science, nor is science philosophy. It is philosophy, not science, that teaches us the difference between right and wrong and directs us to the goods that befit our nature. Man has evolved absolute truths and permanent values, and it is his devotion to these principles that makes a human being more than a dollar's worth of physical substance. It is his ability to distinguish such intellectual concepts as Truth and Value that makes for social progress.

James held the same basic views that Peirce proposed. His

93

philosophy also stipulated that Truth must be judged materially by its "cash value." He also poked fun at what he called "old-fashioned theism . . . with its notion of God as an exalted monarch, made up of a lot of unintelligible or preposterous 'attributes'."[6]

Khrushchev recently told a group of Polish workers, "Your God offers you a better life in the 'next world' but Communism offers you a better life in this one." He did not mention that *freedom* is a *God-given* right, not a Communist-given right, and that the first thing a dictator must do to make slaves out of free men is use his iron fist to replace God with the State. Speaking of the same God (in the same materialistic manner) William James declared that "He [God] gives you indeed the assurance that all is well with *Him,* and for his eternal way of thinking; but thereupon he leaves you to be finitely saved by your own temporal devices . . . The prince of darkness may be a gentleman, as we are told he is, but whatever the God of earth and heaven is, he can surely be no Gentleman."

To be sure, any man is free to speak as he believes in America. The astonishing thing about this philosophy of James is that it so thoroughly permeated American thought and American education—despite the fact that Americans are not now, nor have they ever been, a Godless people.

"If you are not governed by God," warned William Penn, "you will be ruled by tyrants." And, as de Tocqueville long ago observed, "Religion in America takes no direct part in the government of society, but it must be regarded as the first of their political institutions." This was confirmed over and over throughout our history, and as recently as 1954 when a joint resolution of Congress added the phrase, "under God" to the Oath of Allegiance to the Flag of the United States.

There are a number of reasons why the scientific philosophy of James took root in American thought and education. The American character itself was becoming more preoccupied with the nation's ever increasing material abundance. Therefore, a materialistic outlook on life was not so shocking as it would have been a generation earlier. Also, as it has

94

been said, while Henry James wrote novels as though he were a psychologist, his brother William wrote on psychology as though he were a novelist. He seemed to please everyone. There was no right or wrong in his philosophy, no good or bad. He rejected nothing and accepted nothing. In fact, this middle-of-the-moral-road attitude was the basis of his philosophy. As Santayana pointed out, if he had any doctrine of his own it was one of agnosticism.

Nor were the secularistic ideas of James responsible for any particular results. He was not out to change American thought, only America's *way* of thinking. "It is a method only," said this most famous of American philosophers. It was America's own fault that she chose to apply this "method" of thinking to betray her own character.

By the time that James' philosophy was brought out in book form, in 1907, titled *Pragmatism,* intellectuals abroad were already singing, "All Europe knows but one American philosopher." And at home, Josiah Royce ranked him with Jonathan Edwards and Emerson as one of the three nationally representative philosophers of America. The "Pragmatism" of James is considered today according to Crane Brinton, "the most distinguished American contribution to formal philosophical thought."[7]

John Dewey, the most celebrated disciple of James, applied this philosophical materialism to education. It was accepted by American educators and became the most influential factor in classroom teaching throughout the nation. Dewey used the philosophy of James as a basis for his scientific theories about society. He began to experiment with children, believing that they could be "adjusted" through their environment, and that they could therefore be "controlled" and their behavior predicted through a manipulation of environment. The environmental "experiences" of the child became of utmost importance. Since Dewey believed that Truth is a matter of convenience, he felt free to eliminate or revise values according to their immediately useful results. And should a time-honored truth or value prove unprofitable, he felt free

95

to discard it! He abolished the thought that there are basic absolute and permanent ideals and principles.

Dewey needed, and received, some outside help in selling this theory to the American people who, while they were indeed practical, were not materialistic to the point of denying certain moral and political truths which they held to be self-evident and eternal, irrevocable and unchangeable— no matter what a social scientist might do to their environment. Many scientific discoveries, such as those by Pavlov, Freud and the Gestalt psychologists, accidentally conditioned American thought to accept the theories of Dewey, but perhaps the greatest amount of unintentional reassurance was given by Albert Einstein. Just as Deweyism was getting started, the world's most famous scientist published a paper which revolutionized man's image of the physical universe. This paper, his special theory of relativity, described the relativistic nature of uniform motion and the interdependence of space and time. Such things as mass and energy had been considered independent and absolute. Now they were shown to be unified and relative. Dewey's new scientific beliefs about man were thought by many to be an inevitable conclusion drawn from this scientific theory of relativity.

If space is not absolute, reasoned Deweyites, why should Truth be absolute? If energy is relative, why not Value? Though Dewey never did provide proof for such absurd correlations, the genius of Albert Einstein supplied, unwittingly, more than enough prestige.

As wave upon wave of new scientific discovery swept in with the new century, the materialism (which scholars discreetly call Pragmatism) rode the crest of this tide, and the name of John Dewey echoed throughout the academic world as the father of modern American education. It shrivelled the moral and spiritual qualities of American thought. It changed methods of teaching and learning. It changed the subject matter and goals of public education. The philosophy of James and the scientific application of it to education prescribed not only a "new way of thinking" but a new way of

96

life, as we shall soon see. It turned education into a scientific system that has no place for such things as patriotism, tradition, inspirational history, or the very Americanism that made free, public education a reality. And it did all of this without so much as assassinating a single public official, without liquidating a single clergyman, without so much as disturbing a solitary citizen's sleep. It toyed as quietly with the future of American youth as would a cat with a mouse and the end result may yet be as deadly.

CHAPTER 6

THE EFFECT

Scientific Citizenship

❋❋

Any nation that thinks more of its ease and comfort than its freedom will soon lose its freedom; and the ironical thing about it is that it will lose its ease and comfort too.

SOMERSET MAUGHAM

❋❋

IN DIRECT CONTRAST to the efforts underway to replace the traditional philosophy of education with a baseless scientific method, was the work of a committee of leading educators engaged in an extensive study of history teaching in American schools. This Committee of Seven published its findings in a *Report to the American Historical Association* in 1899. Before the study was undertaken, there had not been a major effort by any national association to present the full significance of history, or to provide the teacher with a statement of what might be considered the value of historical study and the place which it should occupy in the school program. A previous "Committee of Ten" had embodied the work of the Madison Conference on History, Civil Government, and Economics of 1892 in its general report, and there had been various conferences of teachers' associations; but the Committee of Seven was the first to undertake a systematic evaluation of civic education.

The task of this committee was, in its own words, ". . . to discover the actual situation, to see what was doing and what was the prevailing sentiment, to localize and establish a modicum of practices and principles, however small and limited it might be; and, having apprehended what was best and most helpful in spirit and tendency among teachers of the country, to seek to give that spirit expression in a report that would be helpful and suggestive, and that would be of service in widening the field of agreement and in laying the foundations for a common understanding."[1]

This report laid the foundation of history instruction in American schools. It arrived at the turn of the century, just as free public education was coming of age. It appeared just *prior* to the new "movement" in education and therefore embodied the original concept of education for American citizenship. Any discussion of the *change* wrought by the new experimental science of education must commence with the first great statement of *Americanism* to issue from the representatives of our schools. It is unfortunate that only a few brief passages of the report can be reproduced here, but even these should suffice to make clear the *original* philosophy that was later exchanged for one of short-term expediency. The Committee of Seven reported:

In the study of American history it is especially desirable that the development of the political organizations be clearly brought forth. Nothing should be allowed to obscure the leading features of our constitutional system. The pupil must see the characteristics of American political life and know the forms and methods, as well as the principles, of political activity. He must have knowledge of the ideals of American life, and must study the principles of American society as they have expressed themselves in institutions and embodied themselves in civic forms. p. 75.

We do not think, however, that economic or social facts should be emphasized at the expense of governmental or poltical facts. It seems wise to say that the greatest aim of education is to impress upon the learner a sense of duty and responsibility, and an acquaintance with his human obligations; and that a manifest function of the historical instruction in the school is to give to the pupil a sense of duty as a responsible member of that organized society of which he is a part, and some appreciation of its principles and its fundamental character. In other words, while industrial and social phases of progress should by no means be slighted, it is an absolute necessity that a course in American history should aim to give a connected narrative of political events and to record the gradual upbuilding of institutions, the slow establishment of political ideas and practices. pp. 76, 77.

. . . the most fundamental ideas in the political structure of the United States may best be seen in a study of the problems of history. The nature of the Constitution as an instrument of government, the relation of the central authority to the states, the theory of state sovereignty or that of national unity, the rise of parties and growth of party machinery,—these subjects are best understood when seen in their historical settings.

But in addition to this, many, if not all, of the provisions of the Constitution may be seen in the study of history, not as mere descriptions written on a piece of parchment, but as they are embodied in working institutions. The best way to understand institutions is to see them in action; the best way to understand forms is to see them used. By studying civil government in connection with history, the pupil studies the concrete and the actual. The process of impeachment, the appointing power of the president, the make-up of the cabinet, the power of the speaker, the organization of the territories, the adoption and purpose of the amendments, the methods of annexing territory, the distribution of the powers of government and their working relations, indeed all the important parts of the Constitution that have been translated into existing, acting institutions, may be studied as they have acted. If one does not pay attention to such subjects as these in the study of history, what is left but wars and rumors of wars, partisan contention and meaningless details? pp. 83, 84.

This same year marked the publication of John Dewey's *School and Society*. At the very time when the Committee of Seven was recommending a de-emphasis of the "social" aspect in favor of extensive study of the basic, inspirational documents and fundamental institutions that serve as a record of the past and a guide to the future, Dewey was urging a de-emphasis of history in favor of the study of the forces and forms of social life. In keeping with a philosophy of day-to-

100

day opportunism he advocated an "indirect sociology" to replace the traditional study of America's past.

"If history be regarded as just the record of the past," said John Dewey, "it is hard to see any grounds for claiming that it should have any large role in the curriculum of elementary education. The past is the past and the dead may be safely left to bury its dead. There are too many urgent demands in the present, too many calls over the threshhold of the future, to permit the child to become deeply immersed in what is forever gone by. Not so when history is considered as an account of the forces and forms of social life. Social life we have always with us ... Whatever history may be for the scientific historian, for the educator it must be an indirect sociology . . . a study of society which lays bare its process of becoming and its modes of organization."[2]

This seemingly mild appeal by Dewey marks the start of a most serious change in United States education. It represents one of the first attempts to enlarge the stature of the new experimental subject of sociology at the expense of reducing the importance of American history. Up to this time, educators regarded American history as the basic subject of the citizenship curriculum. It was believed that: (a) to impart an understanding of, and a groundwork for, coping with the problems of the present, it is necessary to equip students with a well-rounded knowledge of the past; (b) to prepare youth to become responsible, self-governing citizens, they must be taught to understand the governmental operations of their Constitutional republic; (c) to inspire patriotism and loyalty in the young, they must be given full opportunity to learn of the blessings of their heritage, and of the men, events, and sacrifices that secured those blessings.

However, with the rise of a new materialistic philosophy it was considered more "practical" to concentrate on current forms, forces and problems of social life, dipping into the treasury of American history only when the past might pragmatically throw light on a particular problem or circumstance of the present day.

101

Immediately before and after Dewey's influential *How We Think* was published in 1909, a number of circumstances set the scene for a drastic departure from the recommendations of the Committee of Seven. Throughout the nineteenth century and at the start of the twentieth, we were confronted with large numbers of immigrant children who needed to be "Americanized." Educators realized that they had to be introduced to the American way of life—to their new country's history, political structure, and civic principles. When immigration began to ebb after the first decade of the present century, many professional educators reasoned (pragmatically) that subjects such as history, civics, and government had lost much of their importance—that is, their immediate, practical "value"—and were therefore less significant than formerly. Perhaps it did not occur to them that a native American youth is none the more "Americanized" than a naturalized child if he lacks a knowledge of his country's history.

Though the Committee of Seven stressed a formal study of the Constitution in its historical background, this emphasis soon shifted from the formal to the "functional." A book entitled *The Community and the Citizen* (1907) by A. W. Dunn, originated a trend that still has to reach its unknown destination. Prior to the publication of this book schools offered a course called "Civil Government" which centered on a study of the United States Constitution (as the "Committee of Seven" had recommended). This course was quite abruptly changed to "Civics" and re-oriented toward pupil participation in community affairs, stressing the Constitution not as the foundation of our government and the law of our land, but as an instrument which the citizen might find useful under certain conditions.

With the rapid growth of high-school enrollment from 1900 on, and the commencement of the junior high school movement in 1910, the "indirect sociology" championed by Dewey and his followers began to reduce the prominence of American history in the classroom. "Political economy" became simply "Economics," and its historical significance began to

102

give way to its current social interest. The four traditional components (production, consumption, distribution, and exchange) were re-styled to make room for a study of "economic reforms" which meant—and may still mean—anything from socialism to the single tax. American history dropped yet another sizable notch with the introduction of the "science" of sociology in the high schools in 1911. It extracted a potpourri of historical subject matter from its historical background and fashioned the ingredients into a course of study. This course was usually called "social problems"—and it was, indeed, a well-named subject. Every shame of the nation (crime, poverty, racial prejudice, divorce, insanity, bigotry, etc.) was dragged out from under and presented to youth for solution! This muck was "life" and the teen-age student had to be "adjusted" to it.

The changes were underway. About this time John Dewey found a powerful channel for the dissemination of his educational philosophy in the National Education Association, an organization that seemed to dote on his every word. The mutual endeavors of John Dewey and the NEA led each to a unique distinction. Dewey eventually became the most prolific educational writer in the world, and the NEA eventually became, and is today, the largest professional organization in the world.

Since its origin in 1857, the NEA has performed an inestimable amount of services for public education. Perhaps its most admirable quality is a tenacious and rightful crusade to better the lot of the long imposed-upon American teacher—a battle which the NEA has waged valiantly for over a century. When the NEA took up the cause of the new experimental philosophy, with its strictly materialistic interpretation of life, the effect on education constituted a serious national misfortune. Its public endorsement and active promotion of this new, false philosophy influenced thousands of teacher-members to do likewise.

Partly in reaction to the recommendations of the Committee of Seven of 1899, and partly to re-establish its earlier educational prominence, the NEA created a "Commission on the Reorganization of Secondary Education" in 1912, composed of seventeen committees, one of which was a twenty-one-member "Committee on Social Studies." "Reorganization" was truly its goal; the phrase "social studies" itself was little more than a half-dozen years old. The fundamental premise of this committee's policy was that a study of "community problems" was more practical and utilitarian than a study of history. They seemed, along with Peirce James, and Dewey, inclined toward the bidding of Persia's famous hedonist, Omar Khayyam:

> Drink! for you know not whence you came, nor why:
> Drink! for you know not why you go, nor where.

In 1915, the Federal Office of Education (*nee* Bureau of Education) published as Bulletin No. 23 this NEA committee's first report, "The Teaching of Community Civics." From that time to this, the term *Civics* no longer implied the study of the governmental operation of our Constitutional republic. From that time to this, the term Civics has implied the study of social or community welfare. The NEA Committee on Social Studies recommended a field of conglomerate study involving educational topics such as health, occupations, wealth, banking, business, communication, transportation, law enforcement, athletics, hobbies, civic beauty, migration, education, correction, international relations, political parties, social problems . . . and government.

A year later, in 1916, the NEA's Committee on Social Studies finalized its findings in a report titled, "The Social Studies in Secondary Education" (OE Bulletin No. 28). This was the same year in which Dewey's book, *Democracy and Education,* was published. The Committee recommended a new course to be taught in high schools, "Problems in Democracy." It was to present students with problems (in keeping with the Dewey theory of learning through experimentation and socialized recitation) covering trouble areas of social, economical, and political natures. The final report was widely acclaimed by professional educationists—which is to say it

104

was widely acclaimed by the NEA—and established this organization once and for all as the number-one policy maker in American education. It also marked the complete relegation of the American history course to a subordinate position as one component of a panoramic and boundless curriculum called "social studies."

The emergence of "social studies"—or the applied science of society—in American education represents a line of demarcation. On the traditional side of this line the study of American history was more than a mere subject; it was a citizenship curriculum, with social studies as merely one part of the program of Americanism, equal in importance to the studies of geography, economics, and civil government. Social studies was taught within this historical framework, as were the other subjects. On the contemporary side of this line, "social studies" was made the core of the Americanism curriculum, and American history was left to take a minor place within its framework. From this point on, subjects such as sociology, economics and civics were not thought of as studies of the past, as part of American history, but merely as a series of current problems and instruments of various reforms. From this point on, there occurred a steady decline of Americanism in our schools.

The decade of the 1920's witnessed literally thousands of educational experiments. Dewey and his advocates had popularized such slogans as: "Learning by Doing," "The Whole Child," "Life Adjustment," etc., and every teachers' college and normal school thesis seemed to offer a new interpretation of what these hazy phrases meant. There were "child interest" experiments, "problem methods" experiments, "curricula," "psychology of efficiency," and "learning by experience" experiments. Space permits only one example of this experimental circus, but the one selected is typical of countless others.

Teachers College of Columbia University is the main source of educational experimentalism. Our example is *Series No. 209 of Columbia University Contributions to Education:* "Children's

Thinking—A Study of the Thinking Done by a Group of Grade Children When Encouraged to Ask Questions About United States History" by Inga Olla Helseth, Ph.D. (1926) pp. 108-110.

Features of this experiment include: democracy in the classroom, capturing student interest, and helping pupils to study more efficiently. The students are more-or-less left on their own in order to create interest and induce them to think for themselves. Only a few lines are quoted here to give the reader a fair idea of the aimlessness of this particular experiment, and to suggest its preoccupation with method. It is, in essence, an application of Dewey's doctrine of "socialized recitation."

Class Investigated. This investigation was made from September to May of the work by a class which formed a part of a practice school of a southern state college. The class—sixteen pupils of average intelligence and background. Half classified as being in the eighth grade and half in the seventh grade.

APPENDIX I

Extracts from Daily Records of Class Hours to Which Reference Has Been Made in This Investigation.
Key: T. indicates that the teacher is speaker.
  C. indicates that the child is speaker.
  Ch. indicates that the chairman is speaker.
  . . . indicates an omission

493 T. Now, we are ready to talk of plans for studying the making of the constitution itself.
494 C. Study it as we have this first part.
495 C. I am tired. Let us change our way of studying awhile.
496 C. There is no chance, I suppose, to have a play.
497 C. Yes, there is. Why not?
498 T. You might get your English teachers interested in your history play.
499 C. But we want a Christmas play in our English class.
500 C. I can remember things we dramatize. We would have to study the characters.

106

501 T. How many would like to investigate this to see if there is a play in it? (All *except one* raise hands) Can you represent the ideas of the men too? . . .

505 T. I have a book here which I believe will help out on your difficulties. As I read, ask questions if you wish.
506 C. I don't know what prodigious means. (Another explains.)
507 C. I don't see what we are doing.
508 C. We are trying to see if we have material for a play.
509 T. But why am I reading with you?
510 C. You are trying to show us how to study this, since we had trouble with it.
511 T. What value is this I have just read?
512 C. Explains the condition of the country at this time.
513 T. We must know that in order to appreciate the thought and opinion of the men at the convention.
514 C. I saw a cartoon illustrating this same thought . . . *You need to be grouped together to accomplish much.*
515 C. But you stay off to yourself.
516 C. I can study better by myself.
517 T. There is a difference. Are you talking now about being near physically or mentally?
518 C. Some of us stay away from the others. We do not keep up with the thoughts of the class.
519 T. She does not do that. (Teacher continues reading.)
520 C. It's hard sometimes to keep your mind on what you read. Last night I saw that with my history reading. I kept thinking of things that would happen to-day. You can read and not know what it is about.

—A friendly chat, was it not? Still, one can hardly keep from wondering, among other things, about that little boy or girl who *did not* raise a hand when the teacher inquired about the play. There is surely something of *hope* in that small gesture of individualism. Possibly he even muttered something under his breath that the recorder missed (or couldn't print) when his fellow-student recited line 514. At any rate, he wasn't much interested in the idea of a play. Maybe he just wished to learn something about the United States Constitution.

107

In addition to the rash of experiments that began in this decade, the more subtle effects of the new educational philosophy began to spread from the celebrated "Thinkers" outward to the unsuspecting "Indorsers." The whole massive body of educational literature became tainted with pragmatic social-mindedness. The stamp of Dewey appeared on all but a very few textbooks, and perhaps no teachers' text in America was published without it. Books on the social studies (and particularly on American history) evidenced the greatest influence. A representative example is *The Teaching of History* by Paul Klapper, published in 1926.[3]

This text for history teachers undoubtedly manifests many original thoughts and contains much of value. But, like the great majority of his post-war colleagues, Dr. Klapper was influenced by the changes in American thought and education. His *The Teaching of History* is in actuality concerned with the teaching of "indirect sociology" as urged by Dewey. The book is diametrically opposed to four major points made by the Committee of Seven. The contrast is as follows:

COMMITTEE OF SEVEN	DR. KLAPPER
1. A manifest function of history instruction in the school is to *give the pupil a sense of duty as a responsible citizen.*	1. A manifest function of history instruction in the school is to *explain to the pupil why things are as they are.*
2. Economic and social facts should not be emphasized at the expense of governmental or political facts.	2. Economic and social facts should be at all times emphasized.
3. The pupil should study *civil government* in connection with its historical setting.	3. The pupil should study *civics* in connection with its current social utility.
4. The pupil should study the problems *of history.*	4. The pupil should study the problems *of the day.*

108

Here, in the words of Dr. Klapper, is John Dewey's educational application of the Pragmatism of William James:

"Aside from its social significance a fact of history has no value." (p. 123).

It is a simple paraphrasing of James' idea that, aside from its practicality, a "truth" has no "value," that is to say, no truth or value has an absolute worth.

The full paragraph which contains the above quotation is as follows:

"We have come to an impasse in formulating courses of study in history. No progress is possible unless we set aside personal opinion and develop the content of the course by an objective standard formulated in terms of social need. History, we agreed, must explain the present to the maturing pupil; it must instill a social attitude and prepare the mind to have an understanding of social relations and social institutions. Only that must be taught in school history which contributes directly to this social-mindedness. Aside from its social ignificance a fact of history has no value."

This concept of history teaching, advocates the utilitarian or material aspect of history at the expense of the inspirational or spiritual. This interpretation of history means that the value of any historical fact (such as the signing of the Declaration of Independence) is at every moment subject to change—and that it is a truth *relative* to an annual, or weekly, or hourly re-evaluation. In the final analysis, it means that the *value* placed upon *any* person, place, or event by our forefathers cannot be taken as a *true* value because its "truth" depends on the most recent appraisal of its social or utilitarian consequences. Therefore, the great body of truths and values that had erstwhile served to shape American character and inspire patriotism would henceforth be used simply to justify, not shape, the quality of American conscience.

Klapper's book, like countless others, was in the main an argument for changing history into a science of indirect sociology. "Methods of teaching history, the organization of historical data, and the spirit of instruction," he said, "must, in the final analysis, all be controlled by the teacher's conviction of the final function of history." He felt that this final function was the same for history as for all of education: "schoolmen realize, as never before, that the social studies differ from the other subjects in the curriculum because of their content, not because of their aim, for all subjects must be guided and quickened by the same purpose, the molding of a socially minded citizenry." p. 4.

But the function of history is not to socialize the child. The child is socialized through his experience of living, through the whole of his education, home life, religious and community activities. Dr. Klapper would make history the study and analysis of this day-to-day experience which can only be called "living." But true history is not the study of present life; it is the study of past life, important because it can serve as a valuable guide for the best fulfillment of present life, and as a guide for the future.

John Dewey theorized that the goal of education consists of "adjusting" the child to whatever the current trends of "life" happen to be. Dr. Klapper concurred with this theory and applied it to the selection of historical subject matter thusly: "The teacher of history must ever ask, 'Am I giving these young minds a better grasp of the institutional life to which they must adjust themselves?' A negative answer dictates ruthless elimination of the material subjected to this test. An affirmative answer calls for greater thoroughness of treatment and added emphasis of underlying principles because, clearly, the teacher has found subject matter that develops social-mindedness." p. 13.

Formerly, teachers did not judge the content of history in terms of social-mindedness. In fact, before the rise of Dewey-ism, history teachers were not chiefly concerned with "adjusting" students to "life." They were more concerned with imparting a knowledge of the traditional American life, building citizens, inspiring love of country. Students were *expected* to adjust to the America way of life because it was thought to be the best way yet discovered, but they were also free to accept

110

or reject it. They were given the facts and allowed to make their own choice. Teachers were confident that the inherent values and truths manifest in traditional American life were sufficient to outweigh any other way of life. And, most important of all, by discovering the traditional American life, students were enabled to compare it with contemporary life, to note inconsistencies, and to weigh the differences. If the new generation felt that contemporary life held less of value than the traditional, they were not conditioned to "adjust" to these changes but, rather, were equipped with the historical knowledge needed to recover the discarded values and truths of the past. They were, in short, given a set of moral, spiritual, and political standards as a heritage of the past, and these values were to be used to judge and enrich—not merely explain— the present. If history is to explain anything to youth, its function is to explain the institutions of the past, and yet Klapper tells history teachers: ". . . unless the history we teach explains our *present-day institutions* to our pupils, it fails utterly." But history can explain the present only insofar as the past can explain the present. Many of our present-day institutions are not only *not* explained by a study of history, but wholly contradicted by the record of America's past. Far from being satisfactorily *explained* by a study of history, many present-day institutions become utterly astonishing when the past is studied. The great lessons of history are comparisons, not explanations. One need not be a historian to understand that the study of history explains the institutions of the past, and in this capacity serves as a *guide* for the present. Present-day institutions will be fully explained only when they become a part of history, and until they do it is treacherous to consider them as part of this guiding body of knowledge.

History as a "socializing force" required a subordination of nationalism to worldism. This change, begun a generation ago, is the most apparent danger in today's educational philosophy. Patriotism and loyalty are rarely mentioned today for any reason other than to point out how harmful these qualities can be in the character of a lunatic or war-monger.

111

Therefore, in the interest of "peace" it is more practical (or pragmatic) to direct one's allegiance and loyalties toward the world instead of one's country.

Dr. Klapper's personal patriotism shines through many fine passages in his book. But his work stands reluctantly at the threshhold of change and the influence of the new education as a "socializing force" is ever reflected in the light of this change. History, he states, "must be taught because it develops social-mindedness. The great idealist of World War I taught us that America entered the conflict to make the world not merely the United States, safe for democracy. History that is world history and that cultivates a world outlook is history that may hope to achieve its greatest function, the socialization of youth." p. 29.

"Patriotism," in its narrow sense as defined by Dr. Klapper, is not patriotism at all, but a form of jingoism or chauvinism, a sordid attitude. This popular form of ridicule is a half-truth, similar to the truth that an automobile is, in a narrow sense, a weapon for large-scale destruction. But this partial truth led the historian-sociologist of this period to draw dubious conclusions. Dr. Klapper asserted, "At all times we must guard against giving the pupil cause to feel that his country has a monopoly of courage and wisdom." One of the ways to apply this safeguard involves the curtailment of the rich folklore that has grown up with the nation.

"The fundamental purpose of teaching history is to develop socially minded citizens capable of active participation in the highly socialized life of to-day. History must never be used to build up preconceived sanctions and condemnations. [Such as the sanction of inalienable rights, or the condemnation of government by force?] If historic research proves commonly taught facts inaccurate, they must be changed; if cherished statements have been found to be without foundation, then they must no longer hold a place in history. The argument that they have so long inspired American youth that we must not eliminate them does not meet the issue honestly."

Nor does the argument of Dr. Klapper "meet the issue

112

honestly." It is true that inaccurate facts and unfounded statements have no place in history. But that small part of America's copious history which we actually cherish and which inspires American youth is surely not in need of change. We do not cherish chronology; we are not inspired by statistics. We cherish and are inspired by great principles, great events, great men. If these, the sterling nuclei of America's past, are in need of change or elimination, then America itself is misconceived in our minds, and not really America at all!

It hardly seems fair to presume that Dr. Klapper would have us deny youth the harmless and inspiring lore that has become so much a part of the American story—that George Washington should no longer be known to have chopped down the cherry tree, or that we must eliminate the lad who stood below the Liberty Bell and shouted, "Ring, grandfather, ring!"

It is more likely that Dr. Klapper had in mind more serious inaccuracies, such as the one "exposed" by Charles Beard. In his economic interpretation of the Constitution, Beard attempted to show that, far from being a document drawn by patriots and idealists in the name of life, liberty, and happiness, the Constitution was the work of selfish interests whose central purpose was to secure and increase their own personal wealth.

Indeed! *There* was a *change!* Very few Americans today believe that the United States Constitution was motivated by a handful of men for selfish economic reasons. But it wasn't until 1956 that the immeasurable damage was undone, when a young associate professor of history, Robert E. Brown of Michigan State University, published a painstaking refutation of Beard's influential interpretation. Brown went back to original eighteenth-century sources and produced a set of documented conclusions which proved—irrefutably—that our Constitution is honestly and exactly what it purports to be: an open covenant, openly arrived at, for the establishment of a republic by popular choice and acclaim.

"The fundamental purpose of all history teaching," says

113

Dr. Klapper, "is not to use on pupils an instrument of nationalistic propaganda but rather to give them a bird's eye-view of social evolution." And this leads to yet another conclusion: "Nor are we justified in failing to mention the *ills* that beset our growing democracy," among which he mentions a "disinclination to obey the government"! "There is a far-reaching purpose for setting these forth," he continues, "for they become starting points from which we can teach effectively and convincingly . . . that our democracy is not a final stage in political development but rather an advanced step in social-political progress . . ."

It seems proper to point out that *before* the notions of Pragmatism became popular, very few Americans conceived of the constitutional republic of the United States as a temporary stage in political development, or as "an advanced step in social-political progress." One can assert that previous generations of Americans thought and believed that their forefathers had evolved political concepts of lasting value, that the Declaration of Independence and the Constitution contained elements of permanence. There is no question that eighteenth- and nineteenth-century Americans would not have allowed history instructors to teach their sons and daughters this strange version of tentative democracy.

In a chapter entitled, "What Shall Be Taught in Civics," Dr. Klapper lists a number of topics for study. The list coincides for the most part with that of the NEA Committee on Social Studies, and includes such general topics as the family, the home, the school, the street, the neighborhood, sports, departments of local government, foods, water, housing, health activities, protection agencies, education, civic beauty, adequate comunication, corrective agencies, safety, recreation, charities, industry, commerce, transportation and migration.

He writes the epitaph for the traditional course of *civil government* with these words: "Under these topics we find marshalled a variety of information that may be labeled as ethical, hygienic, geographic, arithmetical, linguistic, and governmental; the main ingredients, however, are ethical and hygienic.

114

Those who think of civics in terms of civil government will find little of the traditional data included. Civics is today a subject of generous proportions with elastic limits that encompass any set of facts or activities that teach children how to live." p. 307.

Thus, the "science of society" replaced the study of government. The school seriously jeopardized its responsibility concerning citizenship by usurping many responsibilities of the parent and community.

In the preceding chapter reference was made to the *Dodd Report* which revealed that during the years 1933-1936, "a change in education had taken place from an impetus *outside* of the local community, and that the 'revolution' had occurred without violence and with the full consent of an overwhelming majority of the electorate." Some of the events which led up to this change have already been noted. It might be said, in fact, that the change which the *Dodd Report* attributes to the years 1933-1936 actually began in the year 1898 with William James. We have seen it previewed in the philosophy of James and Dewey, in the work of the NEA and Columbia University Teachers College, in the writings of Inga Olla Helseth and Paul Klapper. These people and institutions were sincere in their beliefs and devoted to the betterment of American education. All made valuable contributions to education during the years referred to. Nevertheless, all were part of a gradual change in the American way of life; all were connected with a transition in thought and education which impeded the existence of *Americanism* in the public school classroom. It would be grossly unjust to condemn James or Dewey or Klapper or the NEA for their part in the change. They did what they thought best for America's children. It is America's business, however, to decide what is best for her children, and had the people voiced an objecting opinion of these changes they would not have survived to precipitate later, more radical and destructive innovations. The late John Dewey was no more to blame for this foreboding betrayal than any one of his fellow citizens. But the fact re-

115

mains, long before 1933 Americanism *was* losing stature in our schools, and great qualities of American education *were* discarded for the sake of new aims.

Several important conclusions may be drawn from the changes of 1900-1930. First, contrary to the opinion of many educators, these changes were not wrought by the Depression. Rather, they were well in progress before the economic upheaval of 1929. Secondly, they were not the temporary effect of Communist, or anti-Fascist indoctrination of the 1930's. These years, popularly referred to as the "Era of Fellow-Travellers," were still ahead. Thirdly, they erupted from within the heart of our own land, a land in which free people, free to choose, had grown soft, and become lazy.

This new "scientific" approach to life was easy to take; as the Italian Papini pointed out, it was "really less a philosophy than a method of doing without one." In a world that was constantly changing, many Americans welcomed with enthusiasm a philosophy like that of James and Dewey which claimed that Truth itself was constantly changing. It was a scientific method that worked well in the field of science. Therefore, it was gradually allowed to take over such fields as education, ethics, law, politics, philosophy and daily living. It was actually thought capable of engendering *scientific citizenship!*

CHAPTER 7

THE CLASSROOM

Battleground of Beliefs

✠✠

The way to protect human rights is not to socialize them.

BERNARD BARUCH

✠✠

As REPRESENTATIVE EDUCATIONAL WRITINGS of the period the works of Inga Helseth and Paul Klapper denote a transition from philosophical and abstract theory to actual changes in teaching and curricula. If William James wanted only to change America's way of thinking, and Dewey primarily her way of teaching and learning, it was evident in teacher-texts like *The Teaching of History* that others desired to go a step further. If science could change thinking, and this new thinking could change education—why then, might education not change the entire social order? A handful of America's most influential educators believed that it could.

The first of these was a man named Harold Rugg. On page iii of the aforementioned *Study of the Thinking Done By a Group of Grade Children*, author Helseth "gratefully acknowledges her debt to" among others, Harold Rugg.[1]

On page 175 of *The Teaching of History* (under the heading: "The Plea for a Unified Social-Science Course"), author Klapper states, "The plea then is not for a correlation of geography, history, civics, sanitation, and ethics but rather for an integration of them into a single subject composed of vital social problems. Assurance is given that after three years of such training in the solution of social problems the pupil will have effective mastery of all that is worth while in the present courses in history, geography, and civics."[2]

117

The plea of Klapper for a fusion of the "social studies" into one subject is a mild variation of the plea of Harold Rugg for a fusion of *all* subjects. The "assurance" of this fusion's effectiveness to which Klapper alludes was given by Harold Rugg. Klapper makes this plain in a footnote on page 181, referring to this paragraph:

"We must rather work out the new course and accompanying textbooks slowly and experimentally, changing content, organization, and gradation according to revealing experiences. Results must be subjected to tests administered under scientific conditions. We must not permit ourselves at present to come to a final conclusion but await the product of the pioneer effort of professionally minded teachers."

The footnote states:

"Harold Rugg, Earle Rugg, Emma Schweppe, 'The Social Science Pamphlets' (Lincoln School of Teachers College of Columbia Univ.)."

As the footnote indicates, the "pioneer effort" mentioned by Klapper was that of Harold Rugg and his associates. Rugg began his pioneer effort about 1921 with several articles in educational periodicals, denouncing the most radical of social studies curricula as too mild and unprogressive.

He continued his pioneering in the *Twenty-second Yearbook* (1923) of the National Society for the Study of Education, under the title: "Problems of Contemporary Life as the Basis for Curriculum Making in the Social Studies." It is probable that this was the article which gave Dr. Klapper his "assurance" that the "solution of social problems" was the solution to building American citizens. Rugg urged that individual subjects be ignored in the selection of curricula material in favor of presenting existing social problems and his peculiar solution for them.

In the same year that marked the publication of Dr. Klapper's book, Harold Rugg wrote, "A Preface to the Reconstruction of the American School Curriculum," This time he fired his revolutionary scheme straight from the shoulder, de-

118

manding the complete socialization of education! "We must," said he, "invent a new synthesis of knowledge and make it the basis of the entire school curriculum. The conventional barriers between existing subjects must be ignored in curriculum making."[3]

This was not merely a call for greater integration of subjects. Rugg proposed, in effect, one gigantic subject that would be composed of a select body of knowledge. The "fusionist" would determine the content of this grand subject according to his judgment of the "needs" of the student. The subject, or the "new synthesis of knowledge," would entail a rejection of traditional methods, and traditional programs of public education, in order to present the student with material of all subjects simultaneously! Rugg's proposal for curriculum reconstruction was, of course, a preface to chaos and confusion. Under the guise of "student needs" he urged that education converge upon the social issues of the day without benefit of system or organization. Educators familiar with the foundation of good education realized that Rugg wanted to build not only a new education but that his blueprints called for construction *from the roof down*. Needless to say, total fusion has never been achieved in U.S. education.

But what was the "pioneer effort" of Harold Rugg and associates of which Dr. Klapper cautioned teachers to "await"? What were the "Social Science Pamphlets" of the Harold Rugg coterie? Dr. Klapper explains in his bibliography that they were "courses of study used in public schools of large cities and in experimental schools. Being helpful to teachers of civics and to students, they planned a unified course in social sciences to supplant individual and separate courses in history, geography, and civics."

In other words, Professor Rugg struck a compromise in his bid for total fusion of the public school curriculum. He became reconciled to the disintegration of subject courses in the social studies only.

Rugg's influence over contemporary social scientists (from whose ranks Dr. Klapper has been selected merely because

119

he typified a great many of them) has already been seen. The popularity of his textbooks was even more startling. As early as 1921 the "Rugg Method," modestly published in mimeographed form, found its way into a few classrooms of experimental schools. The following year more than one hundred school systems used printed books that contained the Rugg system of social studies. Within another year a revised version of these texts, entitled, *The Social Science Pamphlets*, spread to approximately three hundred school systems and remained in use through 1929.

"Hundreds of schools," says Professor Rugg, "located in more than forty states, have purchased and tried out under our direction copies of the experimental editions. In all, more than 600,000 copies of *The Social Science Pamphlets* were used by pupils between 1922 and 1929."[4]

But this was a mere drop in the bucket. Rugg now launched an extensive series of *Rugg Textbooks in the Social Studies* (fourteen "Readers" complete with "Pupil's Workbooks and Teacher's Guides"). From 1930 to 1950, the "Rugg System" was the most widely used of all social science courses. By 1941 Rugg was able to remark, ". . . It is my confident estimate . . . that not less than *five million young Americans* have studied one or more of them."[5]

Did this series constitute a program of Americanism?

Speaking of the first four "Reading Books," Rugg himself assured teachers that ". . . the 'history' and 'geography' necessary to understand modern civilizations is distributed through the four volumes of the course."

However, the first volume "is devoted chiefly to a study of the economic life of the United States." The second volume "introduces pupils to the economic and social life of other lands." The third volume "deals with the economic and social development of the American people." And, finally, the fourth volume, "with their political and cultural growth."[6]

If we are to rely on Harold Rugg's description of these books, it does not seem likely that the history necessary to understand America is distributed through the course. It

120

seems decidedly lop-sided in favor of the economic and social over the political. It is.

An analysis of the Rugg readers discloses one undeniable fact: they do, indeed, contain a wealth of history. They are probably qualified to rank among the most incredible history textbooks ever written. Volume One is the archetype of the rest. It is titled: *An Introduction to American Civilization,* subtitled: *A Study of Economic Life in the United States,* and sub-subtitled: *A Textbook in Geography and Civics with Historical Backgrounds.* This 610-page book contains some of the most distended histories imaginable. It traces the history of "money" back to the salt-cake medium of exchange in ancient China. It traces "barter" back to the Carthaginians. In relating the history of "power" author Rugg drifts far past the beginning of recorded history, some 500,000 years ago, when "man gradually learned to hold things and use his muscles." There are detailed histories of railroads, resources, coal, work, the telephone flight, iron, roads, and so forth. It is literally a "book of knowledge." It would, with slight revision, challenge any standard reference encyclopedia.

On the other hand, it does not introduce the student to American civilization. It introduces him to the history of human existence. If use of the word civics is in any way meant to imply instruction for American citizenship, it is completely misleading. But perhaps the most amazing thing of all is Professor Rugg's claim that the volume is "a study of economic life in the United States." Hundreds of pages are devoted to "the chief factors in the high standard of living of the United States." These are four, to wit:

1. Location in a stimulating climate.
2. Huge size and varied resources.
3. Many people ready to work.
4. Scientific knowledge.

This is a consummate example of the "new philosophy" of education at work. Rugg has "scientifically" scrapped the great value of historical fact that earlier educators so largely drew upon. He seems to have scanned the current horizon,

121

consulted the morning newspaper, looked around to see "what's cooking"—and from this keen observation and wealth of experience he has devised his beliefs, his new, highly practical truths that are so conveniently instrumental in satisfying the pupil's need to know the reason behind America's high standard of living, Apparently, from maps he has learned that the United States is favorably located and that it has a stimulating climate; that it is large and that it contains a wealth of oil and ore. He has found that more people are employed than unemployed; therefore, many people must surely be ready to work. He is aware of the invention of "extraordinary machines" and has deduced that these inventions came about through scientific knowledge. Having established these four useful "truths" Professor Rugg devotes chapter after chapter to their delineation.

He seems not at all disturbed by the obvious fallacy in this materialistic interpretation of America's high standard of living, namely: that there were other nations more ideally located for trade than our country; that other climates were more nearly perfect than our own; that other nations greatly dwarfed the size of the United States; that other countries had similar natural resources which remained latent while America's were tapped; that other populations were multiples of ours; that other nations produced some of the greatest scientists known to the world.

So positive is Rugg of his scientifically produced truths, that he fails to give students the least hint of the real truth behind America's fantastic standard of living. He gives them not the slightest intimation of the value of free enterprise as a cause of economic growth in America. He suggests nothing of the competitive dynamics of our free-fostered political ideology. He leaves the student completely ignorant of the causal effect that freedom had on the tremendous material surge of young America.

Even Rugg, however, cannot totally disregard the world-renowned *American Spirit*. But this spiritual value, this historical truth which is part of the American heritage, seems to

122

embarass the highly scientific sociologist. His 600-page thesis can manage no more than a brief confession that, "Our pep, our energy, is one of the greatest causes of our wealth, and of our comfortable standard of living." He devotes the following space to what he admits to be one of the greatest causes of American prosperity:

We sometimes use a word which is peculiarly American to name this feeling of healthy activity. We call it "pep." We can find better words for that high-spirited, energetic feeling that is essentially American, but "pep" does well enough for everyday use.[7]

The "Spirit of '76," the frontier spirit of hardy individualism, the spirit of independence and equality of opportunity, the spirit of constitutional guarantees to keep the fruit of one's own labor, the mutual spirit of the pursuit of life, liberty and happiness, the never-before spirit of personal freedom—*The American Spirit*—is presented to the student as a salesman might present a vitamin pill. It is explained in terms of sunshine and arresting scenery. The student is led to believe that the American Spirit is a result of his physical environment (*a la* Darwin and Marx), and that the spiritual heritage of American economics is rooted in the vacation-land abundance of nature's biased generosity. (And even this crude interpretation is contradicted when Rugg goes on to introduce the student to the seamier side of American life.)

Harold Rugg and his associates at Columbia University influenced the continuing change that corrupted Americanism in American schools. He influenced the change that fused hitherto separate subjects of history, citizenship, geography, government, economics, sociology, and other distinctive fields of knowledge, into a hopeless maze of information called social studies. He influenced the change of emphasis from historical problems to current economic and social problems.

In order to understand the "Rugg System" we must now take a brief but more critical look at the "revolution" of 1933-1936 documented by the aforementioned *Dodd Report*. It was during this period that a number of leading educators openly

123

launched a plan to create "a new social order" in America through the teaching organization of the public school system. It was intended that certain dictates of social reconstruction should filter through the schools and into the national character from a source at the top of the professional education hierarchy.

The whole scheme was so flagrantly un-American that many distinguished citizens—including congressmen, educators, authors, businessmen, and parents—published their protests in lengthy and accurate critical documents.[8] This criticism stemmed the tide of the "revolution" in education to an extent which, at least, pacified public indignation. Today the "Frontier Thinkers" (as the social planners of this period were called) are usually considered in the *past tense,* as misguided idealists indigenous to leftist uprisings of the depression years.

This present work is concerned only with the notorious "revolution" in education as it falls into the chronological pattern of change that has spanned the past half-century. Therefore, (notwithstanding the volumes of incredible evidence which are available and that constitute a detailed exposition of the entire movement) here but a minimum of comment and a few significant general observations are required.

In a speech given before the House of Representatives on June 11, 1958, the Hon. B. Carroll Reece provided a nut-shell definition of the whole movement in education for "a new social order." He said:

I believe that their sole objective was to reshape the social and economic structure of the United States into a semi-Socialist welfare-state pattern based on group action which most of this small influential group conscientiously considered superior to our traditional individualistic way of life with its elements of risks and rewards.[9]

Harold Rugg was a leader of this small influential group. In light of this fact, his great concern for a "fusion" of the social studies is more understandable. He was conditioning youth to accept change as a relative social value. "We remind the teacher again," he wrote in one of his Teacher's Guides,

124

"that the most important single concept illustrated in the entire course is the concept of 'change'." And, he added, the "momentum of change is rapidly increasing." And again (as Augustin G. Rudd quotes from the booklet introducing the textbooks of Harold Rugg): ". . . the generations shortly to be given the responsibility of self-government must be practiced in the attitude of expectancy of change . . . change in economic and social government . . . and in objects of allegiance."[10]

Why must America be conditioned to change? Professor Rugg supplies the answer:

. . . through the schools of the world we shall disseminate a new conception of government—one that will embrace all of the collective activities of men; one that will postulate the need for scientific control and operation of economic activities in the interests of all people; . . .[11]

This "new conception of government" was little different from the concept being "disseminated" in Russia at about this time. Rugg did not believe in the traditional American way of life.

In 1932, George S. Counts, who was a professor of education at Columbia University and another notable "Frontier Thinker," penned a monograph which asked: *Dare the School Build a New Social Order?* Dr. Counts declared, ". . . if democracy is to survive in the United States, it must abandon its individualistic affiliations in the sphere of economics . . ." p. 45. And, ". . . The growth of science and technology has carried us into a new age where ignorance must be replaced by knowledge, competition by cooperation, trust in Providence by careful planning, and *private capitalism by some form of socialized economy . . .* " p. 48.[12]

That is pretty plain English. If an educator, or any American, sincerely believes that his country should be changed from a constitutional republic into some form of socialistic State, that is one thing; but if, instead of bringing this proposition to the attention of the American people, he seeks rather to foist it on young minds, not yet able to draw mature conclusions—that is another thing.

Dr. Counts was also a Research Director for the 170 pages of *Conclusions and Recommendations* of the "Commission on Social Studies," published in 1934. Perhaps nothing could better indicate the revolutionary character of American education at this time than a comparison of the report of the Committee of Seven with the report of this Commission on Social Studies. *Both* reports were made to the American Historical Association. In 1899 the Committee of Seven reported to the AHA the first great statement of a program of Americanism in the schools. Thirty-five years later, after a steady change in educational philosophy, a Commission on Social Studies was to recommend to this same association:

Cumulative evidence supports the conclusion that, in the United States as in other countries, the age of individualism and *laissez-faire* in economy and government is closing and that a new age of collectivism is emerging.

. . . .

It may involve the limiting or supplanting of private property by public property or it may entail the preservation of private property, extended and distributed among the masses.

. . . .

Almost certainly it will involve a larger measure of compulsory as well as voluntary cooperation of citizens in the conduct of the complex national economy, a corresponding enlargement of the functions of government, and an increasing state intervention in fundamental branches of economy previously left to the individual discretion and initiative . . .

. . . .

In any event the Commission is convinced . . . that the actually integrated economy of the present day is the forerunner of a consciously integrated society in which individual economic actions and individual property rights will be altered and abridged."[13]

And now we know what the *Dodd Report* meant when it referred to the educational "revolution" of 1933-1936. It only remains to point out that this revolutionary plan to build "a new

126

social order" was not merely the dream of a few radical crack-pots. The full weight of the National Education Association (by then over 220,000 members strong) was behind this movement! Other noteworthy "Frontier Thinkers" leading this influential group of social reformers included:

William Heard Kilpatrick, Professor of Education, Teachers College, Columbia University; V. T. Thayer, Educational Director, Ethical Culture Schools; John L. Childs, Professor of Education, Columbia Teachers College; Boyd H. Bode, Professor of Education, Ohio State University; R. B. Raup, Professor of Education, Columbia Teachers College; H. Gordon Hullfish, Professor of Education, Ohio State University; and, of course, John Dewey, Professor Emeritus of Philosophy, Columbia University.[14]

Reflecting upon this outrageous attempt to undermine the American way of life through revolutionary educational doctrine, one is tempted to correlate the change in emphasis wholly with the depression. Certainly the simultaneous presence of these two developments represents more than mere coincidence. However, to conclude that the educational revolution of 1933-1936 was *caused* by the depression would not be correct. Earlier changes in education were leading to a severe distortion of basic American beliefs. The depression simply served as an opportune occasion for launching ideas that would have at any other time in the history of the United States been greeted with public wrath and disgust. The truth of this statement is borne out by no less an authority than John Dewey himself. In collaboration with Professor Childs, Dewey wrote in 1933:

". . . As far as the depression tends to undermine, through its effect on the experience and development of millions of future citizens, what teachers are striving to accomplish; as far as it is a symbol of conditions which are hostile to the realization of educational aims, it is a definitely educational force which teachers have both the right and the duty to face and to reckon with. There is, however, danger that the very obviousness of the illustration just used will narrow our appre-

127

hension of the point illustrated. *Change the instance from the time of depression to times when economic forces are working inequitably even when there is no marked depression, and from conditions which present themselves in the school to conditions which affect the life of children and youth out of school, and the principle still holds."*

He reiterates this conviction in more concise terms: "The demand for a philosophy of education which shall grow out of intelligent acknowledgement of both the conflicts and the new-forming patterns of social life did not find its origin in the present crisis."[15]

In other words, the "new-order" reformers of American education (Rugg, Counts, Kilpatrick, etc.) found in the desparate atmosphere of the depression a perfect excuse for the socio-educational revolution which had been fomenting for three decades. This being the case, the notorious "revolution" in education should be considered as a large link in the long chain of less spectacular changes—and not merely as a climactic or isolated event in the history of our public school system. Like every other link in this chain, its total relevancy rests with the prevailing influences it produced.

The revolution seems to have had three general aims: adjustment of the student to his environment; meeting the immediate needs of boys and girls; and effecting social and governmental reforms. These aims applied to education in general, but were heavily concentrated in the social-studies field. Their realization required a number of peculiar innovations which involved new methodology, experimentation, functional subject-matter, social concepts and character education. Many of these innovations have long since been discarded: others proved highly valuable and have been retained to enrich the schooling of today's youth. Unfortunately, still others were neither valuable—nor discarded. These last are of urgent concern.

The Frontier Thinkers' bid for a *sudden* "social revolution" died with the return of prosperity. Certainly the American teacher of today has little in common with the "social planners" of the 1930's. Nevertheless, it bears repeating that during the new-social-order years specific aims, requirements, methods, materials, and beliefs were purposely injected into the educational system to achieve revolutionary goals. Many of them are present in our schools today. Some of them have been renamed or discretely modified. Some have been more fully developed and have grown in stature! These anachronistic elements should have been buried with the abortive revolution of 1933-1936. They have survived primarily because they are nourished by the materialistic aimlessness of our "new" American philosophy of education. And, like the anti-traditional philosophy which sustains them, they also constitute changes which flagrantly oppose the concept of Americanism that was born on July Fourth, 1776.

Let us examine particular changes advocated by the Frontier Thinkers, and let us take a careful look at their subsequent influence on education. In order to build a new social order definite changes were necessary, new beliefs had to transmute old beliefs. Society, economy, human personality— such haphazard phenomena were to be "planned" scientifically to create a superior culture. It was necessary to condition new sets of attitudes in youth toward free enterprise, patriotism, competition, class-consciousness, world loyalty, private property, vocational ambition, religion, and history. The devised form of these new attitudes was candidly presented to the educational profession (presented to the nation's Inga Helseths and Paul Klappers who had become accustomed to change) by the celebrated handful of "Frontiersmen."

The same year in which Professor George S. Counts' revolutionary *Dare the School Build a New Social Order?* was published, also marked the publication of the Tenth Yearbook (1932) of the National Education Association's Department of Superintendents. Strangely enough, the most notable member of the commission which prepared the NEA yearbook was none other than Professor George S. Counts. The yearbook clarified some of the new changes that were taking place. One can, for instance, clearly observe the germination of secularism in the following quotation:

"The position of the church today is one of confusion and uncertainty . . . Only when it employs the outworn dogmas of the past and appeals to certain of the traditional prejudices of the people does it appear to have confidence in its own pronouncements . . ."[16]

The conclusion appears to be that the school must replace these "outworn dogmas" and "traditional prejudices" with secular "values" pertaining to the student's immediate needs. The principle of separation of state and religion tends to become a policy of separation of education and God.

The new "social education" transcended any clear-cut family ties, or national allegiance: "Loyalty to the family must be merged into loyalty to the community, loyalty to the community into loyalty to the nation, and loyalty to the nation into loyalty to mankind. The citizen of the future must be a citizen of the world." p. 13. To say that one must be loyal to the world, is to mock the very meaning of loyalty. The world, has no set of principles, no common ground of beliefs and ideals to which loyalty might be directed. But this does not seem to matter.

Because of (among other things) the "disintegration of the family [!] as an economic unit," it was felt that ". . . agencies such as the school must assume responsibilities which in the past have rested upon the home and the community." p. 15. It did not matter that the school has no authority to "assume" the responsibilities of the family.

Private property is identified with "the sentiment of patriotism" and is seen as "stimulating the development of the acquisitive and competitive impulses" (p. 25) which, of course, create class conflict—as any Marxist or Communist will quickly point out.

Individualism and traditional history instruction (labelled "chauvinistic") are also at fault: ". . . the emphasis on personal ambition and individual success which was so prominent a part of the schooling of the present older generation is partly responsible for the intensely competitive character of our present-day business life. It is probable . . . that the chauvi-

130

nistic teaching of much of the history of the home country is responsible for a good share of the international friction and conflict." p. 70. This subtle charge negates the traditional teaching of history.

Ownership amounts to "hoarding" and hoarding is an "anti-social act." Thrift, once considered a virtue by men of the caliber of Ben Franklin, becomes a vice "called "unsocial conduct." Likewise, "The profit motive, when expressed in terms of taking from society more than the returns to society warrant, must be looked upon as unsocial conduct..." p. 188.

This comes very close to the Marxian slogan: "From each according to his means; to each, according to his needs."

The traditional concept of moral character—arrived at through such unscientific media as the Ten Commandments and organized religion—was also found lacking. But apparently the NEA was still shopping around for a new concept of moral character to replace the old.

Underlying the new social educationist's high regard for "controlled experimentation" was the same theory of the "conditioned reflex" that had fascinated Charles Peirce back in 1887. In fact, under a chapter headed "Conditioned Responses" the yearbook states that "The entire development of the individual's habit systems, or of his personality or character, is conceived of as taking place after this manner [of conditioned responses]. . . " And, "Conditioning is therefore a process which may be employed by the teacher . . . to build up attitudes in the child and predispose him to the actions by which these attitudes are expressed." pp. 64, 65.

The term brainwashing could be substituted for the term conditioning in the foregoing sentence without changing a single word!

Summing up the new "character education" the Yearbook admits:

"There may well be a curricular revolution implied in the standard which is here set forth. Certainly there are implicit demands for tests of effectiveness radically different from those usually applied to teachers, children, or superintendents. The

131

old structure passes. Religion, morality, business, family, school, and state change . . ." p. 59.

Other Frontier Thinkers concurred and added more changes to the list that transformed the classroom into a battleground of beliefs. Professors Dewey and Childs disposed of traditional individualism in this manner:

We must not only educate individuals to live in a world where social conditions beyond the reach of any one individual's will affect his security, his work, his achievements, but we must (and for educational reasons) take account of the *total incapacity of the doctrine of competitive individualism* to work anything but harm in the state of interdependence in which we live.[17]

They do not mention the fact that a man's work and achievements can be "secured" only through a governmental force that must first deprive him of his individual liberty.

Professor Kilpatrick drew the same conclusion as his colleagues and put it much more bluntly:

On the social side, the theory of education should show how the individual alone is but an abstraction, impossible either to be or be conceived (except partially) . . ."[18]

He also recommended that the Marxist theory of class-conflict be utilized through a new treatment of subject-matter:

The conflicting demands within the social life should be brought to clear consciousness in the consideration of controversial issues, and every effort should be made to help the student form an adequate social philosophy.[19]

Using the popular terminology of the day (for example: the substitution of *laissez faire* for *free enterprise*), Dewey and Childs also realized the value of presenting a distorted "class conflict" theory to young minds:

Monopolistic ownership of land and of values socially created, privileged control of the machinery of production and of the power given by control of financial credit, has created control by

132

a class, namely, control over production, exchange, and distribution. Hence, general and public repudiation of the doctrine of *laissez faire* in behalf of the principle and practice of general social control is necessary. Education has a responsibility for training individuals to share in this social control instead of merely equipping them with ability to make their private way in isolation and competition.[20]

They therefore suggest that the traditional teaching of Americanism be changed to a socialistic citizenship training for a scientifically produced state:

The ability and the desire to think collectively, to engage in social planning conceived and conducted experimentally for the good of all, is a requirement of good citizenship under existing conditions. Educators can ignore it only at the risk of evasion and futility.[21]

A planned society must of necessity be governmentally controlled and governmentally enforced through restrictions of basic personal liberties. Nevertheless, Dewey and Childs insist on a planned Society for America:

The alternatives to such a philosophy as is here projected . . . is likely to be a society planned and controlled on some other than the democratic basis. Russia and Italy both present us with patterns of planned societies. We believe profoundly that society requires planning; that planning is the alternative to chaos, disorder, and insecurity.[22]

Professor R. P. Raup amplifies this socialistic view:

Plan economy has come to stay. The example of Russia has been a stimulus to this end, but even without Russia our own conditions would have brought it about. The bulwarks of conservativism, economic and political, are crumbling all around. New conceptions, new visions, new ideals, new world and local cultures require to be born.[23]

Raup feels that a change in educational method from the

133

traditional to the "project" method will aid in bringing about this new social order:

In Russia the project seems to have come into its true character, a whole society moving ahead, the spirit of the project as taken up in the schools becoming therein a true spirit of adventure with life significance. (And) . . . The "project" idea is, then, not properly a substitute for a tradition, a gripping culture, but rather it is a method by which we arrive at a new tradition.[24]

The project idea is a "functional" method attuned to the immediate "needs" of pupils. The traditional curriculum was not at all functional enough for Professor Kilpatrick's vision of the new social education:

. . . we cannot approve the traditional treatment of subject-matter, still strong in most teacher-preparation institutions. In this ordinary way of teaching, the probability is great that even as "subject matter" what is learned will not *function* in the life of the learner . . .[25]

And the Frontier Thinkers truly had the "functioning" of his life cut out for the unsuspecting learner:
. . . he must rise [said Professor H. Gordon Hullfish] to a method of action which naturally brings old values up for reconstruction as changing conditions necessitate new attitudes. [as for the teacher] . . . He needs to realize that as a member of the social order he has an obligation to bring about its steady reconstruction.[26]

These "old values" were to be replaced through experimentation, according to Dewey and Childs:

The great problem of society is to combine a maximum of different values, achieved by giving free play to individual taste and capacity, with a minimum of friction and conflict. The experimental method solves this problem as no other method can.[29]

The "great problem" amounts to material utility. The "experimental method" solves this problem as no other method can by simply rearranging the meaning of *Value* to correspond

134

with *Practicality,* thereby ruling out any consideration of right or wrong, or of the past or the future in its plan to reconstruct present society.

Endless volumes have gone into the body of literature that supports a "planning" of American life through educational indoctrination. The foregoing excerpts from this vast writing can hardly be considered a complete citation of all changes proposed by the Frontier Thinkers, nor anything more than a brief sampling of any particular one of them. They do, however, suggest the general circumstance of American education in the early 1930's. There *was* an attempt at revolution. The public schools *were* the vehicle for the achievement of this revolution. It *did* entail major changes in traditional American beliefs concerning religion, the family, patriotism, parental responsibility, private property, free enterprise, competitive enterprise, individualism, the classless nature of our nation, the teaching of history, the profit and loss theory, moral character, limited government, the method and matter of teaching, change as a means, truth as an end, permanent values, and American tradition itself.

How many and how much of these fantastic changes infected our system of education and remain today to betray our own children? We discovered that many of the changes originated long before this period. It is also apparent that these and additional changes were given a hard sheen of respectability by the depression. It now remains for us to determine exactly how much of this veneer is left in the American classroom—and to scrape away this deceptive gloss wherever it is found—to face, once for all time, the grim ultimatum of surviving changes which are destroying Americanism in our educational system.

CHAPTER 8

THE COMMISSION

Educating Tomorrow's Citizens

❖❖

Nothing shall ruin the country if the people themselves will undertake its safety, and nothing can save it if they leave that safety in anyone's hands but their own.   DANIEL WEBSTER

❖❖

PART I.   THE IDEOLOGICAL REVOLUTION OF 1933-1936—which activated through the school a program of scientifically "engineered" living, a Godless ethic, a "planned" social order, and a State "controlled" economy—continued to dominate the thinking in education until World War II. With the war came a new surge of patriotism and renewed appreciation for American tradition.

The Frontier Thinkers and their followers were forced to back down under the mounting pressure of both internal and external criticism. They found it necessary to dilute their "calls" and mandates for a new social order with a semblance of respect for time-proven American institutions. Goals which formerly had been widely published and openly avowed were henceforth concealed from unsympathetic teachers and parents. Gradually, this radical segment of education regained academic respectability by making minor and intermediate steps of their original goals, their new and only professed goals.

Thus, deceptively watered down, the revolution continued. And, by 1947, it began to be less of a "movement" than a set of accepted attitudes and an unquestioned body of educational thought and activity.

There still remains a hard core of zealous policy makers, including a small "inner core" of the original Frontier elite.

But today they stand more as guards or "keepers" than makers. There is simply little "policy" left to make. The earlier climate of fanaticism, flagrancy, and sensationalism has given way to an easy, conditioned lassitude, an apathy which has enveloped the nation.

The "frontier" has finally been cleared, the hatchet work finished. The national character has at last caught up with the "trail-blazers" of 1900 and the "pioneers" of 1930. The foundations of change have all been laid. The machinery is running smoothly and quietly. The Ruggs and Countses and Kilpatricks understand very well that it is now only a matter of time.

The moral and spiritual attributes of America are well in the process of becoming based wholly on material need—a goal of the Frontier Thinkers.

The concept of man as a social unit rather than as an individual person has already caused large-scale intellectual and social leveling in America—another goal of the Frontier Thinkers.

Vast economic control and bureaucratic competition with private industry by the federal government is expanding at an incredible rate in America—the chief goal of the Frontier Thinkers.

Thirty years ago goals such as these were considered so radical that even their formulators called them "revolutionary." The Frontier Educationists openly admitted that these changes were intended to revolutionize the American way of life. The fact that we have today partially succumbed to their changes does not make them any less revolutionary.

There is no evidence that the general American public (We, the People) has lost faith in the American way of life, or that the people actually desire to replace it with an experimental version of Marxian socialism. That is to say, there is no evidence that the people of the United States—by, for, and of themselves—have wilfully demanded the state of subtle revolution now existing in America.

This book was written on the assumption that a large majority of Americans have, on the contrary, a deep-rooted faith in their country and do not want to destroy the principles upon which it was founded. Holding this to be true, it does not follow that the youth of America should be educated, in considerable ignorance of these principles, to accept and further a new revolutionary order.

This situation underscores the entire American crisis considered in the first part of this book. And its correction underscores any possible solution. There is to be found here, however, a queer paradox of difficulty. Oddly enough, it is the trouble, not the solution, which poses the greatest difficulty. Corrective measures (such as a program of Americanism) may be easily ascertained by any thoughtful American. On the other hand, it is exceedingly difficult to believe, and extremely difficult to accept the fact, that our children are being educated for a kind of citizenship that may ultimately bring about the ruin of our country. Due to the incredibility of the situation itself, the most difficult aspect of its correction is to first establish its existence. Consequently, the greater part of the solution here proposed consists of the evidence needed to support that existence.

Any meaningful weighing of the evidence must proceed under the further assumption that when the people of the United States instituted a public system of free schools, they also conferred upon the educational profession a high, civic commission. Public education was authorized and expected to prepare American youth for intelligent and responsible citizenship. It was therefore intended that boys and girls should thoroughly acquire:

1. Knowledge of their inalienable rights and of the corresponding responsiiblities.

2. Knowledge of their constitutional republic, of the obligations therein established, and, the individual rights therein guaranteed.

3. Knowledge of their economic system of free enterprise and its basis of private ownership of property.

138

4. Inspiration for loyalty, and patriotism toward their country and faith in their national heritage and purpose.

During the first three decades of this century an educational philosophy and movement arose which imposed a directly conflicting body of knowledge on America's school children—knowledge diametrically opposed to that which the people authorized, expected, and intended to be taught. A version of this "new" education exists today.

"The individual," said William Kilpatrick, is "an abstraction."

"The old structure passes," said the 1932 yearbook of the NEA Department of Superintendents, "Religion, morality, business, family, school, and state change . . ."

Incredible?

"To draw a straight line from the NEA'S 1932 Yearbook to today's educational system," wrote Mary Helen Brengel (former *Facts Forum* editorialist) in 1958, "and to project it but a short space more to the oblivion of America requires no prophet nor seer, nor even a geometrician. A simple examination of the facts is sufficient."

The straight line to which Mrs. Brengel alluded is, essentially, a projection of the broad, basic, line of adverse *change* which extends back sixty years to the pragmatic materialism of the Peirce-James-Dewey philosophy. We have already traced it to the juncture mentioned in the above quotation. In this chapter we shall continue to follow it—through a simple examination of the facts—to its present position.

From 1934 to 1944 much of the "new order" propaganda was dumped into the educational stream by two monthly magazines, *The Social Frontier* and its successor *Frontiers of Democracy*. The initial October, 1934 issue of *The Social Frontier* contained an introductory editorial revealing the basic proposition of this and future issues:

"For the American people the age of individualism in economy is closing and an age of collectivism is opening." p. 3.

This viewpoint was enlarged upon in the next November, 1934 issue of this uninhibited "educational" instrument:

139

. . . The Social Frontier will throw all the strength it possesses on the side of those forces which are striving to fashion a form of collectivism that will make paramount the interests of the *overwhelming majority* of the population. p. 4.

However, "teachers" and "laymen" were urged to inform this same "overwhelming majority" as to what it was that the overwhelming majority was "striving to fashion":

. . . The mistaken notion that democracy and freedom are identical with the institutions of property and profit should not be allowed to go unchallenged. On the contrary, teachers and laymen should make clear by all means at their disposal, that a collectivist social order is not only necessary in a world of large scale production, corporate control, and human interdependence, but also that under these circumstances only social ownership and democratic control of the means of production can secure a free and democratic life. p. 9.

It should not come as a surprise that Dr. George S. Counts was an editor of *The Social Frontier,* nor that Dr. William H. Kilpatrick was chairman of the board of directors.

Other Frontier Thinkers were making "progress" as members of the "League for Industrial Democracy"—a new name given to the "Inter-collegiate Socialist Society" in 1921. The LID was founded specifically to help bring about "education for a new social order based on production for use and not for profit." Its officers included Director Harold Rugg, Vice-President John Dewey, and Treasurer Stuart Chase.

The revolutionists grew bolder and bolder. Three years after the publication of the Tenth Yearbook of the NEA Department of Superintendence, for example, Stuart Chase delivered a speech to this Department, warning these educators:

"If we have even a trace of liberalism in our natures, we must be prepared to see an increasing amount of collectivism, government interference, centralization of economic control, social planning."

And John L. Childs, who had been much less overt in his earlier collaborative writing with Dewey, penned in this Department's 1935 Yearbook:

140

". . . Under present industrial conditions democratic control can be made a reality only by the collective ownership of those industries whose coordinated administration is essential to the success of a planned economy."[2]

Also essential to the success of this socialistic plea was the public school classroom and effective indoctrination of young students and their teachers. The preliminary steps had been carefully laid by Harold Rugg and others who had effected a "fusion" of citizenship subjects into a general course of social studies. Now it was only necessary to slant this consolidated material, through the rewriting of textbooks, toward a reconstruction of society along socialistic lines. Thus, in 1936 Professor Howard David Langford called for a consolidated "program" of ". . . education—in action and in theory—of the masters and builders of the society of the future . . ." in the preface of his book, *Education and Social Conflict.*

"The program outlined in these pages [of Langford's book] for the schools and the teacher-training institutions call for the rewriting not only of most of our educational theory but of the psychology, the sociology, and the economics upon which it is based, and of nearly all our textbooks in most subjects of instruction."[3]

Counts had already pronounced that teachers ". . . .must oppose every effort on the part of publishing houses, business interests, privileged classes and patriotic [sic] societies to prescribe the content of the curriculum."[4] Was the content of the curriculum to be left alone? By no means. Who then was to prescribe the content of the curriculum? Apparently it was the exclusive handful of Frontier Thinkers who were "reconstructing" education; for, as Harold Rugg advised, ". . . a necessary . . . step in educational reconstruction lies in the remaking of the curriculum."[5]

Perhaps we can better grasp the significance of this move in 1936 for slanted textbooks by considering the attitude of one of the "followers," rather than one of the Frontier "leaders." A southern elementary-school principal, James M. Shields, said of this new edict:

141

It fairly staggers one to consider the tremendous task ahead in revision of our existing instructional literature if it is to be of any use at all in a collectivist society. Hardly a public school textbook now in use but is saturated with the profit psychology. Arithmetics are permeated with profit and loss, gain, 'making' money. One would hunt in vain through their pages for an incentive to economic cooperation. Even geographies are replete with production for gain. And as for histories! No wonder the Russians started from scratch in creating an entire new educational literature under the Soviet system. Almost we may have to discover America anew.[6]

James M. Shields was not the only teacher taken in by the Frontier Thinkers' scheme to turn teachers into "engineers of social change." A 1936 survey entitled, "The Social Attitudes and Information of American Teachers," conducted by the "John Dewey Society," (and published in this "Frontier" society's first yearbook in 1937) was circulated among 9,300 high-school teachers. Here are a few of the 106 questions asked, along with the rated replies:

Our national health would suffer if physicians were made civil servants like the public school teachers and placed on the Government payroll.
No: 69%

Persons who wish to bring about a "New Social Order" make poorer teachers than those who adhere strictly to their own specialty.
No: 65%

A satisfying life for the masses of people can be secured without introducing important economic changes.
No: 75%

We need a Government marketing corporation empowered to buy and process farm products and to sell them here and abroad.
Yes: 47%

And the most startling of all:

An improved American nation will result from step-by-step advances in the socialization of the means of production and distribution.
Yes: 74%

142

Certainly teachers had a right to hold such opinions in America. But did teachers have the right to foist these opinions (such as that the socialization of our economy will improve America) on young minds? In 1938, the year following publication of the above survey, John Dewey told teachers that indoctrination is a permissible "education procedure."

"If teachers," said Dewey, *"who hold that there is an intrinsic relation between actualization of democracy and social planning of economic institutions and relations hope to bring others to the same conclusions by use of the method of investigation and free cooperative discussion, I see nothing undemocratic in the procedure.* [Italics in original.]

It looks to me like an education procedure, and, moreover, to be of the same sort that teachers who have been led to accept the conclusion *might then use with their own students."*[7]

It is characteristic of Dewey to judge indoctrination according to its qualification as an educational procedure. To his credit (despite a philosophy which excluded God, the soul, immutable truth, a fixed natural law, and permanent moral principles) John Dewey rarely allowed his socialistic political views to override his primary interest in *educational* reform. In the final analysis, Dewey was more interested in revolutionizing the school than reconstructing society. He was more concerned with the education of the child for adjustment to his environment than with the child as an instrument for ideological revolution.

Harold Rugg and his disciples, on the other hand, seemingly were interested not in the child but in the *changes* which could be effected through a brainwashing of the child. In 1939, Rugg once again explained to his teacher-readers what must be accomplished through their profession:

A large-scale sustained-yield economy can be operated here [he wrote in *Frontiers of Democracy*] if a practicable social design and an efficient and socially acceptable scheme of control can be provided . . . comprehensive enough to cross any boundaries, either of State or personally owned properties . . . that, it seems to me, is what we must teach.[8]

143

In this year, the Progressive Education Association took over *The Social Frontier* and renamed it *Frontiers of Democracy*. It was thought to have become milder in tone and less extreme in its viewpoint. However, in the following year, 1940, *Frontiers of Democracy* revealed little change from its predecessor's point of view. In the January issue, for instance, Theodore Brameld and Dr. Harry Elmer Barnes, two of the most radical Frontier Thinkers expressed their unwise opinions. Said Brameld: We need an American design which encompasses and unifies the partial, contradictory, often destructive plans of our traditional economy. We need a design where nature's goods at last are consciously, *collectively* controlled by the majority of our people.[9]

Professor Barnes repeated this theme, and unwittingly exposed the disastrous significance of his own proposal!:

The only way to plan is to plan. It is impossible to graft a planned economy on to a competitive economic order and still hope to preserve the latter. Planning is compatible only with a considerable amount of *collectivism and economic regimentation.*

Friends of planned social change might as well recognize this fact and . . . be prepared for *the regimentation of economic life* and the *restriction of complete intellectual freedom which effective planning must entail . . .* We cannot have social planning without paying a price therefore in terms of some *curtailment of pioneer individualism and freedom.*[10]

In 1941, five months before Pearl Harbor, the first session of the eighth International Conference of the New Education Fellowship took place. The conference, attended by delegates from fifty-one countries, stated on page 2 of its program:

. . . it can be said with justice that upon the whole the older type of education was a part of the *old social order,* whose bankruptcy constitutes the present epoch of history. A *new social order* must be built and a new type of education must be worked out as an integral part of the construction of this inclusive human order.

Does this new-social-order propaganda sound familiar? Well, American representation included three very familiar gentle-

144

men, each a notorious Frontier Thinker of the period. Dr. Harold Rugg *presided over the session*. William Kilpatrick was a guest speaker, as was Professor Goodwin Watson, who had three years earlier ". . . begged the teachers of the nation to use their profession to indoctrinate children to overthrow 'conservative reactionaries' directing American government and industry."[11]

So we find that throughout the 1930's and up to the eve of World War II there was: (1) an attempt to revolutionize American society through the public school; (2) persistent effort by educational leaders to realize this goal; (3) wide endorsement by professional educators and general acquiescence by school teachers; and (4) tolerance or unawareness by most laymen and parents.

With entrance and engagement in World War II there evolved a revision of both public and educational attitude. The war did not put an automatic end to the revolution in education (just as the depression was not the source of its beginning), but the fact that thousands of our young men were suddenly fighting and dying for a "cause" led the nation to a reconsideration of what that "cause" actually meant. The war returned prosperity and renewed faith in a free-enterprise system that had cast a shadow of doubt over the nation after the economic collapse of 1929. But Americans realized that the "cause" they were fighting for involved a much wider faith than this. The noble concept of free individuals united under the sacred banner of Liberty once more came to the fore. It was a time of honest national introspection; America looked in on herself with a critical eye. During the course of the war it occurred to many people that their faith lay not in the "new order" prescribed by Harold Rugg and George Counts, but in the truly *new order* established by that small group of patriots in 1776. The founders had established a new nation because they had had their fill of "social planning" by the British crown. During World War II, Americans once again came into contact with the inevitable results of the "planned" State. Italy had accepted the idea of social planning. America

145

was given a firsthand look at the bitter Fascist results. The world bore witness also to the "social planning" of Adolf Hitler, including his extremely efficient system of horror chambers. Even the "great experiment" of Soviet Russia was beginning to show signs of social deterioration and political tyranny.

Consequently, the small, active minority of Americans that had consistently opposed the planning of a new social order began to grow. Newly organized groups (such as the American Education Association, and the Guardians of American Education) brought public attention to the fallacy of "indoctrination for social reconstruction." And a body of critical literature, including Dr. Robey's exhaustive analysis of six hundred social-studies textbooks, challenged every facet of the educational revolution.

Under national pressure, the Frontier Thinkers gradually ceased to represent official educational policy. In time they came to signify *an* educational movement rather than *the* educational movement. It became clear that there would be no sudden, "spontaneous" change in the social, economic, and political institutions of America as the decade of the 1930's had seemed to forecast. The depression was history. The nation had survived. There was a war to be fought. The spectacular Frontier movement lost some of its glamour and glitter when these facts struck home to many young radicals and social-idealists.

The shift in attitude is fairly perceptible in an incident that occurred during the war years. In 1942, Harold Rugg (at that time one of the most illustrious personages in American education) launched a dramatic plan to wage a "war-at-home over a free, abundant, and creative world"—for "full employment at abundance level"—through State "interjection of social capital into the system." This "war" was announced in open letters to President Roosevelt, the U. S. Commissioner of Education, and superintendents of the nation's public schools. Dr. Rugg envisioned a federal office of education that would have "a budget running into billions if necessary, to

146

reach ten, twenty, thirty million Americans day after day, week after week, without let-up" through an "all-out campaign over every trunk line of communication in this country, a nation-wide barrage of ideas and attitudes that will reach every city, town and hamlet . . ." Moreover, he and his colleagues craved "a chance to teach these great ideas to their high school youths and to the prospective teachers . . ." and ". . . write them into the new textbooks that will be made to herald the new day."

"This campaign," wrote Rugg in December, 1942, "requires a pamphlet-bulletin-article-book-writing program that would dwarf anything that has ever been dreamed of . . ." wherein authors would be ". . . drafted to write. Drafted, I say."[12]

One can detect an underlying note of desperation in this plea, an almost audible urgency to get on with the "revolution" before it burned itself out. Rugg had evidently felt the shift of national opinion, but it was too late. One month later (January, 1943) he warned, "There may not be time enough . . . to silence the isolationist, exploitive back-to-normalcy, die-hard right and their vicious press."[13] Bitter words from one committed to the *objective* education of youth!

The incident came to a close when Rugg announced shortly after: "I am unhappy to report that the hoped-for attack from Washington has not been forthcoming."

The shift in national attitude caused a corresponding shift in the social viewpoint of education, made fairly manifest in 1947. In a general sense, this view has prevailed up to the present time. But before we examine the later attitude, let us briefly consider the situation as it stood when the attempt at "formal" social revolution began to fail. There are three aspects to consider: the position of the Frontier Thinker, the position of the educator *not* affiliated with this movement, and, most important of all, the classroom results in terms of education for citizenship.

The National Association of Secondary School Principals and the National Council for Social Studies, both departments of the NEA (which had been one of the major organi-

147

zational forces behind the Frontier Movement), indicated in 1944 that the educational task of "rebuilding the social order" was by no means given up. In this year the aforementioned NEA agencies published jointly a book to "... serve teachers as resource material." Written by Oscar Lange and Abba Lerner, it was entitled, *American Way of Business*. It is impossible to say how much harm this book has done to the teaching of basic Americanism in our schools. Here is a small sampling from this "source material" for teachers, who are advised that:

. . *public enterprise* must become a major constituent of our economy, if we are really going to have economic prosperity. [and] . . . it is necessary to have *public ownership of banking and credit* [investment banks and insurance companies] . . . A publicly owned "banking and credit system alone is compatible with the flexibility of capital value necessary to maintain competitive standards in production and trade. [and] . . . it is necessary to have *public ownership of monopolistic key industries*. . . . The legal basis for public ownership of such industries should be provided by an amendment of the anti-trust laws . . . [and] . . . it is necessary to have *public ownership of basic natural resources* [mines, oil, timber, coal, etc.]. [and] . . . special economic courts [enjoying the same independence as courts of justice] might be established [and] . . . That *the economic courts be given the power to repeal any rules of Congress, of the legislatures, or of the municipal councils* . . .

Is it any wonder that today government intervention and domination in the area of private enterprise is rapidly transforming America into a welfare state!

Lange and Lerner were admittedly Frontier extremists. But even the most sincere and scholarly teachers of the social studies had been swayed by the years of intense, "new-order" propaganda. Perhaps no professor of education of this period was *less* impressed by the Frontier movement than Dr. Edgar Bruce Wesley, an esteemed and prolific author who, for many years, taught at high schools and teacher-training institutions. Dr. Wesley, belonging to that portion of the profession who were first and foremost educators, felt neither the need nor the inclination to indoctrinate youth for a remolding of American society. Due precisely to this fact, it may well be that Dr. Wesley and his colleagues are more significant to this study than the avowed social planners of this time.

One may charge that Harold Rugg disseminated subversive ideas through the public schools. The charge would not be denied because Rugg did so openly and wilfully. But to charge that an innocent educator of high dedication, in this instance Dr. Wesley, was an instrument of subversive thought is an altogether different matter. The Frontier Movement may be criticized, *but the influences of this movement which have been widely accepted apparently must not be questioned.* Once a revolutionary doctrine has been toned down and dignified and incorporated into the general fund of educational material taught in our schools, it seems henceforth to be considered immune to critical analysis. This complacent tendency — conformity to group-trends in education — is the crux of the controversy between those who charge that brainwashing and subversion exist in our schools and those who vehemently deny it (as did the superintendents surveyed by the Independence Hall Association and quoted in Chapter Five herein.

Dr. Wesley was neither a brainwasher nor a subversive. Nevertheless he *was* influenced, as all social studies teachers have been, by the Frontier philosophy and movement, and his writings *do* contain elements of Frontier thought. His book, *Teaching the Social Studies* (the revised, 1942 edition), shows a number of moderate derivations from the concepts originated by the new-social-order people. For example, the pragmatic concept of our constitutional republic as a tentative political structure can be discerned in Dr. Wesley's outline of "A Philosophy For Social Studies Teachers." He states, "Democracy, being more than a form or a structure, requires constant study, criticism, and constructive efforts."[14] If he were speaking here of "democracy" in the broad sense, rather than as a synonymous term for our clearly defined "republic," the statement would be acceptable. But the implication regarding our permanent, constitutional form of government is clarified by a further

149

statement that, "The quibble over the words republic and democracy should not confuse anyone as to the essential elements of a democracy." p. 247. As will be clearly pointed out in the chapter to follow, what is here called a "quibble" is not a matter for quibbling at all. Democracy is a word that means one thing. Republic is another word, the meaning of which is altogether and importantly different. To consider these concepts as interchangeable is no more logical than to call a glass of water an ocean. As Dr. Wesley himself explains, "Whatever be the form, a government can be infused with the democratic spirit and process." *(op. cit.)* A government can be democratic whatever its form, be it a monarchy, communistic, socialistic, collectivistic, republican, or what-have-you. One of the most damning innovations of the Frontier movement was its abolition of the proper noun *Republic* in favor of a vague and cunning application of the common noun *democracy.*

The new interpretation of man as a social integer rather than as a human being of individual significance is inferred by Dr. Wesley's statement: "Social good takes precedence over individual success." p. 17. A practical application of this "democratic" view, regarding the family, is seen in the pronouncement that, ". . . the parents must ask the children about buying a new rug, moving to a different house, readjusting the budget to fit the income, and making other decisions which affect the welfare of the whole family. In brief, the family must be democratized." p. 275. The effect which this sort of abdication of parental authority has had on the youthful population in America does not require comment.

The reconstruction of the social order had required a change in emphasis from historical problems to current, unsolved problems. This Frontier innovation is also reflected in Dr. Wesley's book:

"The successful teaching of current controversial topics, such as evolution, sex information, socialism, and pacificism . . . is worthy of great attention; to a considerable extent they are the only materials that reserve the highest quality of peda-

150

gogical effort. So the answer to the question, "Should teachers deal with controversial issues?' is that they should, after performing their routine obligations, deal with nothing else." p. 434.

A federal government, definitely limited in power by a written constitution, a threefold division of power, and a vigilant electorate, was believed by our forefathers to be the prime safeguard of individual liberty. The Frontier Thinkers, on the contrary, openly called for unlimited government power as a prime instrument of the evolution of a new social order. Their influence can be clearly seen in Dr. Wesley's teacher-text. He describes the traditional emphasis on limited government by a discreet assertion that, ". . . negation rather than positive action was regarded as the great safeguard of democracy." p. 252. In 1942 he stated that limited federal power is old-fashioned: "An active, strong, and vigorous government was considered the antithesis of democracy. And even today many people still cling to this outmoded concept." (op. cit.) In his revelation of an up-to-date concept of government planning and control, Dr. Wesley veers closer to the Rugg-Counts concept than anywhere else in his book. "Rugged individualism [individualism is always "rugged" to those who oppose it]," said Dr. Wesley, "and unplanned economy result in waste and exploitation; the general welfare requires social control and deliberate planning." p. 18.

The agnostic philosophy of William James holds that Value must constantly undergo change and that the values of one generation will not serve another. Hence the pragmatic educator must keep an open mind for new ideas, no matter how radical or disloyal they may appear to be. It is not pragmatic, for instance, to commit oneself to a judgment on the basis of historical hindsight; the pragmatist does not judge a movement for a new social order as good or evil, but simply says, "Let's wait and see." In this connection it is interesting to note several comments made by Dr. Wesley regarding the "Frontier movement" and one of its leaders.

The periodical *Frontiers of Democracy,* from which we have quoted Rugg, Dewey, Barnes, etc., Dr. Wesley says: "This

151

courageous monthly magazine constantly discusses problems of democracy, education freedom, and teachers' responsibilities." p. 263.

The School Can Teach Democracy, by George S. Counts: "This little pamphlet carries an emphatic and much needed lesson." p. 262.

The more notorious *Dare the School Build a New Social Order?,* by Counts: "An appeal to the schools to assume a more aggressive role in promoting social reform." p. 91.

Unlike Professors Rugg, *et al.,* who have afforded us a picture of the Frontier "leaders"; unlike Professor Paul Klapper who served to represent the position of the Frontier "followers"; Dr. Wesley should fairly clarify the attitude of the "non-Frontier Thinker" of the period in question. Had this last group been a little less "open-minded" toward the fate of American education, the effects of the revolutionary years might well have been nullified in later years.

It remains to be examined how well the commitment of education to prepare future citizens was being met. What had happened in the classroom? How were the children faring? An indication of the effect of the new-social-order education is very evident in an "educational exploration of the future of democracy," directed by Brameld and discussed by him in 1945.[15] Students of a typical Mid-western high school were given a number of propositions to either affirm or deny. A portion of the "rated" propositions follow:

There should be Government ownership and control of radio stations.
(Affirm)

Liberal interpretation of the Constitution has permitted too great expansion of the powers of the Federal Government.
(Deny)

Family life is in need of no change in its traditional form.
(Deny)

What this country needs is more TVA's.
(Affirm)

152

The Constitution needs some radical modifications.
(*Affirm*)

There is need of a change in our constitutional pattern which would eliminate State boundaries and set up a system of representation based primarily on economic and geographical regions. (*Affirm*)

There is too much bureaucracy in Government already.
(*Deny*)

Our economic base must be shifted from rugged individualism to economic planning.
(*Affirm*)

Without individual competition for profits, our economy would slow up and soften.
(*Deny*)

These excerpts were taken from Shafer and Snow's *The Turning of the Tides*, which concluded:

The indoctrination is subtle. During the student year it is a detail of the work. It is an item to be done. No talk is raised; no sound is heard. Yet here, fitting significantly into the pattern of the whole, its warning rings out like a trumpet call.[16]

Children involved in this "educational exploration" were not merely hypothetical units of a survey. At the present time they are about thirty years of age. They are among the young adults of today who are faced with the serious responsibility of preserving the heritage of America through wise and vigilant self-government. Will they? Were they educated for this difficult task? From the views expressed on government, the Constitution, the family, and the American economy, it is apparent that they were taught a form of socialism, not Americanism.

And so it may be said that only the *external* war was brought to an end in 1945. America has still to win the war that wages within her very soul—the public-school classroom.

153

PART II. "WE SHALL MAKE NO COMPROMISE," said Harold Rugg in 1947 and, "we cannot take a middle road."[17]

Nevertheless, a compromise was made. Following World War II, the "social aims" of education were broadened and couched in words that could be acceptable to teachers and reformers alike. The social emphasis shifted from a reconstruction of America to the establishment of a "genuine international authority"—reconstruction of the whole world. Earlier emphasis on the destruction of our free-enterprise system shifted to the engineering of a new "ideal" system of international economics. Educational reformers had come to "think big" in terms of government, economics, and society. The new idea, the idea which is at this present moment predominant in American schools, was the development in our schools of "world citizens." Patriotism and national allegiance are "narrow" and "dangerous." National sovereignty is a "myth." A "new tradition" must be fashioned and youth must not be allowed to succumb to the old out-dated traditions of their forebears. Thus, the old "revolution" was broadened and given a new coat of euphemistic paint.

This new compromise was formally adopted November 29, 1947, at a meeting of the American Education Fellowship in Chicago, Illinois. The statement of the "New Policy for the AEF" was prepared by Theodore Brameld. It included, ". . . two great constructive purposes [which] have first claim for active support."[18]

1. The reconstruction of the economic system in the direction of far greater justice and stability; a system to be secured by *whatever democratic planning and social controls* experience shows to be necessary: . . .

2. The establishment of a genuine world order, *an order in which national sovereignty is subordinate to world authority* in all crucial interests affecting peace and security . . . an order in which *international economic coordination* of trade, resources, labor and standards parallels the best practices of individual nations; an order geared with the *increasing specialization and public controls* now developing in England, Sweden, New Zealand and certain other countries . . . an

154

order in which ' *world citizenship*" thus assumes *at least* equal status with national citizenship.*

Through information such as this, the classroom teacher is to form "convictions" and these convictions are, in turn, to be "shared" with the students. A false type of "academic freedom" would be thus utilized to engineer a new world order. "In implementing the above outlook," warned the AEF statement, "there should be no attempt to indoctrinate for any political party or for any given economic system." But the teachers should ". . . make sure that the process will lead to conclusions. This can be done by *informed* teachers who have *convictions of their own*—convictions which they do not foist upon their students but which at appropriate age levels they *share* with students."

The development of "world citizens" meant to the AEF a complete overhauling of traditional beliefs and allegiances. The schools should:

. . . study and endorse the United Nations to be sure; and that is helpful. But they seldom face the contradiction between high-minded objectives for all nations and the still dominant power of sovereignty for each nation. Students are taught that internationalism is desirable; they are also taught that the United States is supreme in its own right.

Therefore, that a "genuine international authority" might not be foiled by a sovereign United States, teachers were urged to ". . . push for recognition by the United Nations of the need to lift UNESCO above its present purely advisory status."

UNESCO, which should be lifted above an "advisory status" reports in the first of a series of volumes called, "Towards World Understanding":

A Model Plan for the Analysis of Textbooks has been drafted. After

* Expressions which appeared in the first draft, but not in the final statement included: "international planning of production and distribution," "chaotic planlessness of traditional 'free enterprise'," "natural resources . . . owned and controlled by the people," "outmoded economic systems," "diseased nationalisms," and "reshape the culture of America and the world."[19]

155

it has been checked by experts in different countries, UNESCO will *suggest* to its Member States that they review their own textbooks in light of the recommendations."[20]

Obviously, the only reason why UNESCO may do no more than "suggest" governmental review of textbooks is the fact that it has *not* been lifted above an "advisory status."

Have American parents and citizens commissioned educators to "push" for an increase of the power of this international educational organization? Do our people want a world government and/or the national government to analyze and review textbooks in the light of world citizenship? One of our country's strongest beliefs has been the *local operation and control* of public schools. Isn't a "Model Plan" devised by a world organization and "checked" by foreign "experts" a long, long way from home?

This relatively new "world citizenship" indoctrination in our schools is a frightfully important matter for consideration by the American people. Surely, no one would argue against education for international understanding. But just as surely no American intends that it be taught at the expense of American tradition, sovereignty and allegiance! It is therefore vitally important that the citizenry of the United States understand exactly what some educators mean when they use the simple phrase, "education for international understanding." There is evidence which indicates that it is really indoctrination for world government.

Public Law 471, HR 8067, enacted by the eighty-third Congress and signed by the President, is a specific directive against the teaching of *One World Citizenship* or *One World Government* in the schools of this country. Hence, it is not likely that One World advocates would operate openly. And it is unlikely that a controversial world organization like UNESCO would admit to a more ambitious goal than world "understanding."

As the *Eleventh Yearbook* (1951) of the John Dewey Society ironically points out: "The one phrase which most nations seem to be willing to use is 'education for international under-

156

standing' as attested to by the adoption of this phraseology by UNESCO after long and heated debates. These words imply a less ambitious approach and one which most governments are willing to approve."[21]

But nevertheless: "Nothing short of a transformation of our educational system is likely to produce the kind of results which are needed to build a world society." p. 230.

It is a fact that this transformation involves a gradual change in the feelings, appreciations, attitudes, loyalties and behavior characteristics of American children. These changes consist of orientation away from the nation and toward the world. As was the case in the old "revolution," these changes are to be effected through curricula and textbook revision, and through increased emphasis on new goals of education.

The NEA is the largest organized representative of teachers in America. Its publication, *Education for Internal Understanding in American Schools,* is a comprehensive policy statement for our teachers to follow. Now, as mentioned previously, the American people not the NEA, is the commissioning body of public education. Of each of the following excerpts from the NEA book on international understanding, the question must be asked: Is this what the American people want for their children? And if it is not what we want, we must say so *now*.

It is "imperative," states this NEA report, that our children:

. . . be trained in the art of judgment that will be ultimately reflected in the public decisions that constitute the foundation of official governmental policies. Since it seems evident that the firm establishment of a world organization and the achievement of a world order will be a slow and gradual process, the children in our schools will be called upon to sustain, and strengthen this movement, and to lend their efforts to its advancement.[22]

Underneath the double-talk this statement clearly implies that "the children in our schools" are to be "trained" to make "public decisions" on our own "governmental policies" through which the "advancement" of "this movement" toward the "establishment" of a "world organization" will be "ulti-

157

mately reflected." Do we, the American people, want our children taught to build a new world order through a world organization? Or is this a new goal of education set by a handful of Americans? We did not accept the idea of building a new "social order" through education, and it is highly likely that we do not desire the building of a new "world order" through the public school system.

The "new world order" people are not making the same mistake that the "new social order" people made in the 1930's. This revolution is not to be sudden. Rather, it is to come about gradually, painlessly:

. . . we cannot expect to revolutionize our thinking overnight. Established habits of thought die hard, national prejudices are usually quite deep-seated, and long-range goals are sometimes difficult to keep in view . . . we cannot afford the assumption that meeting the challenge now will guarantee a world order perhaps even within our generation. p. 9.

If a "prejudice" is "national" it must be that a majority of the people hold it. And, as no one considers his own principles to be "prejudicial," it must be the minority of "non-prejudiced" people who see these beliefs as national "prejudices." Can it be then that some of the "prejudices" referred to by this reporting minority are, in fact, national beliefs or widely accepted traditions? The question is not whether America contains prejudices; every nation does. It is whether or not the educational leaders under our commission have the authority to decide which beliefs are "prejudices" and what "established habits" must be washed from young brains. Do the American people desire teachers to "revolutionize" their children's thinking? Is this "long-range goal" for a "world order" what the American public wants for tomorrow's citizens?

. . . the school program must include experiences designed to tap all the sources that go into producing the desired behavior characteristics of the world-minded American. Actual changes in behavior is the goal, and any modification in behavior entails changes in attitudes. p. 83.

158

. . . As has been emphasized above, factual information alone will not make a world-minded citizen. He must . . . have world-oriented feelings, appreciations, and attitudes.

At a time when solid Americanism is urgently needed, this is the direction that citizenship education is taking. The school program must be revised to *change* behavior. It is certainly apparent that the behavior involved here is one of loyalty and allegiance, inasmuch as the change sought requires the re-orientation of feelings, appreciations, and attitudes. Those familiar with this movement are aware of this constant plea to replace "narrow" patriotism with "world understanding." Though the effort was begun little more than a decade ago, the success of this movement is already perceptible. The statements above amount to an approbation of indoctrination for world citizenship; and once again we must ask ourselves whether this is by commission of the American people.

The NEA "international understanding" policy statement reveals a number of methods of achieving the new educational goal. For example:

This will certainly involve curriculum revision and the *recasting of many time-honored educational policies and practices.* p. 9.

UNESCO offers a direct means through which the *power of education* may be channeled for the *gradual* achievement of *its* over-all objective. p. 37.

UNESCO is devoted to formulating and carrying out on a world-wide scale a positive program for promotion of international understanding through education. . . . Among these activities and projects . . . [is] collection, study, and improvement of textbooks and teaching materials, particularly those which relate to international understanding . . . p. 37.

It is very plain that one of the time-honored educational policies and practices which One-Worldites would recast is the very *source* of American education's "over-all objectives." Surely, in our country the *people* are the "means through which

159

the *power of education*" must be channeled, not UNESCO. *Edu-cational* changes as fundamental as this are certainly not the sole responsibility of professional educationists. And the "improvement" of American textbooks and teaching materials is positively not the responsibility of the United Nations Educational, Scientific and Cultural Organization.

The world-minded American knows that unlimited national sovereignty is a threat to world peace . . . p. 13.

The America-minded citizen, however, knows that the loss of national sovereignty would be a much more deadly threat to individual liberty. Sovereignty is a condition of supreme political authority. It is "unlimited" by definition. America may either keep her sovereignty or surrender it to a sovereign world government, but she cannot become nine-tenths sovereign, or 99.9% sovereign. It is a decision that rests with the American electorate. But it is incredible to find that our youth are given alternatives of national sovereignty *with war,* or world "peace" through a world authority. Even though the American people have in no way indicated that they want to relinquish their sovereignty, our teachers are further advised:

Both world history and American history can contribute to the young American's appreciation of the facts that "unlimited national sovereignty is a threat to world peace" . . . p. 175.

Thus, we are told of a major means whereby the second "great constructive purpose" of the American Education Fellowship is to be carried out, namely, "The establishment of a genuine world order, an order in which national sovereignty is subordinate [not "limited"] to world authority . . in which international economic coordination . . . increasing socialization . . . [and] 'world citizenship' " exist!

We are told that American history can contribute to the discouragement of national sovereignty. Never! Not if it is taught factually by teachers devoted to their country. American history, on the contrary, is in itself the story of a sovereign people and a record of the great accomplishments that grew

160

out of this individual right and responsibility to rule. An appreciation of America's history is the common denominator which has changed sovereign individuals into a sovereign nation; the heritage which has inspired the people of this nation to perpetuate the American way of life—and it will never "contribute" to America's destruction unless it is perverted by motives foreign to the ideals of our sovereign Republic.

While "world-oriented feelings, appreciations, and attitudes" are instilled in the child, another suggestion advises:

"If history books used in England or Canada can be obtained, students in American history classes will find it of interest to compare these books with their own texts with respect to their treatment of the American Revolution and the War of 1812." (P. 142)

But that is just one "learning experience" through which the child may develop disrespect for his country. The authors continue:

Many similar learning experiences can be developed if textbooks from other countries can be made available to U. S. students. Translation of textbooks used in the Soviet Union will be found in *New Russia's Primer* (Houghton Mifflin, Boston, 1931) and *I Want to be Like Stalin* (John Day, New York, 1947). P. 142.

The translator of *New Russia's Primer* prefaces this text with such remarks as, "What child could resist the appeal . . ."— "No one can read the last chapter without being moved by the great social vision . . ."—and "To American teachers and students of education this little book should prove both suggestive and challenging."

The translator, incidentally, is Dr. George S. Counts.

An indication of the extent of brainwashing that can be achieved through this sort of "learning experience" is also provided. An account of a study of Russia by a sixth-grade group, ". . . illustrates the direction which much of our study of other peoples may take." The teacher who gave the account is quoted; and in, turn this teacher quotes a student who wrote a story about Russia, "as a final evaluation check-up":

161

After studying our unit on Russia [wrote this sixth-grade student], my way of thinking has changed. In the beginning, I felt that this was a country . . . [with] . . . different thoughts, and different way of living Now I feel better acquainted with them . . . I think their government should let more books be written about the Russian people and how they live today . . ." p. 163.

Is it fair to our children, even in the name of "international understanding," to teach them that Russia is a country with thoughts that are not different from our own, and *a way of life* that is not different from the American way of life?

Teachers are given, "Still another approach" through a description of a program called "Looking at China." After this program, "When the lights go on again . . . the Chinese flag and other decorations have new meaning. And it is the Chinese Flag the [American] children face as they sing the Chinese National Anthem "Chi-Lai." p. 164.

Is this sort of educational practice generally accepted by the American people? We are given the answer by those who recommend the "approach":

Symbols of international ideas—songs, flags, slogans, posters, and the like can be expected eventually to contribute focal points for developing international loyalties [*sic*], but few such symbols *have as yet been generally accepted.* p. 176.

This would seem to prove that the majority of teachers, parents, and citizens of America prefer the development of loyalty toward the Land of Liberty, not a *world order*.

When this new educational goal was launched in the post-war years there was considerable opposition voiced by teachers and laymen. However, this army of patriots made hardly more than a ripple in the "new world" advance. And this was a prophecy come true, for the NEA's *Defense Bulletin No. 35* warned in 1950:

The enemy in this campaign that seems to be impending is stronger than he looks. If we get our combat team together, however . . . even a stronger army than this one would make hardly more than a ripple in . . . our advance. [23]

162

The NEA got its "combat team" together, and the strategy used was very simple. The enemy of indoctrination for One-Worldism, in the eyes of this powerful organization, became a part of, ". . . a general attack on public education in the United States . . . recruiting and training his forces, building up his stockpiles, filling his war chest, and organizing his propaganda units."[24]

The strategy is very effective. How many teachers (or laymen, for that matter) could afford to belong to such a wicked and ruthless army as this described by the NEA? A blow struck for national loyalty and patriotic citizenship, thus becomes a blow against "public education in the United States."

As these professional educationists were forming their "combat teams," the Frontier Thinkers not only continued their movement for a "new social order," but they fell easily into step with the new-world-order movement. In 1950—years after the so-called "temporary revolution" in education had "ended"—one of the original Frontier Thinkers was still urging teachers:

We must [wrote John L. Childs] develop a more positive regard for cultural aspects of human existence, and be prepared to support a vastly extended program of community services. This, in turn, means *frank commitment to the welfare state'*, and to the *planned organization of the productive enterprises* of our country.

Because the Frontier Movement was no longer *the* movement in education, Dr. Childs spoke rather of a "group" of educators who desired "a reorganization of our economy." And he candidly described this group's connection with the present movement toward a new world order through the schools:

This group of educators also believes that there is an *intimate connection* between the *domestic effort* to achieve a more *socialized economy* and the *world effort* to develop a democratic system of *collective security.*[25]

It would be a mistaken and dangerous assumption to consider the influence of the Frontier Thinkers as unimportant

163

in the decade of the 1950's. As recent as September, 1958, a supplement of the monthly *Educational News Service* carried this paragraph:

"On any list of foremost educationists, ranked on the basis of prominence and influence, the name of George Sylvester Counts will appear in the top ten. On many lists the name will be one of the top five."[26]

In 1952—the year in which *today's eighth-grade students* began their schooling — Columbia University Teachers College proudly published a book entitled *Education and American Civilization* by George S. Counts, Professor of Education. After acknowledging Dewey, Childs, Beard, Henry Steele Commager, and others, Counts proceeds to reiterate the same un-American call that he had made to the teachers of the nation a generation before. Although in 1952 he doesn't openly demand a "socialized economy" as he did in 1932, he does so indirectly with such euphemisms as: "Some measure of general planning, direction, and coordination is clearly necessary. Whether this can or should be achieved by a far-reaching fiscal policy, by the *direct assumption on the part of existing governmental agencies* . . . by the creation of some special *federal* organ . . . by the *socialization* of certain strategically situated branches of economy . . ." Etc.[27]

The reader of this volume is told by the author of the *Forward,* Stephen M. Corey,* that:

We cling tenaciously to a *host of myths* that are contradicted by the most significant of contemporary events.

This clinging blindly to the past, Mr. Counts believes, is the surest way to lose the future. p. vi.

We are told that Dr. Counts offers a "new American way of life," which must rest upon a new synthesis of values. The truth is that he offers an *old* way of life, one wherein the government rules the people. He offers the way of life that existed

* Executive Officer, The Horace Mann—Lincoln Institute of School Experimentation. This Institute, wrote Corey, ". . . is proud to add *Education and American Civilization* to its list of published studies."

164

in America prior to 1776. His proposal rests on the antithesis, not the synthesis, of the American thesis of values. America believes that the individual is of greater value than the State. Professor Counts offers to reduce the individual's value by eliminating his sovereignty through a welfare state. "In terms of economic welfare," he writes, "an age is opening that will mark a revolutionary break with the entire civilized human past." He predicted this years ago—for the first half of the twentieth century—but the revolution failed. Now, in this book, he attempts to sell this "new American way of life" to another generation of teachers. *Now* it is, "During the next half-century [that] we are going to modify profoundly our economy, our social structure, our cultural institutions, and even our outlook on the world." p. 215.

Corey speaks of "what he [Counts] believes to be the American heritage," and Counts speaks ironically of the "urgency of reconstructing conceptions and attitudes inherited from the past . . ." (p. 307) Indeed, "We must cease casting nostalgic eyes toward the past," says Counts just as Dewey (whom Counts ranks with "Socrates," "Jesus," and "Jefferson" p. 284) had proclaimed a generation before.

It cannot be over-emphasized that this book was written only eight years ago, by an American educator, for American teachers of American children in school today. In it Professor Counts offers to the American people a "new American way of life"—not openly through the Congress of the United States— but through the vulnerable young minds in the public-school classroom.

It amounts to the same old condemnation of fundamental American attitudes and principles. It carries the same old message to undermine the traditional American way of life, and proves that there is still an influential Frontier movement attempting to sell a foreign ideology to our teachers.

But—perhaps most important of all—it reveals the "intimate connection" between "the domestic effort to achieve a more socialized economy, and the *world effort* to develop a democratic system of *collective security.*" (cf. fn. 25)

165

Dr. Counts sees the logical relationship between the building of a new social order and a new world order, the former being a mere preparatory step to the latter. And so he tells our teachers, "The contraction of the earth has been accompanied by the laying of the physical foundations of a *world community.*" And that, ". . . the struggle to build a *world community of equal peoples* will be long and difficult."

(Dr. Counts says of Communism: "Wherever it goes it destroys the last vestige of individual freedom and subjects men to a tyranny far more terrifying than that of the worst of tsars." But is not this very Communism he speaks of, a "struggle to build a world community of equal peoples" by destroying "the last vestige of individual freedom"?)

Like the educationists mentioned earlier, Professor Counts advises teachers to condition their students to accept world sovereignty and surrender their heritage of popular sovereignty to this "world community."

"Men must," says Counts, "acquire knowledge, develop the *loyalties,* and make the sacrifices [*sic*] necessary to discharge the *political* responsibilities required for the establishment of an international order." Here we have a much more direct interpretation of "international understanding." We learn now that the establishment of an "international order" is a *political* responsibility. In other words, the "knowledge," "loyalties," and "sacrifices" required of us are for the construction of a world polity or government.

Dr. Counts tells our teachers: "The myth [*sic*] of national sovereignty is still deeply rooted in our pores." (p. 198). And teachers are advised to pass this information on to our children, because:

The younger generation must understand the changed foundations of sovereignty and be prepared to make sacrifices to the building of a genuine *world order.* p. 427.

Is this Americanism or Worldism? Is this education for American citizenship or for World citizenship? Is this preparation for victory or defeat in the battle against communism?

166

While this educator would have our youth believe that national sovereignty must be sacrificed to a world authority, an advocate of the UN would have us believe otherwise. A Public Affairs Pamphlet, published in cooperation with The Institute for International Order, claims that sovereignty is not an issue of the bid for world organization:

Large-circulation American newspapers and magazines warn against the UN's "world government" ambitions although its Charter, without a hint of equivocation, guarantees the sovereignty and interdependence of every member nation.[28]

Why, then, should our children be taught that national sovereignty should be surrendered? Is the UN Charter and Declaration of Human Rights preferrable to our own Constitution and Bill of Rights? The answer is *no*. Note, for example, the wording of Article 29 of the UN Declaration of Human Rights:

"In the exercise of his rights and freedoms, everyone shall be subject only to such limitations as are determined by law . . ."

Is this consistent with our concept of God-given rights that are to be secured rather than limited by law? Compare this Article 29 of the UN Declaration with the First Amendment in our Bill of Rights:

Congress shall make no law respecting an establishment of religion, or prohibiting the free exercise thereof; or abridging the freedom of speech, or of the press; or the right of the people peaceably to assemble, and to petition the Government for a redress of grievances.

This amendment, as well as the rest of the Bill of Rights, our Constitution, and our way of life, is protected *by the sovereignty of our nation*. And our sovereignty is, in turn, sustained by citizens who have been taught the meaning of their heritage, who have been given an education enriched with spiritual and moral concepts of loyalty, duty, devotion, and allegiance to the United States of America. Without the preparation for

167

patriotic and responsible citizenship which they are entitled to, tomorrow's citizens may surrender their popular sovereignty to an international order. And only after it is too late to matter, will they grasp the meaning of what they have lost, and realize how seriously we adults betrayed them in their youth.

The change is very subtle. The method is a blurring or a merging of loyalties until the student may eventually recognize no significant difference between his international understanding and his American citizenship.

A recent federal Office of Education Bulletin listed as a principal guide for program planning, the idea that, "Citizenship education moves out to state, national, and world situations by way of the experiences which pupils have had in school and community. As they move outward, pupils should be led to see and understand the connections . . . One therefore finds no sharp divisions of the social studies into courses on the community and courses on national and world affairs."[29]

One can perceive a steady deterioration of Americanism education which began decades ago and still persists. Under Dewey's influence history was turned into an indirect sociology. The citizenship subjects were blurred into a social studies curriculum by Rugg and others. And here is a further blending of important distinctions, wherein one finds "no sharp divisions" of community understanding and loyalty, national patriotism, and the student's relationship to the world.

These changes have been made, and are being made, in the name of universal social reform. The schools are considered experimental instruments through which the world may be improved according to the test of experience, not the test of truth and value, or of good and bad. Thus, in 1956, we find the distinguished educator Ernest O. Melby stating in a national news weekly:

"In this human-centered universe, there is no perfect hierarchy of truth, there are no criteria beyond the realm of experience. . . . Anything to be learned must be lived . . ."[30]

168

A reform movement for an international order, based on this false, pragmatic philosophy, should not, *must not*, replace Americanism in the classroom. The fallacy of this new version of citizenship education is clearly explained by Robert M. Hutchins:

If we are going to talk about improving men and societies, we have to believe that there is some difference between good and bad. . . . We cannot tell this difference by any examination of the effectiveness of a given program as the pragmatists propose; the time required to estimate these effects is usually too long and the complexity of society is always too great for us to say that the consequences of a given program are altogether clear. We cannot discover the difference between good and bad by going to the laboratory, for men and societies are not laboratory animals. If we believe that there is no truth, there is no knowledge, and there are no values except those which are validated by laboratory experiment, we cannot talk about the improvement of men and societies, for we can have no standard of promoting or judging anything that takes place among men or in societies.

Society is to be improved, not by forcing a program of social reform down its throat, through the schools or otherwise, but by the improvement of the individuals who compose it. . . .The individual is the heart of society.[31]

While the orientation for world citizenship continues, there is evidence that the teaching of fundamental Americanism has greatly suffered. Dozens of recent polls and surveys have turned up shocking facts about the civic ignorance prevailing in many classrooms. There is evidence that American youth is not receiving an adequate grounding in American history, the Declaration of Independence, the Constitution, the Bill of Rights, and other basic cornerstones of the foundation of our republic.

In February, 1959, the *Ladies' Home Journal* reproduced examples of written work of high-school students in an article which asked, "Is This American Education?" Theodore Guerin, the author of this alarming article, explained:

I have hundreds of similar papers that I have collected in high schools in which I have taught and from teachers in other high

169

schools. When I show them to my neighbors, they are amazed But another teacher is likely to say, "why, I have worse on my desk right now!"[32]

One example consisted of an assignment in a twelfth-grade history course which called for the spelling of states. The misspelled names of states listed below were taken from a list of thirty-five turned in by a senior who graduated—and who is now in college preparing to become a teacher:

Wasington, Califoria, Taxes, Florda, Montanna, Main, North Decoda, Oaklihoma, Kanses, Kentucky, Rode Island, Kiniticate, South Decoda, Pensilvania, Vermount, Illinoise, Alibama, Arisonna, Missouii, Massachucits, Luisianna, Carilina, Origan and Conniticate.

Even more shocking and pathetic are the following excerpts from history tests given to eleventh-grade students:

Washington fairwell agress a speech which said, what will go on, and what will be needed to beguin like stay away from Europe.

Francise, Scott, and Key   Please tell me
The 13 - 14 - 15 Amendments. 13 is know slaieves in the U.S. 14 is that colored people are [citizens?] of the U.S. and 15 they have the right to voot.

3/5 Compromise that is if the house has 3/5 and senat has 3/5 and Congress has 3/5 that the bill can passed.

22 Amendment is that beer can not be sold or made or anything like that.

Undoubtedly, the above are extreme examples. But they are not rare examples. Citizenship education is vital to the survival of our nation. Whether a student is dull or bright, he is destined to take part in the government of America. Whether a student is dull or bright he must receive a fundamental understanding of the foundations of his country. And this understanding must take priority over social reform, over

170

international understanding, over life adjustment, over curricular experimentation, over all temporary expediency. Americanism is basic to American education. And today, with the deadly shadow of Communism already stretched across half the globe, Americanism is more urgently needed in our schools than at any other time in the history of our country. Yet, at this very moment, citizenship education is being oriented *away* from this basic understanding and toward a vague re-ordering of the world.

Henry Steele Commager, one of America's best known historians and an influential educator, presented a paper at a recent, three-day Conference on the American High School. In this paper (included in the 1958 publication of *The High School in a New Era*) he asked, not for a return to traditional Americanism, but for the continued discouragement of it. He conjectured that at the present time, ". . . perhaps the greatest need is to understand other countries and other cultures. . ."

"The young," Professor Commager believes, "do not need more nationalism, but less . . . nor do they need to have their enthusiasm for something called vaguely 'the American system' whipped up artificially. There is no reason to suppose that the compulsory study of American history in the elementary school and again in the high school necessarily makes good citizens."

In his opinion, and deplorably so, ". . . the schools, instead of encouraging the young to challenge old shibboleths and to develop broader and more spiritual loyalties, tend to join in the parade of ostentatious patriotism."[33]

We are not now listening to the words of a "radical" or of an educational "revolutionist." Henry Steele Commager is a dedicated, respected American with a genuine interest in the education of today's youth. He is quoted with necessary brevity here and, of course, "out of context"; there is no intention to delineate his exact stand on citizenship education. Simply mark the tone of the quoted remarks—other countries, old shibboleths, broader loyalties, artificial enthusiasm, ostentatious patriotism, a vaguely called American system.

171

What is this new fashion in language? What kind of round corner are we backing ourselves into? Of all that Americans have fought and died for, of all the valour and heroic deeds that have gone into the building of America—is this sort of equivocal solicitude all we have left?

Doubtless there is great need for mutual understanding in the world today. But this need does not alter fact. It is axiomatic that our youth—soon to rule three million square miles of human liberty—must be educated to understand their *own* complex country and their *own* democratic culture. This is a requisite of their American heritage. This need must be given priority over the need to be introduced to fifty or sixty other countries and cultures.

The enthusiasm of students for "the American system" is not going to be whipped up—"artificially" or any other way —until they understand through the study of its history— "compulsory" or otherwise—what the American system is.

There is no reason to suppose that the study of history makes good citizens because it is compulsory. On the other hand, there is every reason to believe that the study of history is compulsory because it is basic to the making of good citizens. It is fundamental to the development of loyalty and devotion toward the principles and spiritual guides of our land, and as such, it is compulsory by commission of the people.

Good will toward the world is one thing—a very splendid and important thing—but loyalty is another, It has carried a particular meaning for thousands of years. The standard definition of loyalty is very clear and concise:

Faithful adherence to one's government or sovereign.

To broaden our children's loyalties, it is either necessary to make them wholly meaningless, or to re-direct them away from America and toward an alien government or sovereignty. That is the plain truth. Nevertheless, the old American "shibboleth" of loyalty is being challenged today. It is a change in process today. It marks the present direction of a long line of changes in traditional educational philosophy and goals concerned with citizenship. Scarcely a dozen years old,

172

this latest change amounts to a gradual shifting from Americanism to Worldism. This new movement in direction is steadily gaining momentum. The American character is leaning toward it. American youth are being conditioned to accept it.

As we have seen, the establishment of this "genuine international authority" became a formal educational policy at the 1947 AEF Convention. We also examined some of the main implications of this policy. A brief "progress report" seems appropriate at this time.

A recent, major "milestone" of this movement occurred several years ago in the form of an NEA bulletin published in December of 1956. Much more panoramic than the 1948 volume, this *International Understanding Through the Secondary School Curriculum* is also better organized, more specific, more fearless—and more frightening.

There is still the ticklish problem of what to call this new goal of education, but the selection of terminology has grown larger:

Many terms are used at present to designate the type of education which is needed. Some of the disagreement over these terms originates in differences as to *objectives*. Some of the disagreement arises from differences as to strategy [sic]. Among the terms now being used to designate this new dimension are the following:

Education for World Citizenship or education for a world society. Persons who use these two terms usually feel that the world has reached a stage of development where one can speak of a world society or world community, no matter how much it may be torn asunder by differences . . .

There are other and better terms to designate the type of education we are examining in this volume and which do not carry *unfortunate* connotations to most people . . .[34]

The suggestions which follow include: Education for living in the world community, Education of world-minded persons or persons with world horizons, Education for living in an international community, Education for world-minded Americans, and the selected heading, "Education for international understanding," which is "the most commonly used title."

173

Teachers are told in the beginning of the first chapter that, "Education for international understanding should be one of the *chief goals* of every secondary school in the United States."

The excerpts to follow are taken from "14 characteristics of an effective secondary school program in international understanding."

Where opposition does arise, those in charge of such programs need to analyze the reasons for such resistance, call on parents and local groups for support, present their case to the public in a variety of ways, keep other administrative officials informed of developments, *and conduct an open battle for their program if opposition mounts to such a point . . .*

If necessary, teachers are to carry out this program of international understanding against the will of parents and citizens of the community. But this is not a matter of technique or method which might better be decided by a teacher than a layman. In the words of the bulletin, it is a matter of whether or not this kind of training is to be *"one of the chief goals"* of our schools. Democracy rests on the belief that the people are the best judge of what the people want and do not want. In our country, if the people do not want their children to be educated for "international understanding" on the terms set by these educationists, and even if these professionals are convinced that they know what is best for our children, the right of the people must be recognized.

One of the primary characteristics of re-orienting a child toward world understanding, involves the conditioning of a new set of attitudes. The NEA bulletin provides some "findings" which may help the teacher internationalize his students. There is no mention of "brainwashing" but nevertheless the word comes to mind. Here are some of the findings, "From what we know at present":

B. Attitudes can be changed at any age.

C. It is difficult to change attitudes by working on individuals; change is best effected by involving groups.

174

F. Information is less important than usually considered, but carefully selected information from reliable sources (especially if the changes have selected the information themselves) and general reading of a non-conformist nature prepare people for change.

K. Appeals to pride, to one's practical nature, and to idealism are often effective.

It does not say how one may change the *world citizen* back into an American citizen in the event that the new attitudes prove treasonable.

Under another "characteristic," the teacher is advised that this education should be: "Carried on continuously, cumulatively, and comprehensively." For instance, "What is needed is the permeation of every subject and of every related activity by the philosophy of education for international understanding, with high priority given to this goal." It does not say what it should be given priority *over,* but inasmuch as Americanism is the only logical alternative perhaps that would seem redundant!

In a chapter entitled, "How Can the Principal Promote International Understanding?" the NEA bulletin refers to a secondary-school principal and his feelings about this subject. The principal reveals quite candidly exactly what is happening to the fundamental subject matter that has traditionally served to educate youth for American citizenship. To wit, it has become expendable:

The principal must assist such teachers in understanding that there is room for selected problems only and that one of the most critical areas is that of international problems, . . . *In the development of social studies courses, teachers must do some very severe pruning to permit important current items to be taught.*

Perhaps the whole of *International Understanding Through the Secondary School Curriculum* is most accurately (and most disturbingly) summarized by an openly un-American statement appearing on page 231:

"International Society" or "World Community" may not be a

175

reality to young people, or to many teachers. "Community" connotes some type of unitary government and structure, with laws that are binding on its members and with symbols of loyalty and authority. It involves people and places that are primary to one's experience, and anything beyond the nation may seem "out of bounds." To some, "World Community" is a utopian dream; to some others, it can never exist. "World Community" is, in fact, as much a state of mind as a concrete fact, and we should work toward this state of mind by concretizing the realities of international cooperation . . . .

Is there any power in this mighty American Republic of ours endowed with the authority to tamper with the *state of mind* of a solitary American child in the name of a *utopian dream?*

This final quotation is taken from Chapter 4, "How Can the Social Studies Promote International Understanding?" It is in the manner of confident flippancy, but there is something tragic about it:

"But professors, and various learned sirs," the social studies teacher may bemoan, "do you want us to spend *all our time* making students conscious of the big, wide, messed-up world that may burst into flames at any moment. Should we ignore the respected traditions of our predecessors who taught history in this very school before I was born,—and teach about the past *and* the present and what it means for the future? Should we abandon our sacred mission to fill our pupils' notebooks with historical knowledge (that may be very useful to them—sometime) in favor of something of the type recommended in this chapter?"

You, gentle reader, may answer for yourself. The author can only murmur—"certainly."

Yes, the reader may answer for himself, and so may the author; but who will answer for our children?

CHAPTER 9

THE OMMISSION

Russia's Real Sputnik

✿✿

Our greatest asset is the youth of America, and whoever or whatever wins youth wins the future of America. It is among the youth that Red Plague bearers do their most concentrated work. Teach your child the truths which have made this nation great, and you will have done much to combat the virus of Communism.　　　　J. EDGAR HOOVER

✿✿

SUPPOSE, FOR A MOMENT, that none of the facts cited in the four preceding chapters are important. Let us assume—in order to ascertain the seriousness of the American crisis—that pragmatic materialism has not contaminated the American character; that the change from a traditional citizenship curriculum to an experimental course in social studies has not affected educational Americanism; that the "revolution of 1933-1936" bred no lasting influences; that the current movement toward "world understanding" will have no ill effects on the citizens of tomorrow. In short, let us assume that we are educating citizens as well today as we did in the Nineteenth century. If this were true, *and it is not,* could we then continue along our complacent way?

The answer must be a resounding "No!"

Today, we are engaged in the deadliest war ever waged. It has no precedent in military history. It is a war that has made bullets and bombs virtually obsolete. Today, the whole world is divided into two camps by a crucial war of ideas, in a grim contest of the human mind that will be won or lost in the classroom. The Communists have sworn repeatedly that they

177

will not stop short of complete global conquest. If America fails to lead the free world to victory, Moscow will reduce it to despotic slavery.

No, it is not enough to build adequate citizens anymore; our schools must prepare soldiers of human liberty, ready to defend the rights of all men, articulate spokesmen for freedom, justice, and the fundamental dignity of every human being that inhabits this earth. Our youth must be prepared to meet falsehood with truth. They must understand the conflicting doctrines of Individual Sovereignty vs. the Totalitarian State, and be ready to defend the one and refute the other.

"Let truth and falsehood grapple," said Milton, "who ever knew Truth put to the worse, in free and open encounter." But we must never forget that the weapons of Communism are *treachery and deceit*. We must realize that a great task of our schools is to make this ideological war a free and open encounter. And we can only do this by affording our children a set of values, principles, and moral and spiritual beliefs which we hold to be true. To fight world Communism they must be given every opportunity to grasp the full significance of our own governmental system, our own economic concepts, our own glorious history.

Communism is on the march. It is advancing along every level and facet of life. J. Edgar Hoover recently warned that we "are face to face with a tyranny more monstrous, more devious, less understood and more deadly than any which has threatened civilization heretofore." And we now know that America is not dealing with some vague and primitive force. The Soviet machine has become a world power, a fact we shockingly learned when Sputnik I took the world by surprise. The extent of their technical advances was somberly brought home to us, and the American public began immediately to ask why the Russians beat us to outer space with a man-made satellite. All fingers seemed to point at the schools, the consensus of opinion being that the schools were not turning out enough high-grade scientists. Enthusiasts of federal aid to education used the Sputnik scare to push House Bill 12630 through Congress, allowing the federal government to spend a few more hundred million dollars of our money, and the problem was considered well met. The shock of Sputnik has already worn off.

Unfortunately, and disastrously, we have failed to recognize Russia's real Sputnik.

That small disc orbiting the earth did not symbolize the real threat of Communist tyranny. It is not that we are producing too few scientists, engineers, and technicians. Our failure goes deeper. We are producing too few men who are prepared for the responsibility of active participation in the so-called "cold" war between freedom and bondage—too few Americans. Our failure is one of *omission,* the omission of values that are a vital requisite in this world war of words. A strong foundation of Americanism has been grievously omitted from the public school system and, innocent though it may be, it constitutes a selling out of our own children.

"When values are clearly stated," says Professor Boarman of the University of Wisconsin, "students are free to agree or disagree with them. But where values are concealed in the name of a specious objectivity, students will be brainwashed without being aware of it; they will be hood-winked even though unintentionally."[1] If we turn out scientists who regard loyalty as a "myth" and patriotism as something "narrow" or "old-fashioned," what have we gained? If they believe that free enterprise is something to attack, and that the "welfare state" is something to serve and meekly obey, what good will their scientific expertness do America? If allegiance is dead and devotion is for the dollar, what will keep their discoveries out of the international auction house?

The Sputnik we must face does not fly through the air: it creeps into the mind. Its shadow is made up of warped intellects which force their lies into the minds of innocent young Russians, Chinese, Hungarians, and other Communist-oppressed youth of the world. We have only one defense against this ideological Sputnik; we know of but one light source

179

powerful enough to wipe this shadow of deceit from the world, and that is the exemplification of Americanism by the 180 million individuals who daily share in its blessings.

Lunacharsky, the Soviet Education Commissar, is quoted as saying, "We hate Christianity and Christians, even the best of them must be regarded as our worst enemies. They preach love for one's neighbor and pity, which is contrary to our principles. Down with the love of one's neighbor; what we want is hatred. We must know how to hate, for only at this price can we conquer the world."[2]

There is your Russian Sputnik!

The Communist has no more respect for right and wrong than the beast of the jungle. The aim of the Communist educator is to poison the minds of little children, to turn them into shock troops for the advancement of a ruthless scheme to conquer the world. When these young victims grow up and become active adult Reds, what chance will Americans have unless they are thoroughly cognizant of their priceless American heritage? Whenever and wherever the democratic message of Americanism fails, the truth-twisting specialists of the Soviet regime are there to profit by our omission. Every Communist is an accomplished propagandist, an expert preacher of the party line. But how many Americans could successfully debate Americanism?

Dr. Margaret B. Luszki, who spent three years in East Germany, has revealed the blood-chilling fact that Communist indoctrination begins with the kindergarten tot and infests every aspect of learning. The following is quoted directly from her description of a Communist kindergarten teacher:

"She begins to make paper dolls, with much show of enthusiasm. 'Look, I have already finished six FDJ boys.' [FDJ, or *Freie Deutsche Jugend,* is the Communist Youth Organization.] She continues, 'Do you remember why they all marched to Berlin? Yes, for peace. Those capitalists and bad people in the West always want war. But we want peace, don't we? Look, now our FDJ boys are marching to the Brandenberg Gate. Let's all sing!'"

180

In concluding her report, Dr. Luszki states: "This is the kindergarten under Communist influence. Such events may seem trivial in themselves, but they assume tremendous importance when one thinks that even the smallest incidents in the kindergarten are reigned over by an inflexible will that aims at total control. This will has taken hold of even the child's world, so that instead of being able to play happily in the healthy atmosphere of freedom, children are being molded into regimented members of the state."[3]

There, in that kindergarten, is Russia's real Sputnik. It should alarm every American citizen. It should turn every parent and teacher into a full-time American patriot with a resolute desire to put citizenship education back at the top of the list of our educational goals. For every seed of Communism that Russia plants in young minds, America must produce a "soldier of democracy" ready to defend liberty and justice to the last.

Another example of Russia's iron-fisted educational system was witnessed at the recent Seventh World Youth Festival held in Vienna and sponsored by Communist front organizations. Seven thousand Communist youth attended seminars and mass rallies, sang and chanted their Godless hymns. These "captive" delegations always were seen in groups, never isolated, always being led. Always there were older leaders among them, who often moved into smaller group discussions to correct points of doctrine clever dialecticians who could take over a youthful conversation and preserve the Marxist line. Non-Communists in attendance described this supposedly democratic convention as "a spectacle of hatred, not friendship, toward those who don't think on Communist lines."

Communist students were guarded, isolated, herded by bus to cultural events, and not allowed to converse with delegates from non-Communist countries. Young Hungarians were made to report at a given place every hour. If anyone failed to do so, an immediate search was ordered. This is the Communist concept of liberty.

Where regimentation and restriction were not enough, vio-

181

lence was used. American literature was swept from the tables at this "democratic" festival of Frienden Fraumschaft (Peace and Friendship). A Glasgow delegate who joined a group of American anti-Communists told of being struck in the face. "Then I was kicked in the back. I fell down. Someone else kicked me in the stomach and I passed out. I came to in the emergency hospital."

That is yet another view of the deadly, ideological Sputnik which Khrushchev and his henchmen have launched.

Power-mad dictators leave no stone unturned in their nefarious attempts to build a "super-race." Hitler set up camps to produce pure-bred Nazis. In his insane plot to build an empire of perfect physical specimens, he reduced German youth to the level of military units. The Communists, on the other hand, are preparing their children for a different kind of war. They are specialists in propaganda, semantic warfare, and the the "art" of lying. The Communist teacher is an expert at producing mental robots. In the words of former Attorney General Herbert Brownell, "He starts off with the intention, not of teaching, but of twisting and torturing the truth. Since he is committed by oath and disciplined by obedience to conform to the 'Party Line,' he lacks the capacity to engage in honest inquiry and of rendering an objective judgment. Since his own mind is enslaved how can he possibly be sympathetic to, or concerned with, stimulating an open, searching, free mind in his students?"[4]

This army of hypnotized State worshippers grows daily. Its combat front has pushed out from Moscow into every part of the world.

Only the loud, clear voice of Freedom can match this mighty propaganda machine.

Only individuals who stand firmly for something far better, can crush the reaching tentacles of this Communistic octopus.

Communist rule is established under the same familiar language of this Freedom it would subjugate. When they conquer a country, they announce the "liberation" of its people. They proclaim this new extension of despotism to be a "people's democracy; the new dictatorship becomes a "guardian of equality." The Communists have stolen the language of Liberty and have successfully perverted it to serve their own methods of conquest and subjection. They steal our own price-less words to enslave innocent people. This "semantic warfare" is one of the Communists' strongest weapons, used whenever and wherever possible. The calculated distortion of key words is the Red method of destroying values of patriotism, initia-tive, individuality, and moral precepts. Communist definitions of peace, truth, democracy, patriotism, capitalism, etc., hover constantly in reach of our youth. Unless they are taught *our* meanings for thcsc words, they will be weaponless against falsehood and deceit.

"The beauty of this type of warfare, as far as the Commu-nists are concerned, is that once a synonymous or false mean-ing of a word has been established, each person who unwit-tingly accepts the verbal prostitution becomes a semantic 'Typhoid Mary' reinforcing the reaction each time the word is used, thereby spreading the mental infection."[5]

The Communist idea of "peace" is unresisted aggression. It is no wonder that the Soviet leaders speak of "glorious peace," for to them it means the total surrender of the free world. They eagerly sell their idea of "peaceful co-existence" because to them it means one-sided war. Shortly after World War ii, simultaneously with their concerted efforts to enslave the world, they established in America such organizations as: American *Peace* Appeal, American *Peace* Crusade, American People's Congress and Exposition for *Peace,* American Youth *Peace* Cru-sade, East Harlem Women for *Peace,* Young People's General Assembly for *Peace,* Committee for *Peaceful* Alternatives, Mid-Century Conference for *Peace,* National Delegates Assembly for *Peace,* National Committee to Win the *Peace,* New York *Peace* Institute, *Peace* Information Center, Veterans for *Peace,* World *Peace* Congress, and new similar names are constantly cropping up. The semantic strategy of this effort is to conceal the undeniable fact that the present ideological war is more treacherous than the bloodiest battles of yesterday. We have

183

been told by the Soviet Premier that the Communists will bury us. The Kremlin logic is that we can avoid "war" by accepting this "burial"—"peacefully."

American youth will be prepared to challenge the subtle poison of Communism—to recognize it as revolutionary warfare rather than a "peace crusade"—only if they are fully aware of moral, spiritual, and political concepts rooted in the American way of life . . . only through an understanding of America's history.

Neverthless, a recent poll by a Purdue University Opinion Panel, conducted among teen-age students, revealed dangerous omissions in their understanding of basic Americanism. Among other things, one out of four youths would be willing to permit search and seizure without warrant; thirty-four per cent believe that free speech should be denied to certain people; forty-one per cent do not believe in complete freedom of the press; and over fifty per cent—every other student polled —accept the Communist thesis that most people are not capable of deciding what is best for them. These fundamental errors indicate a shocking misconception of our Constitution and the history of our free republic.

Adults as well as youngsters show signs of citizenship miseducation. Last Fourth of July a number of newspapers sent reporters into the streets to seek public signatures on typewritten documents. These documents were variously worded to test the Americanism of "the man on the street." One such paper, printed by the *Rochester Democrat & Chronicle,* read in part:

We, the undersigned American citizens, believe that whenever the government becomes destructive of the equality and rights of the people, it is the right of the people to alter or abolish the government and set up a new one.

And when a long train of abuses and usurpation show a design to reduce the rights of the people under absolute despotism, it is the right and duty of the people to throw off such government.

Of twenty-one persons stopped, seventeen refused to sign,

184

and the other four did so only with great wariness and doubt. Some of the comments were: "Sounds Communistic to me." "That's goofy." "What are you trying to pull?" "I'm not signing anything."

The words, written by Thomas Jefferson, are from the Declaration of Independence.

This deterioration of Americanism has recently become so apparent in our country that an editorial in the March 31, 1958, issue of *Life* magazine warned the American public:

"Cut off from any but the most obvious contact with his tradition, e.g., an occasional project visit to the local courthouse, the student has lost his sense of history, at a time when his country needs this most." [6]

While our enemy is turning its youth into precision instruments with which to "bury" our children, we are toying around with knowledge that is of crucial importance. "Because adolescents go out on dates," reported professor Arthur Bester in a national news weekly, "one pompous educational commission in my own state, Illinois, seriously recommended that, as part of their work in history, high-school students be asked to 'make studies of how the last war affected the dating pattern in our culture'." [7]

Even more discouraging are some of the new "gimmicks" used by the experimentalists to create "student interest." For example, a high-school principal from Saratoga, California encouraged teachers, in an *NEA Journal* article, to stimulate interest by drawing cartoons on the blackboard. This "gimmick" is directed to the young, impressionable minds of grade-school students. The idea seems to be this:

The teacher is to draw a funny picture of a man on the blackboard. This comic is given certain "tags" (such as an umbrella or a bow tie) and a queer name so that the children may easily identify him whenever he appears on the board. Then, in the case of American history, Mr. "X" is made to appear at all sorts of historical events, accompanied by famous men of history. Thus, the student may find this comic character holding "the kite for Benjamin Franklin . . . and almost

185

gets electrocuted . . ." Or, perhaps, collecting the ballots in the East Room of Independence Hall to make a joke out of this solemn event with his "interest creating" buffoonery.

Not only does Mr. "X" appear on the blackboard as a cartoon character, but so do all the great men of our past.

Undoubtedly this "student interest" gimmick works splendidly in the classroom, just as it does in advertisements and television commercials. Admittedly, boys and girls never get enough of such funny looking characters as Mickey Mouse and the like. If the teacher is particularly proficient at the art of cartooning, it is likely that the boys and girls will get a good laugh out of "funny" George Washington crossing the Delaware, or the humorous cartoon of Lincoln at Gettysburg.

But if the inspiring history of America is to be taught through cheapening cartoons, perhaps the teacher should add one more "funny" object to the pictures on the board—Russia's Sputnik—the real Sputnik—for there is where it belongs.

As Norman Angell, Nobel Peace Prize recipient, recently cautioned, "The real lesson of Sputnik is that we of the West must take as much pains to make the case for freedom understood by every citizen as Russia takes to make Marxism understood by every child passing through her schools. Every Russian student knows thoroughly the philosophy of Communism." In contrast, the leading British author estimates (perhaps too conservatively) that "not one American or British schoolboy in a thousand" could explain the philosophy of freedom. "If this contrast continues to exist," he concludes, "Moscow will eventually triumph."

There is further evidence that we have drifted so far from the traditional, original concept of Americanism that many youth literally do not know the form of government of the United States. Going back, momentarily, to the post-war policy statement of the American Education Fellowship, some of the "problems" which the AEF outlined for teachers included "economic problems such as the place of private property in an evolving democracy." By an "evolving democracy" was meant the United States. Now, for nearly two centuries the

186

United States has been a constitutional republic. To anyone curious about the difference between an "evolving democracy" and a constitutional republic, a glance at the foregoing AEF quotation as it appeared in the *original* draft should be of help. It originally read:

". . . economic problems such as the place of private property in an increasingly socialized order."

How shall we describe our government to the student; as a republic, or as a democracy meaning a socialized order? Educators have chosen the word "democracy" in application to very nearly all aspects of American life. In Counts' *Education and American Civilization,* for instance, *Democracy* is given twenty-five separate listings in the index; *Republic* is given none.

The extent to which "democracy" has replaced "republic" in the classroom is particularly astonishing in light of the fact that our government *is* a republic, and *is not* a democracy. And it is still more astonishing when one considers that the Communists have stolen the word "democracy" to describe their dictatorship. It is true, though very hard to believe, that a notable text-book author made the following confession in a speech which appeared in the *Congressional Record:*

At this point I wish to explain the use of the term "democracy" in the title of our textbook on Democracy Versus Communism. Personally, I would prefer to call our American Government a "Representative Republic." This is more in keeping with the thought of the fathers of the Constitution. But after hundreds of talks with schoolmen, politicians, and scholars I am persuaded that any textbook or new course in the curriculum under any other name than "democracy" would have little or no chance of adoption in the American school system.[8]

In speaking of the "thought of the fathers of the Constitution " it may be that this textbook author had the words of James Madison, one of the principal architects of the Constitution, in mind: ". . . democracies have been spectacles of turbulence and contention; have ever been found incompatible for personal security, or the rights of property and have in general been as short in their lives as they have been

187

violent in their deaths. A republic, by which I mean a government in which the scheme of representation takes place, opens a different prospect, and promises the cure for which we are seeking."

Possibly these thoughts of Madison, which clearly set forth the thinking of the founding fathers, "would have little or no chance" in the American school system either.

A republic is a form of government wherein representatives of the people make all laws, and whereby no law may be made except with the consent of the people acting through their representatives. A democracy is one in which the people act directly. It is interesting to note that while our republic has lasted almost two centuries, the contemporaneously created democracy of the National Assembly of France in 1789 was, as Madison said, short in its life and violent in its death. Even more pertinent is the fact that neither the United States Constitution nor any of the state constitutions uses the term "democracy." On the contrary, the federal Constitution guarantees that every state shall have and retain a republican form of government.

Regardless of these facts, many students go through their entire education without learning the difference between the two, namely that one signifies the form and the other the spirit of our government. For past generations this distinction might have been relatively unimportant. But today, with Communists and Socialists shouting the glories of their "democracies" it is senseless to misapply this same term to our own Republic. If we continue to deceive the rising generation by perpetuating this fallacy, they may very possibly follow in the footsteps of the young Bolsheviks of a generation ago. They may demand a "democracy," get a "democracy," and find themselves eventually slaves of the "democratic" State. As the founders of our Republic pointed out time and again, rule of the people in a democracy resolves itself into rule of the majority, and ultimately into the rule of the stronger, which is exemplified in the Marxist doctrine of "the dictatorship of the proletariat." The founders were determined to

188

protect the rights and human dignity of the individual from any coercive governmental power. For this reason they created not only a republic, but a unique republic having a government of law, imperishable and immutable.

"We are not," says Verne P. Kaub, "as some may believe, in a 'trap' merely because the Communist-Socialist propagandists are so adept at using the current terminology to describe their own evil purposes. It is our own fault insofar and so long as we insist upon using terminology of the Communists' own choosing and liking."

It is true that many of our greatest statesmen have used the word "democracy" to designate our form of government. But it is equally true that the meaning which they gave to the word was synonymous with that of "republic." Today its meaning is more nearly synonymous with "socialism." Today, democracy applies not only to government, but to every phase of life. It is the "great equalizer," the leveller which will do away with all individual differences among men. Socialists love to use the word "democracy" because, as the penetrating mind of DeTocqueville observed, "Democracy and socialism have nothing in common but one word: equality." Socialism is economic "equality" in that no one owns more than anyone else because everyone owns nothing. Socialism gives to every individual "equality" of freedom because every man is shackled with the same amount of State control. "But," says DeTocqueville, "notice the difference, while democracy seeks *equaliy in liberty,* socialism seeks *equality in restraint and servitude."* And that is why the socialists, and Communists, are forced to hide their despotic intentions under the once-beautiful term of *democracy.*

This is a simple Communist tactic through which our children should be able to see. And yet few students have a clear understanding of *equality* as it has been conceived by Americans to enrich their way of life. There is little stress made in our schools of the high spiritual concept of this basic precept, while every effort is, or seems to be, made to nurture the false, materialistic interpretation of equality.

189

The principle of the Declaration of Independence which states that "all men are created free and equal, and are endowed with certain inalienable rights," is a pillar of our republic. It is the cardinal argument against State supremacy over the individual. Our whole way of life is the manifest expression of this profound idea. It makes a common cause of individual rights, by proclaiming the equality of rights as a free gift of the Creator. It lifts the lowliest members of the human family to the level of the highest and inspires them "with the elevating consciousness of equal human dignity."

There is only one alternative to the principle of equal rights. That is the arbitrary despotism of enforced privileges . . . the so-called "equality" of Communism and socialism. It is an artificial equalitarianism that usurps human rights in the name of justice, that tramples over equality before the law to obliterate human individualism and eradicate the special distinctions between man and beast.

And each time we allow the federal government to take on responsibilities of the individual citizen, each new move toward the "welfare state" made by collectivists and advocates of "big government," is a step toward equalitarianism and a step away from the principle of equality of rights. The great majority of our youth fail to learn this vital, simple truth in our schools. Our educators are reluctant to set aside their "social vision" and teach students the real meaning of the basic terminology of the American Creed. While the Communist "freedom" fighters are eager to offer their definitions of "democracy," "equality" and "human rights," we are busy introducing their strange terminology, like a "new world order" and "integrated economy," to our youth.

We are not preparing our children to *hold their own* in the present world of ideological chaos by undermining the traditions of their own country.

"Competition is to many a threat to well-being."[10]

Thus reads a 1958 U.S. Office of Education bulletin entitled *Educating Children in Grades Four, Five and Six.*

The American economy is based solidly on competition.

190

Communism is the antithesis of our competitive system. But there it is, in a federal government publication—Competition is to many a threat to well-being.

"It is comradeship the ten-year-old boy wants," says Gasell (a "human development" researcher), "not competition." p. 14.

May we still argue this point with the government? Might it not lead toward the foreign concept of equalitarianism?

"Comradeship" versus "Competition" — how does that sound to you?

". . . one teacher reported twenty-eight children using twenty-eight different books." p. 53.

The Office of Education bulletin calls this "individualization carried to the furthest degree." It might better be called enforced privilege, a blow against competitiveness, an intellectual equalitarianism as near perfectly executed as possible. It is not hard to imagine what would happen to the American belief in *incentive* under these conditions. But this too is taken care of, on the very next page:

"Another comment that seemed to have significance was to the effect that a job once started should be completed if it concerns the group but not necessarily completed if it concerns the individual only."

What business has the federal government to publish such jejune remarks? Or is this yet another glimpse of the real significance of Russia's ominous Sputnik?

In a thoroughly documented article entitled "Semantic Warfare," Gene Wicks explains how many important words are twisted or given false synonyms by Communists to further their cause. Patriotism is one such word. "Its meaning," says Wicks, "has been transferred to other words that not only do not stimulate love of country, devotion to duty, respect for the flag, and other attendant emotions that impel a man to defend his country but the connotations given the replacement words actually act to inhibit these emotions. The replacement for 'patriotism' is 'nationalism.' The Junior Scholastic Magazine, given free to public school children, says of 'nationalism':

191

" Nationalism—imperialism—cold war. Any of these might lead to another war. ("Your Key to World Words" p. 25). Thus, nationalism, imperialism, and cold war become synonymous."[11] And patriotism becomes something narrow, provincial, and prejudicial.

Further evidence of the decline of American patriotism in the public school system was compiled in a report prepared by a group of parents in Fairfax, Virginia. The group submitted their report to the State Board of Education, stating that the Fairfax County schools followed a pattern calculated to produce a generation of Virginians:

". . . who believe that patriotism is a form of jingoist provincialism; that they are citizens of the world first and of their own country second (if at all); that they owe a higher duty of loyalty and allegiance to the United Nations than they owe to the United States."

When it is so vital that citizens of the United States understand their own form of government, it is difficult to find a justifiable reason for the recent educational obsession for teaching the "universal law" at the expense of our own. Surely, educators must realize that an understanding of the United Nations Charter will not aid the student's grasp of his own Constitution.

Even a cursory comparison will bear this fact out:

UNITED STATES CONSTITUTION	UNITED NATIONS CHARTER
1. Provides for limitation of the powers of government.	1. Provides for the vast expansion of government power.
2. Provides for separation of powers.	2. Provides for the centralization of power.
3. Provides for elected officials.	3. UN officials are appointed.
4. Protects property rights.	4. Omits mention of property rights.
5. Protects right of trial by jury.	5. Omits mention of trial by jury.

192

| 6. Provides for our common defense. | 6. Admits known enemies into our councils. |
| 7. Was written by American patriots. | 7. Was written in part by Alger Hiss, Harry Dexter White and Vyacheslav Molotov. |

The objection is not to the study of the United Nations; it is to the tendency toward placing America second best in the teaching of national and world government. In his critical documentation of popular American history textbooks, one of the conclusions drawn by Dr. Root lends considerable weight to this objection:

"The authors [of the American history texts], as we have seen, make vivid much of the real or fancied evil of the American story, but one wonders why the story is not balanced with its glory, as historical proportion requires. The authors can illustrate virtues when they want to. Every picture in this volume [*America's History* by Lewis Paul Todd and Merle Curti] which deals with the United Nations is vividly idealistic! The U.S. is played down, the U.N. is invariably played up."[12] (italics in original.)

We began this chapter by making certain suppositions, certain *false* assumptions. Now let us take a look at the cumulative facts. The twentieth-century materialistic traits of the American character are playing havoc with our traditional American values and time-honored truths. Clearly defined, thoroughly taught subjects of history, civil government, economics, and American citizenship have been seriously impaired by emphatic changes in curriculum and methodology. The un-Americanism of the Frontier Thinkers influenced lasting distortions of the goals of citizenship education. The present trend away from Americanism and toward Worldism is gradually increasing. Communist youth are being indoctrinated for global conquest and trained to use any means, no matter how treacherous, to achieve victory. American education has taken no significant steps to offset this growing ideological threat to this and future generations of Americans.

193

There is still time to save our Nation from decay and ultimate slavery. There is still time to return to responsible, sensible, fundamental teaching of Americanism, and patriotic practice of Americanism. We still have the choice of doing our duty or surrendering our heritage. But we must make the choice *now*. Either we govern ourselves as individuals today, or we will be ruled over by an all-powerful State tomorrow. Either we preserve liberty through the classroom now, or it will be lost to our youth forever.

"Despotism, while it is gaining ground," wrote Helvetius, "suffers men to say what they will, while they suffer it to do what it will: but once established, it forbids all talking, writing, or thinking."

So let us do our talking, writing, and thinking now. Let us solve the American crisis before despotism gains another inch of ground.

CHAPTER 10

THE SOLUTION

A Program of Americanism

✠✠✠

If America forgets where she came from, if the people lose sight of what brought them along, if she listens to the deniers and mockers, then will begin the rot and dissolution.

CARL SANDBURG

✠✠✠

WITH GREAT WISDOM AND FORESIGHT, Thomas Jefferson long ago offered a solution to the crucial problem we face today. "I know no safe depository of the ultimate powers of society but the people themselves," said the author of our Declaration of Independence, "and if we think of them as not enlightened enough to exercise their control with a wholesome discretion, the remedy is not to take it from them, but to inform their discretion by education."

Take not the power of government from the people, but rather educate them that they may wield their power wisely and justly. This is the alternative to an authoritarian state.

The men who fought for American independence taught their sons the meaning of self-government, and they in turn repeated the story of American liberty, equality and justice to their sons . . . and they to theirs. The great message of Americanism has come down to us as part of our heritage. Nine score and four years of struggle and achievement, of bloody wars and industrial revolution, of undreamed of wealth and urbanization through free enterprise, have made possible today a vast system of public education. Modern education owes a debt to millions of Americans who contributed to its

195

realization. Every school has a solemn obligation to reflect the way of life that made its fine, free institution a reality. Every classroom carries a grave responsibility to the founding fathers, to the nation, and to the forty-five million children of the United States. Every child has a right to the message of Americanism that has passed from father to son, from teacher to student, from generation to generation, since the beginning of the American Republic.

A program of Americanism must once again be established to provide every American youth with the opportunity to promote, practice, protect, preserve, and perpetuate those fundamental and divine principles of liberty, equality and justice—to the end that an American need not fear any man, nor envy any man, but instead enjoy peace and individual dignity under God. The urgency of such a program is predicated on the historic proposition that American liberty and private enterprise cannot endure unless the young people have full opportunity to learn why our form of government and economic system have proved better than any other form or system known to mankind. Further, if individuals, as part of their education, are prepared to exercise self-government and to show independent, thoughtful initiative, alien philosophies of Statism will be intelligently rejected by them as they mature to responsible adulthood. American youth, if imbued with a spirit of loyalty to the family, community, and country, and with a sense of duty, will be able to take its place in the professions, business and industry, and to carry on the traditions established in 1776.

The success of any effective program of Americanism depends entirely on the degree of positive, patriotic action taken by individual local communities. The federal government, state commissions, and national professional organizations, combined, could not accomplish as much good for a given school as one courageous teacher or a single citizen acting under local *control.*

No matter how hard professional educationists push for centralization in education, the fact remains that our public

196

schools originated in the local communities to fill obvious needs. And the period during which education in the United States was strictly under local control produced the generations of young people who successfully built the United States into the most productive country in the world. The simple principle underlying local government in the nineteenth-century also served as a guide for educational policy. It was believed that the people who built and supported the schools, who sent their children to the schools, knew best what the role of the school should be. It was held that common sense had a central position in the educational scheme and that therefore the traditional custodian of common sense—the intelligent lay public—knew at least as much about the large goals and general nature of education as the professional theorists and national policy-makers.

Before the National Education Association and its affiliates established a huge organizational bureaucracy, teachers were not turned into guinea pigs for testing new theories and philosophies in education. History teachers simply taught children history; teachers of civil government taught civil government, and so forth. Teaching was considered (and is) a noble and highly responsible calling. Teachers were looked upon (and truly are) noble beings.

Today, the majority of classroom teachers are sincere and hard working persons. They are often forced into teaching practices objectionable to themselves, as well as to many parents and citizens aware of the facts. Good teachers are aware of their obligation to the community which they serve and to the young minds in their charge. No teacher dedicated to his or her calling would hesitate to espouse a program of Americanism if such a program were commissioned by the parents and citizens of the community. However, no teacher can return patriotism to the schools without the active support of the community. The essential task of putting Americanism back ino the public school system require the concerted efforts of teachers, parents, tax-paying citizens, the clergy, the press and other influential members of the community.

197

Lay people such as these have recently shown increased interest in schools throughout the country. Few of them have as yet turned their attention to the need for a program of Americanism; nevertheless, this renewal of public interest provides a symbol of hope. Presently, there are citizen's committees at work in over 18,000 communities. These local groups help get out the vote for school bond issues, conduct surveys of trends in population, help present architectural plans for the new schools in their communities, recruit teachers, and so on. If individuals and committees such as these, together with local school boards and administrators, are once made aware of the far more serious problem of properly educating citizens, the American crisis may yet be faced, and the nation saved.

An example of what can be done on the local level was recently shown by the successful campaign of a city newspaper to refurbish Americanism in the local schools and direct state-wide attention to the place of American history in the curriculum. For many years American history tended to be slighted in the New York state school system. The recent increased emphasis on this basic subject by the State Board of Regents is the fruit of a long and energetic campaign to that end by the Buffalo *Evening News*. As a more immediate result of this newspaper's patriotic crusade, ninth-grade students of the Buffalo public high schools are scheduled to receive enriched preparation for citizenship this year through a new course called, "The American Ideal of Freedom and Self-Government." This new unit traces the development of self-government and personal liberties in the United States, *contrasts* the American and Communist ideologies, and emphasizes the ideals, privileges and duties of American citizenship.

Here was a case where the local paper brought the issue of citizenship education out into the open, where the local citizens, teachers, and prominent educators got behind the crusade and helped to make it a success. Ten years ago the history syllabus offered by the New York State Board emphasized "world backgrounds" so extensively that actual American history study was limited to six weeks. It was then that the campaign for Americanism began.

"Buffalo's academic high schools are not following—will not follow — the State Board's suggestion," said Frank J. Dressler, Supervisor of Social Studies.

Buffalo's Dr. Selig Adler warned that if the trend away from actual history persisted, ". . . our high school pupils won't know any American history at all."

"Our high schools should give them the facts of our nation's development, of our past problems and how successfully they were met," added John T. Horton, head of the University of Buffalo history department. Pointing out the fallacious emphasis on "contemporary problems," he concluded, "Then these students themselves will be able to understand the problems that eventually confront them on the basis of what's gone before."

The struggle for a full program of Americanism is still going on in Buffalo. Another semester of American history was added to the curriculum this year, and as the *Evening News* proudly reported in a recent editorial, "The Buffalo School Department is working to assure even greater emphasis in this field in the future."

This example of community action is one of the best answers to the familiar question: "But what can *I* do?" A return to Americanism calls for modern pioneers to blaze trails between the home and the school; it calls for modern Paul Reveres who have formed opinions based on facts and who are ready to place their opinions before the public; it calls for "full-time patriots" to take one step forward voluntarily.

Buffalo needn't be the only city to prove, that when local citizens are willing to unite and demand to be heard, *it can be done.* In the last analysis all but a very few Americans want to see the American way of life preserved. As quickly as they realize that it is up to the individual American and not "the other fellow" (the other fellow being the undefined "general public"), the great majority will pitch in and do their part. For Americanism is not in any way a new proposal or a goal of some special minority or political interest, as devotees of "Worldism" education often brand it. A program of Americanism is the expressed desire of the people in every state of the Union. With the exception of two states, all *require* the teaching of American history in their schools, and the two exceptions require instruction in the United States Constitution. Twenty-eight states require the teaching of civics, twenty-two require courses in state and local history, and twenty-six require additional social-studies courses beyond the requirements of the three preceding subjects. True, the time requirements for these courses often fall short of the mark, and some of the social studies subjects required by state law discourage rather than encourage Americanism—but the underlying significance of these citizenship subjects lies in the fact that they were made compulsory by the people through their state representatives. They are part of the state curricula by commission of the people. Note this excerpt from a typical State Law:

If citizens, teachers and laymen acting together, in every state did nothing more than carry out a law such as this, every boy and girl would be assured of a solid education in Americanism. The goal of a program of Americanism could not be better expressed than as an "object of producing the highest type of patriotic citizen." But today we are paying lip service to state requirements like the one cited above. Not one school is a thousand is producing the highest type of patriotic citizen today because social studies "experts" have filled the citizenship curriculum with a new set of goals designed to produce the most *un*patriotic kind of citizen possible.

It is the duty of the citizens of every community in America to examine and evaluate the current programs that supposedly constitute Americanism in their schools. If the social studies are fused into a meaningless conglomeration of irrelevant subjects and concentrated on contemporary problem-solving, it is the duty of citizens to take positive action.

If loyalties are being directed away from the nation and toward the world, it is time for honest individuals to express

200

their objections. This may be done through the press and radio, through formal and informal discussion, through correspondence with responsible officials, directly through the board of education or indirectly through board elections. The citizen who is willing to give active support to a program of Americanism will soon find that the opportunities are unlimited.

If the curriculum is based on the "felt needs" and "immediate interests" of the child, it does not constitute a program of Americanism. Simply because the typical student does not feel a *need* for history (how could he, if he knows nothing about it?) and because his daily concern (like that of all of us) tends toward that which takes place within his immediate view, the curriculum "expert" has no right to replace sound history instruction with the *Reader's Digest.* For the great majority of communities containing this sort of citizenship curriculum in their schools, there is no better advice than that given by Dr. James J. Lynch, distinguished member of the Academic Senate at the University of California. In the course of an address entitled, "This Is the American Challenge," Dr. Lynch told his audience:

"If you, as members of the intelligent lay public, would set about to reform the curriculum, you could not do better than to begin by destroying the whole present concept of the social studies. In their place should be restored the ancient and essential disciplines of history, geography, and civics (or political science) . . ."

In that brief remark, Dr. Lynch disclosed the essence of the problem facing social studies teachers today. They have no choice but to try to inculcate citizenship without the basic curricular tools that citizenship training requires: the fundamental subjects of Americanism. Throughout the nineteenth-century and up until the experimentalists and social "scientists" too over, the subject of American History served teachers as the organizing core around which relevant materials of all the social studies subjects were assembled. History was emphasized to connect and coordinate the citizenship course because of its predominant involvement in past poli-

201

tics, past economics, past sociology, and past geography—because only through the common ground of history can these subjects be meaningfully brought up to the present time and projected into the future. All of the separate citizenship subjects were approached historically. They were thereby made more significant by study of the particular subject of American History, and in turn enriched the meaning of American history by their complementary perspectives. In this way the entire "social studies" became a study of American history with the specific subject of American History as the master key of the citizenship curriculum. And therein lay the basis for an effective program of Americanism.

In terms of the foregoing observation, American history has an educational meaning, not only as a subject *per se,* but as a broad course of study with a definite reservoir of knowledge, a fixed method, and a clear viewpoint. It was this broad educational meaning that was forced out of our schools by the emergence of the modern concept called "social studies." It is this broad meaning of American history, as a curriculum rather than as a subject, that must replace the unproven experiment of concentrating on current problems and events. If we are to initiate a program of Americanism, "current events" must assume its former status—that of a subject—and cease to exist as the core of the citizenship curriculum. Not until we restore traditional American history to its rightful place in American education, will the teacher be equipped to develop and bring out clearly the story of our political, governmental, economic, geographic and social institutions. Only then will the young student acquire love and respect for the great Americans who carved out of an unfriendly wilderness, our palatial national abode. Only a sincere appreciation of the men and events of history can lead to the patriotism, loyalty, and devotion to duty that our country is in such dire need of today.

The task of American adults is clearly indicated in the findings of a Fairfax, Virginia, citizens committee (typical of similar patriotic groups in other communities) which revealed:

202

We started collecting old textbooks and comparing them with the textbooks in use today. . . . We found those old books to be well planned and complete, and that they lead the pupils through a thorough course of study in each subject. . . .
Beginning with books copyrighted in the late twenties, however, we noticed that the standards were being lowered and more emphasis was being placed on social objectives and "life adjustment." . . . They do little more than touch on the skills and fundamentals which are scattered willynilly throughout the books. . . .

Add to this general watering down of fundamental information in public-school textbooks the material "slanted" in history texts and social-studies texts to debunk the traditional American way of life, and the urgent need for civic action can be seen. We must keep in mind that if five per cent of a book is propaganda it is *heavily* loaded. The most dangerous books are nearer to two per cent. Un-American material is always more effective when it is concealed under high-sounding principles!

Local school boards and lay-committees, as well as parents' associations and civic groups, should take note of patriotic examples such as this one set by the Education and School Committee of a Kern County, California, grand jury after examining textbooks used in their school:
[The Committee recommended] That the books cited in this report be rescinded from use in our county tax supported schools, and that the County Board of Education set up a lay committee for screening school books for subversive materials. This committee should include in its examination pocket editions available on racks in college book stores. . . . Tax money should not be used for propaganda.[1]

It is a sad commentary on the conditions that exist in our schools when there is need, not only for re-establishing Americanism in the classroom, but to rid the school system of existing anti-American materials and procedures.

But let us start now to strive for a positive program. Let us not only defend patriotism in the school curriculum but demand that it be increased and expanded wherever possible.

203

Americanism should enter into the spirit of the school and become part of its character. Educators should borrow some of the stirring atmosphere generated by football heroes and basketball stars who have become part of school legends, and apply it to the heroes of Lexington and Concord and to the "stars" of Independence Hall and the Continental Congress. Our "cheer-leaders" and high-school bands know the slogans and music of the playing field—but they should also be inspired by the immortal shouts and meaningful hymns of the American battle-fields, and the field of glory upon which our priceless liberty was won.

With a wealth of great authors like Whittier, Irving, Hawthorne and others, we should no longer allow their place of honor in our history to be usurped by modern mud-slingers whose writings have not yet stood the test of time. American literature should reflect American standards and ideals, not berate them. The extent to which literature courses can convey the American spirit and serve to inspire youth is particularly apparent in the following outline of an eleventh-grade literature course proposed in a New York City curriculum bulletin:

THEME: *The Individual and the American Heritage.*

1. Westward Ho!—the Pioneer Spirit.
2. Great Americans and Their Legacy to Us.
3. Let's See the Funny Side: American Humor.
4. The Regions of America Contribute to Her Heritage.
5. America in Song and Story.
6. Guideposts to Liberty
7. The Union: Storehouse of Treasures from All Lands.
8. Tell All the People: Mass Media.
9. American Literature: Ideals in the American Heritage.
10. New York City: Focal Point of American Culture.
11. Secession versus Union: A Drama of Human Relations—
    Many Became One.

Any youngster introduced to the best of our national literature in a framework similar to that suggested above would

204

find little reason for trading his American sovereignty for an "international order." Local curriculum committees would do well to take note of this outline and compare it to the literature courses offered in their own community. "Patriotism, like everything else," says Senator Dilworth, "has to be taught and to be taught effectively it has to permeate all our books . . ."

Despite admonitions such as this, a large number of educators openly avow that "world understanding" takes precedence over Americanism. The argument is that the interdependent nature of modern civilization has widened the responsibility of Americans from that of a "narrow" nationalism to the extending of the blessings of freedom throughout the world. It is an excellent argument, for no thoughtful American would want to refute this high objective. But if America is to help secure human liberty for the world, which is more important as a goal of our schools: an understanding of the *world,* or an understanding of human liberty?

Americans who understand the foundations upon which liberty was erected, realize that a "world order" is the greatest enemy of individual freedom, not a means to achieve it. Our message to the world should be the same message we should have passed on to our children, that true freedom depends on local self-government, on effective access of the people to their individual rights, and *not* on a distant and powerful world government. Our idea of government is directly opposed to any such ultimate centralization. In the words of Robert A. Taft, "The whole idea is based on the union of the thirteen colonies in 1787. But those colonies were made up of men of similar origin, similar methods of thought, similar ideals with similar forms of government. They lived approximately the same kind of life, with similar standards of living. Even then, one single difference resulted in a violent civil war about seventy-five years later which almost destroyed the Union. Here we would be attempting to unite peoples who do not even understand how their new fellow citizens begin to think; we would join democracies with dictatorships, Moslem states with Christian states, the Brahmin with the Rotarian, men who speak only Japanese with men who speak only English. We would attempt to unite the most highly civilized with the aborigines, the workman who earns twenty dollars a day with the coolie who earns twenty cents a day. The difficulties of holding together such a Tower of Babel under one direct government would be insuperable. . . . Furthermore, if it could remain in existence at all, it would not remain democratic—if a state including dictatorships like those of Russia, Communist China, Argentina and Yugoslavia could ever *have been* democratic."[2]

No, it is not an understanding of Russia, or Red China, that will best secure freedom for the world; it is an understanding of freedom and how it can be won or lost that will lead to its triumph over despotism. If we want our children to influence other nations on behalf of building a better world, they must first understand America. The great influence that Communism has had over the world in recent years came about because Communists understand Communism. Communism will not be defeated by an understanding of the idea behind it. It will be beaten by an understanding of a far better idea with which to replace it. In the ideological war between Communism and the free world, America has the opportunity and obligation to supply the most potent weapon known to man—the truth. And this is what we must teach our children to bring to the backward and enslaved nations of the world. If an innocent man has fallen into a pit, it will help little to understand how he got there or what it is like to be in a pit, if there is no understanding of how to get him out.

This fact was never more evident than in Major Meyer's expert analysis of why so many American soldiers succumbed to Chinese Communist brainwashing during the Korean war. When this military expert on psychological warfare was asked what specific educational lacks were shown by American captives, he replied:

A returning prisoner often made reference to the fact that he was given by the Communists a very intensive education about America. A Communist viewpoint of history which evidently emphasized every possible defect in our development and our attitudes, and the soldier would confess that his own knowledge of the American system—of our history, our politics, our economics—was insufficient to enable him to refute this Communist version, even in his own mind.

The Communists, with obvious wisdom, did not try to sell Communism, but instead they 'unsold' America and its institutions. From the very beginning they told these soldiers that they merely wanted to show them the truth as they saw it, and that they wanted to enlist these soldiers as fighters for peace. In this endeavor, the Communists added, these men could be of greatest value to mankind if they would return home and tell the truth as the Communists had taught it to them. It was Fantastic.[3]

The fallacy of "world understanding" as it is approached in our educational system, was clearly brought forward by this record. No matter how well you understand an enemy you cannot defeat him without weapons.

Only through an understanding of their own country will our youth be prepared to contribute to world peace and universal freedom. And from another, much more urgent, viewpoint, only through an understanding of their own country—through a sound program of Americanism—will our youth be able to keep America from internal destruction. Today, they are being allowed to complete their education with no sense of basic value. The attempt to establish relative, baseless, pragmatic values has failed utterly. This moral and ethical vacuum is in effect the greatest challenge facing the nation's teachers today.

A system of values means simply a set of standards by which things or events or persons are judged as good or bad. The American Creed is an example of a system of values. It holds that such things as freedom, freedom of worship, individual worth, and rights such as life, liberty, and the pursuit of happiness are valuable to all men of all times. They are basic values "relative" to nothing less than human existence. The creed of America holds that men must have such values.

207

The illogic whereby our youth are deprived of value judgments is amazing. Because it is necessary to eliminate value judgments from scientific inquiry, and because the "social studies" are an application of "social science," the classroom is somewhat likened to the physical science laboratory. Values are turned into hypotheses that children may reject or accept. The traditional value of personal achievement is no longer considered a valid part of the American character. It is superseded by group conformity, belongingness, and togetherness. The value of past experience and consideration of the future is subordinated to a materialistic, present-time orientation. The value of thrift has been changed from "a penny saved is a penny earned," to "buy now, pay later." The value of hard work with just compensation has been minimized by the idea that the government is responsible for economic security. The value of personal virtue has been given a new statistical meaning: morality consists of what the "group" thinks is moral. The value of equality of opportunity has evolved into a pursuit of mediocrity.

These are but a few of the many traditional American values that have been made meaningless under the new philosophy of education. But such fundamental and traditional values must serve as the foundation of the program of Americanism so vital to good citizenship education.

* * *

There is no pat answer to the problem, no automatic button to press. Every citizen must appraise his local public school system and determine his own community's needs in terms of education for Americanism. Every member of the teaching profession, notwithstanding the organizational pressures that descend from national educational policy-making, must take a positive stand on citizenship education in his or her school. Every administrator, pedagogical philosopher and professional organization must re-examine attitudes and positions that have been taken for granted in regard to major goals of education. Every school in the nation must take active measures to return *American history* to its traditional status in the general curriculum, once again to accept it as the material format vital to a program of Americanism. For only when American history becomes the medium through which specific citizenship subjects are coordinated and taught, will the classroom again achieve the great American goals to which it has been dedicated. Then, and only then, will America be able to present her children with a program based on these historic attributes of Americanism:

1. SPIRITUAL CONCEPTS.

Every young American has a fundamental right to know all the facts connected with the spiritual origins and official customs of our nation. To overlook, ignore or eliminate any of them from his education is to leave him defenseless in an age that is dominated by materialism. He must understand that a person without spiritual qualities is but a shell of a human being.

2. MORAL VALUES.

Every American boy and girl is entitled to know that his country was founded and nourished on the idea that there are some unchangeable Truths and Values valid for every individual person inhabiting this earth. He and she must be shown that morality is not in perpetual state of pragmatic flux, but founded on the immutable, timeless laws of the Creator.

3. THE AMERICAN CREED.

America has the solemn obligation to perpetuate her heritage, to teach children to understand the meaning of the Declaration of Independence, the Constitution and Bill of Rights, and other basic documents. The obligation does not end when the teacher has taught as much as possible under the time allotments of the present curriculum. Knowledge of the foundation of our way of life must be allotted as much time as students need to thoroughly acquire it. And this knowledge must take precedence over a knowledge of present-day problems.

4. WORLD RESPONSIBILITY.

America's school system has a relatively new obligation toward the world inasmuch as every youth must be prepared to spread

209

the message of Liberty to all peoples as an earnest repudiation of the world-wide indoctrinary propaganda of Communism. Children must be fortified for their inevitable participation in this ideological war through an understanding of the truth as the American people see it, and by a truthful comparison of the good that can be achieved through freedom with the evil that must result from Communist enslavement. They must be made to understand that their responsibility toward the world is consistent with the American ideal of human relations, that the ultimate solution lies in individual liberty and not world government.

5. AMERICAN INSTITUTIONS

It is not necessary to "color" the story of our American way of life. But the schools have a positive commitment to approach the subject of America on the specific premise (or value-judgment—to which every American adheres) that America's constitutional republic has been up until this very moment, the greatest system of government and social existence known to mankind. American youth should be encouraged to understand and appreciate the history of limited federal government, the sovereignty of state governments, the safeguards of local rule, the unsurpassed success of our competitive, free-enterprise economy with its emphasis on risk and rewards, and the incentive value based on the right to private property. Youth should be thoroughly exposed to our fundamental social concept that every individual is a free and sovereign person whose rights are not gifts of the government; that, on the contrary, the authority of government exists only by common consent of the people, and its power emanates from the only source of power recognized in these United States—the individual citizen.

6. AMERICAN CITIZENSHIP

Patriotism, loyalty, firm allegiance, and devotion to duty, are vital traits of the American character, vital to the survival of the nation. Every youth must be taught to respect the great symbols of his country: a firm allegiance to his country's Flag, a deep loyalty toward the sovereign Union of his nation, a reverent admiration for the founding fathers and selfless heroes of America's past, and a vigilant devotion to his duty as a self-governing citizen of the

210

American republic. Every textbook on American history government, economics, citizenship, and allied subjects, every lecture and every discussion, every assignment and supplementary tool of citizenship education should reflect the unique spirit that has guided and enriched the American way of life.

This synopsis of Americanism is nothing new. It has been stated many times, more succinctly and in greater detail. But in these half-dozen brief attributes of an education for American citizenship, the essence of traditional American history instruction may be seen. It is an outline of that important body of knowledge which serves our people as a *common denominator,* and which the majority of American parents expect the public school system to provide their children.

And it is more. It represents a body of knowledge that stands on solid ground, that stands as an irrefutable challenge to expedient changes which serve only to *betray* the youth of America. It represents a means by which the traditional character of Uncle Sam can be saved by and for the future generations of Americans. It is nothing more than a copy of the original blue-prints by which the American republic was built. This concept of Americanism turned out to be the solution to the American crisis of 1776. If we may rely on common sense, it is the only logical solution to the American crisis of today.

So you see, the program of Americanism that we need in our schools and that has been proposed here, cannot be patently explained as a new "dynamic course" or a progressive innovation that will enable "Johnny" to read better or spell correctly. It is a program based on four little words, *The Spirit of* 1776. It involves the children, the teacher, the school-board, indeed, but its real success or failure will depend on you and me. There is so much that we can do, and so much that needs to be done.

You must establish an opinion, as soundly based and firmly held as possible. You must see that this opinion is given expression in public. You must help to rekindle the national spirit we have allowed to die through our easy-going folly, our self-indulgence and get-rich-quick attitudes. Many of the things we should deplore in our schools are the same things which we adults popularize outside of the schools. These tendencies, such as our social and intellectual acceptance of conformity, and our willingness to recognize group acceptance as the mark of success, must be shed by our own generation before we can correct them in the next.

We must be willing to reach beyond the three absolutes of citizenship (regular voting, jury service, and armed service in time of war) to reclaim the spirit of the past. American history must become a part of *our* life if it is to have lasting significance for our children. Together with our children we should celebrate Constitution Week (Sept. 16-21), Flag Week (June 14-20), American Education Week (Nov. 10-16), Thrift Week (Jan. 17-23), Conservation Week (Apr. 1-7) and similar periods set aside to enliven great concepts of American history.

There are special days of the year when American History should permeate the school, the home, and the community, and spread a glow of patriotism across the face of America . . . the birthdays of Washington, Jefferson, Lincoln, Franklin . . . the anniversaries of Independence, Old Glory, Memorial Day, Pearl Harbor . . .

There are symbols that leap from the pages of American history, symbols that will find a place in the heart of youth only when they are seen to be respected by us elders . . . the Liberty Bell . . . the red, white and blue . . . *Uncle Sam* . . . the covered wagon . . . the Statue of Liberty . . . the tombs and memorials of our honored dead . . . the yellow parchments that have survived the wear of time to reveal the record of America's struggles . . . and the great words that inspired our fathers and their fathers before them:

Liberty! Justice! Equality! Opportunity! . . . *E pluribus unum* . . . Our liberties we prize and our rights we will maintain . . . the Land of the Free and the Home of the Brave . . . these are words that we must once again fit into our scheme of values if they are to retain meaning for the generations to follow.

If our children are to love their country they must see in

212

us a reflection of the great Promise of America as it is revealed in our lives, in the Law of our Land, in the traditions of our nation, in the literature of America, in these words written by Thomas Wolfe:

—to every man his chance

—to every man, regardless of his birth, his shining, golden oppor-

tunity

—to every man the right to live, to work, to be himself, and to be-

come whatever his manhood and his vision can combine to
make him

—this seeker, is the promise of America.

PART THREE

An American Inheritance

"I cannot understand why men should be so eager after money. Wealth is simply a superfluity of what we don't need."

"What constitutes the bulwark of our own liberty and independence? It is not our frowning battlements, or bristling seacoasts, our Army and Navy. These are not our reliance against tyranny. All of these may be turned against us without making us weaker for the struggle. Our reliance is the love of liberty which God has planted in us. Our defense is in the spirit which prized liberty as the heritage of all men, in all lands everywhere. Destroy this spirit and you have planted the seeds of despotism at your own doors."

ABRAHAM LINCOLN

This masterpiece is not a picture on canvas, it is a living influence of the greatness that was his.

216

Introduction

AMERICA IS MOST OFTEN SEEN *"in miniature" through the personal telescope of daily material existence. Each of us has his own special focal point, his own familiar dot called "home" on the map of the United States. The America we know best is bounded by the private sanctum wherein we reside and carry on the business of living. This is one perspective of America—and an important one for it provides us with individual roots and personal reality.*

But there is another perspective of America which is equally important, for this one supplies the roots that unite millions of strangers in a common brotherhood, and lend reality to the very concept of nation. A broad, spiritual vision is required to see this America; it calls for a vision that can penetrate the past as well as the present, focus on places to which we've never been, events that took place before our time, eras of another century, men of other generations.

To know America—to appreciate, honor, and defend her as good citizens are obliged to do—we must look at her with more than the human eye; we must see her with the clear vision of our heart and soul. We must be able to see America through the lens of our only common denominator—her history.

American history is not merely a classroom subject. Much of our past is a part of the living present. When we dismiss, as a glorified obituary, the story of our country's past it is because we see it in a false perspective. The moral and spiritual threads of American history are caught up in the basic meshwork of our national life; in our language, culture and physical environs. Our lore, arts, customs, the streets we live on, the bridges we cross, the flags and monuments we pass: all are part of the magnificent historical vision that we call America.

217

Every aspect of life in America today is, in some way, symbolic of the past. Accordingly, knowledge of the past gives greater meaning and significance to these symbols which surround us, adding depth to our national life and ultimately enriching our personal lives. Some of these symbols, of course, hold greater meaning than others. The field of Gettysburg stimulates keener emotion than the field of the Wright brothers. Old Glory elicits greater inspiration than the whole of the Smithsonian Institute. But all of our historic reminders, be they local or national, of small interest or great value, help form our common heritage, the Spiritual visin of America.

These final chapters are a glance at this larger perspective of America. They sketch a vision of something we Americans share in common, something capable of raising us above our kitchens and offices and binding us together as a nation. These last few pages are a brief story of a sacred symbol, the original fountainhead of American freedom.

This symbol is a permanent part of our American inheritance. To those who have never looked at America with the eyes of an American, it is just another location on the map. But to those who see in America the history of a great nation, this symbol looms in the foreground of their vision, for it is the revered shrine of their country—the Birthplace of their land and liberty.

To some Americans the very name quickens the heart. To others the name means nothing. To some this symbol dramatically brings to life the heroic men and deeds of 1776. To others it is merely mortar and brick. But this shrine continues to stand while generations pass. It has inspired untold millions of our ancestors and will inspire ourselves and children if we but raise our spiritual vision to its lofty level. It is one immortal monument among many national reminders of our past, all able and ready to enrich our lives, but it is also the first portal through which the patriot must pass, the one door which opens onto the vista of Spiritual America, and which leads to other doors. These chapters, then, are an account of America's foremost shrine. But they are also the story of a certain spirit born in 1776, which has come down to us as part of our national inheritance. The spirit and the symbol have become almost indistinguishable with the passing of time because they are both so much a part of this hallowed relic called Independence Hall.

218

APPENDIX A

INDEPENDENCE HALL

Birthplace of Our Nation

✣✣✣

Independence Hall! How impressive are the associations that cluster around this sacred temple of our national freedom! They inspire the thoughtful patriot with veneration—they enhance devotion to the institutions of our country.

D. W. BELISLE

✣✣✣

PRIOR TO THE WAR FOR AMERICAN INDEPENDENCE, the colonists lived as British subjects accountable to provincial governors appointed by the Crown. This situation led to many infringements, or outright denials, of the basic rights which we today take for granted. One such instance, involving the famous trial of John Peter Zenger, occured in New York in 1734.

The issue was freedom of the press.

Zenger had fearlessly printed bold denunciations of the corrupt administration of Governor William Cosby. The infamous royal official had hastily arrested Zenger and had him thrown in jail, and it seemed a foregone conlusion that the printer would pay the full price for his "crime" of printing the truth. Popular opinion was in the form of a question: What jury, what defense counsel (several lawyers had already been disbarred for merely offering to defend Zenger) would defy Cosby's hand-picked judicial bench and risk the governor's notorious wrath? On the day of the trial there arrived in New York an old gentleman, white-haired and ailing, leaning heavily on his walking stick after an exhausting journey from Philadelphia. This stranger was Andrew Hamilton, one of the most able attorneys in Pennsylvania—and the first of

219

many great men associated with what became known as Independence Hall.

Hamilton had heard of Zenger's plight. A man fiercely dedicated to the cause of individual liberty, he had secretly arranged to defend this fellow-champion of the rights of man.

The ensuing trial was to become a milestone in the annals of civil law. Despite the ranting of Attorney General Bradley and the underhanded intervention of the Bench, the wizened frame of old Hamilton never flinched; and slowly, methodically, without once raising his voice, he proved that to call the truth a libel "is a sword in the hands of a wicked king and an arrant coward, to destroy the innocent."

But the prosecution refused to accept his reasoning and responded with indirect threats of chastisement.

"Then, gentlemen of the jury," said the sage Philadelphian, "it is to you we must now appeal for witnesses to the truth of the facts." And turning his back on the Royal Bench, he quietly put the case of John Zenger before the people. With arduous passion he laid bare the injustice of the court, concluding, in the dignity now of a silent aura of respect and with every eye intent upon him, "The question before you, gentlemen of the jury, is not of small nor private concern; it is not the cause of a poor printer, nor of New York alone, which you are now trying. No, it may in its consequence affect every free man in America. It is the best cause. It is the cause of liberty. Every man who prefers freedom to a life of slavery will bless and honor you as men who have baffled the attempt of tyranny and, by an impartial verdict, have laid a noble foundation for securing for ourselves, our posterity and our neighbors that to which Nature and the laws have given us a right: the liberty both of exposing and opposing arbitrary power by speaking and writing Truth!"

It took the aroused jury but a few moments to return their verdict. John Zenger was found *not guilty* of the charge of libel. Governor Cosby (described by an early historian as an ex-army colonel who "was rapacious and came to the colony to make money") was foiled in his attempted despotism, while

220

the courage and wisdom displayed by Andrew Hamilton two centuries ago remain to this day our foremost precedent regarding man's right to freedom of the press. A generation later, in paying tribute to Hamilton, Gouverneur Morris wrote, "The trial of Zenger, in 1735, was the germ of American freedom—the morning-star of that liberty which subsequently revolutionized America."

The tyrannical charge against John Zenger provides a fair idea of the condition of freedom as it existed before 1776. It also provides an indirect introduction to the man who designed Independence Hall; for Andrew Hamilton, humble defender of liberty, was none other than the amateur architect who created "the forge on which the sword of liberty was shaped."

As one of three commissioners appointed by the Provincial Assembly of Pennsylvania to superintend the financial end of constructing a State House, Hamilton not only designed the building but was also put in charge of its actual construction. It seems most fitting that as Speaker of the first Assembly to occupy the State House, he also became the first presiding officer of the room in which the Declaration of Independence was destined to be signed.

The site that was chosen by Hamilton and his fellow committeemen was a wooded patch of land near the (then) western limits of Philadelphia, extending from Chestnut Street halfway to Walnut, between fifth and sixth streets. With an almost prophetic sense of its eventual significance, the provincial authorities wrote into the deed that the yard was to "remain a publick greene and walke forever"—a condition which has never been broken.

According to the records kept by architect Hamilton, the original cost of the State House was $16,250, a handsome sum in colonial times. Money was not a plentiful commodity in America two hundred years ago; a dollar was worth a dollar and consequently there were fewer of them. Hence, it was not until the issue of paper currency in 1729 that the members of the Assembly found it possible to "unanimously resolve that

221

2,000 of the 30,000 pounds to be emitted in paper currency should be appropriated toward building such a House . . . for the purpose of accommodating legal business, the disposition of Colonial statutes, and the transaction of various other matters." The actual construction was begun in 1732, about a month after the birth of George Washington, the man who would one day stand in this very hall before the Continental Congress to accept his appointment as General and first Commander-in-Chief of the American army.

Except for the wings and tower, the State House was completed by 1735, and a year later the Pennsylvania Assembly met for the first time in its new home.

Without exception, descriptive literature on the State House tends to become quite elaborate whenever it treats of architecture or design. No detail seems too trivial for mention. "The Hall of the Signing," confides one author, "is thirty-nine feet and six inches wide, by forty feet and two inches long, with a height of nineteen feet and eight inches," whereupon he discards his tape measure and surmises, "the intent having apparently been to have it precisely forty by forty by twenty." Another author reports: "Four drain spouts." And so on.

No detail about the birthplace of our nation can be completely irrelevant. On the other hand *men* and not fixtures immortalized this building. It seems, therefore, more revealing to curtail the customary lists of amounts and measurements and to add in their stead a few relatively insignificant names to the "fund of minutiae" about the State House. According to the *Annals* of John Fanning Watson:

Edmund Woolley did the carpenter work, John Harrison the joiner work, Thomas Boude was the brick mason, William Holland did the marble work, Thomas Kerr, plaster, Benjamin Fairman and James Stoopes made the bricks. The lime was from the kilns of the Tysons . . . and the glazing in leaden frames was done by Thomas Godfrey . . ."

Like Andrew Hamilton, who died long before the Revolution, these men had no way of knowing that they were con-

222

tributing their skills to a hallowed monument. (No doubt carpenter Woolley would have been more careful in his measurements of the Hall of the Signers had he known.) Yet these obscure craftsmen—carpenter, bricklayer, plasterer—these unfamiliar names linked to the future Independence Hall, came forth from among the ranks of the people. And every American, be it Thomas Jefferson the Statesman or James Stoopes the brick maker, is of equal importance as an individual under the laws of our land and of our Maker. Yes, it is a good thing to remember that ordinary people built the State House, and that these people were individuals with names and occupations. It is a fine thing that history has retained the individuality of the builders—for it was within this Hall which they built that our own individuality was born and guaranteed.

The builders did their job well, with a vocational pride that dates back to an age when the tradesman was judged by the quality of his work. There is today the clean, fresh look of soap-and-water about Independence Hall, a radiant look of neatness, of American wholesomeness. Its beauty eminates from a dignity that is more spiritual than material. Viewing at a distance, one is instantly struck by the unexpected pattern of clear colors:

The red, scrubbed-looking brick front; the white stone trim and tower, set against a background of blue sky.

It seems almost as though Hamilton had *planned* this combination of red, white and blue!

The Hall consists of two stories and adjoining wings. Entered from Chestnut Street, on the left is the Declaration Chamber, originally intended for the Provincial Assembly. On the right is the West Room, or Judicial Chamber, where the Supreme Court of Pennsylvania held its sessions. On the second floor, the vestibule is flanked on the right by the Governor's Room and on the left by the Chamber of the Clerk of the Assembly. These are in the rear of a long room called the Banquet Chamber. The wings, now museums, were used by various provincial officials. In the early years of Independence

Hall's existence an out-of-state visitor would have found little cause to stop and enter. It was a State House and nothing more.

The beginning of the evolution from "State House" to "Independence Hall" occurred with the purchase of our grand old Liberty Bell. By mid-century sufficient funds had been secured to add a tower and steeple to the Hall. The next step was to acquire a bell. But as the people had already provided a "great public necessity" by placing a clock in the west end, there was some opposition to the measure on the grounds of extravagance. The bell was not considered extravagant in itself, but the idea of having to send to England for one, at added expense, was an irksome matter. The home government held an exclusive monopoly on almost every facet of manufacturing, thereby forcing the colonists to rely on the mills, looms, and furnaces of England for most of their purchases.

After a good deal of heated argument it was decided (with much of the credit going to Speaker of the Assembly Isaac Norris) that the State House was entitled to a bell. In November of 1751 Norris wrote to the Colonial Agents in London:

Respected Friend, Robert Charles,

The Assembly having ordered us [the Superintendents] to procure a bell from England to be purchased for their use, we take the liberty to supply ourselves to thee to get us a good bell, of about one hundred pounds sterling, or perhaps, with the charges, something more, and accordingly we have enclosed a first bill of exchange . . .

We hope and rely on thy care and assistance in this affair, and that thou wilt procure and forward it by the first good opportunity, as our workmen inform us it will be much less trouble to hang the bell before the scaffolds are struck from the building where we intend to place it, which will not be done till the end of next summer or beginning of the fall. Let the bell be cast by the best workmen, and examined carefully before it is shipped, with the following words well shaped in large letters round it, *viz:*—

224

By order of the Assembly of the Province of Pennsylvania, for the State House in the City of Philadelphia, 1752.

And underneath,

PROCLAIM LIBERTY THROUGH ALL THE LAND TO ALL THE INHABITANTS THEREOF. LEVIT. XXV. 10.

As we have experienced thy readiness to serve this Province on all occasions, we desire it may be our excuse for this additional trouble from thy assured friends.

ISAAC NORRIS.

THOMAS LEACH.

EDWARD WARNER.

Thus, was the "Great Announcer" of our independence and freedom acquired. It arrived in August of 1752, with hundreds of people on hand to watch and cheer as it was unloaded from the ship. The bell, cast by Thomas Lister in London's Whitechapel, weighed over a ton. It was hooked onto a temporary armature in the Square to be tested, but "upon its being hung up to try the sound, it was cracked by a stroke of the clapper without any other violence."

It had to be re-cast of course but, rather than send it back to England, the superintendents decided to experiment. "Two ingenious workmen [the Messrs. Stow and Pass] undertook to cast it here," wrote Norris, "When we broke up the metal, our judges generally agreed it was too high and brittle, and cast several little bells out of it to try the sound and strength . . ." When the re-cast bell was rung, in April of 1753, it rudely clanged forth its evidence of too much copper. Although Pass and Stow had "made the mould in a masterly fashion," they were "so tiezed with the witticisms of the towne," they agreed to cast it once again The third one — which has come down to us as the Liberty Bell — was hung in the belfry in June of the same year, to everyone's satisfaction. Speaker Norris remarked, "They made a good bell, which pleases me much that we should first venture upon and succeed in the greatest bell, for ought I know, in English America—surpassing, too, the imported one, which was too high and brittle."

The scriptural verse, "Proclaim liberty through all the land to all the inhabitants thereof," so prophetically suggested by Isaac Norris, was not changed, but it was placed above the accompanying line this time. The second line was revised to read: "By Order of the Assembly of the Province of Pennsylvania [sic] for the State House in Philada., Pass & Stow, Philada. MDCCLIII."

Although the Liberty Bell's triumphant career started in 1753, independence was still a long way off. In this year George Washington was but a diplomatic courier involved in the Ohio Territory dispute. Thomas Jefferson was a scraggy, ten-year-old farm boy. Benjamin Franklin had just been appointed deputy-postmaster for the English-American Colonies. John Hancock and John Adams were still students at Harvard. Patrick Henry was a 17-year-old inn-keeper, and that heroic youth, Nathan Hale, was not yet born.

Still, the epic struggle for independence and liberty can be said to have begun with the placement of the Liberty Bell in the modest steeple of the State House. Almost immediately its clear, firm ring became the familiar signal for public assemblies in the Square to uphold the cause of freedom. The seed of the Spirit of '76 was planted the very next year, when Dr. Franklin proposed his Albany Plan of Union—a plan surprisingly similar to the Constitution which he was to assist in framing three decades later. It was rejected, chiefly because it was pre-mature. There was too much democracy in it for the "Lords of Trade and Plantation," and too much prerogative in it for the colonial assemblies. But the novel idea of union was not forgotten by the people.

The trickle of colonial grievances evolved into a flow in the next few years and the bell was called upon to "proclaim liberty" so regularly that "divers inhabitants living nearby" petitioned against the noise. They described it as a "lethal weapon" and asserted that "from its uncommon size and unusual sound, it is extremely dangerous and may prove fatal to those afflicted with sickness."

But by this time the ring of the Liberty Bell was no longer

226

just a sound; it was an angry, revolutionary voice that could not be silenced. In the February chill of 1761 it beckoned thousands to the State-House Yard to denounce the repulsive Writs of Assistance. The fiery tongue of young James Otis lashed out on behalf of discouraged Americans. Referring to the arbitrary power of the Writs, he began his speech with, "A man's house is his castle," and concluded with a startling avowal:

I am determined to sacrifice estate, ease, health, applause, and even life, to the sacred calls of my country, in opposition to a kind of power the exercise of which cost one king his head and another his throne.

. . . To my dying day I will oppose, with all the power and faculties God has given me, all such instruments of slavery on one hand and of villany on the other.

"Then," said John Adams, who had witnessed this speech, "the independence of the colonies was proclaimed."

Independence was first looked upon as an alternative, but gradually it was seen to be inevitable. The colonial situation had changed mightily since the year when ground was broken for the State House. At the time, England's sagacious Walpole had opined, "I will leave the taxation of America to some of my successors who have more courage than I have." And twenty-five years later the great Pitt was heard to say, "I will never burn my fingers with an American stamp tax."

But the Ministry of 1763-65 was far less visionary. Their Sugar Act was received in America with unprecedented opposition. While angry throngs engulfed the State House, within its chambers it was formally resolved: "that no impositions of taxes against natural and legal rights would be tolerated." Six months later infuriated merchants gathered in the Square and adopted a resolution to boycott British merchandise—an open retaliation against the obnoxious Stamp Act.

The Stamp Act was to go into effect on the first of November, and on that day the Liberty Bell tolled a steady funeral knell while the people observed fast and abstinence! They had appealed to the King in vain; now they appealed to God. Revolution was in the offing.

227

The inevitable repeal of Parliament's tax acts brought a temporary release of tension to the colonies, but by 1768 conditions were once again unbearable. And once again State House Square was filled with men who refused to live in servitude. They flatly asserted, "The Parliament of Great Britain had reduced the people here to the level of slaves."

The tea tax, and subsequent closing of the port of Boston, was the final prologue to war. More than two months before the infamous "Tea Party" a public meeting had been held at the State House, during which the people protested taxation by parliament in eight terse resolutions. They denounced as "an enemy to his country, anyone [who should] aid or abet in unloading, receiving, or vending the tea." Further, any pilot who would dare to bring a British tea ship to Philadelphia would be hanged!

When on Christmas morning, 1773, British Captain Ayres attempted to dock and unload his tea ship, *Polly*, he was met four miles below the city and forced to return to London with his rejected shipment of tea. The good captain was quite indignant over the affair; it is to be supposed that he lived out his remaining years wholly unaware that his sea-faring neck had come within four miles of a waiting noose. The incident was the first act of defiance against the hated tea tax. Henceforth, as the small band of colonists well knew, there would be no turning back.

After the violent demonstration in Boston, it was generally conceded throughout the provinces that unity of action was essential. "There is no time to be lost," declared the Boston *Gazette*, echoing the public sentiment, "a congress or a meeting of the American states is indispensible; and what the people will shall be effected."

Any misgivings they may have had were undoubtedly dispelled on April 24, 1775, when a wary, somber-faced stranger named Paul Revere reined in his lathered horse at Philadelphia, requesting to see some members of the Committee of Correspondence. His story was indeed startling, but it came as no great surprise.

Six nights earlier, General Cage had sent eight hundred men, under Major Pitcairn, to seize a secreted store of munitions at Concord. At dawn (April 19) the British force reached Lexington and there found Captain Jonas Parker—backed by seventy grim-faced farmers—standing in the middle of the green with his hard eyes squinting against the sun and his gleaming rifle-barrel pointed straight ahead.

Pitcairn rode forward and barked a command: "Disperse! Disperse, ye rebels! Down with your arms, and disperse!"

Not a man moved. The strange tabloid stood defiantly so until at last there was fired *the shot heard 'round the world.*

Upon hearing this news, the Assembly publicly agreed to assemble for the purpose of defending "with arms their property, liberty, and lives." Eight thousand angry outraged men gathered in front of the State House to cheer and applaud the announcement.

Now that the first blood had been shed in the name of Liberty, the Provincial Assembly of Pennsylvania unhesitatingly offered its chambers to the Continental Congress. On May 10, 1775, the Congress took over and it became the destiny of this unpretentious, two-story brick building to serve as the historic seat of our American heritage. Delegates from each colony (except Georgia) gathered in the East Room, now known as the Declaration Chamber, to discuss the immediate future. A full account of recent events in Massachusetts—the chief target of the King's vengeance—was laid before them. A written inquiry from the province under discussion had been sent, "asking advice as to the form of government to be adopted there, and requesting the Continental Congress to assume control of the army at Cambridge." The other colonies were sympathetic to the cause of Massachusetts. The most popular slogan of the moment capsuled the situation thusly:

THE QUARREL WITH AMERICA FAIRLY STATED

Rudely forced to drink tea, Massachusetts in anger
Spills the tea on John Bull—John falls on to bang her;
Massachusetts, enraged, calls for neighbors to aid,

229

And gives Master John a severe bastinade.
Now, good men of the law, pray who is at fault,
The one who began or resents the assault?

Immediately, a Committe of the Whole reported, and the Congress resolved, that war had been commenced by Great Britain. Committees were appointed to prepare formal addresses to the people of Great Britain, Ireland, the Assembly of Jamaica, and "the oppressed inhabitants of Canada."

On June 9, Congress spoke for the first time of the "United" Colonies, in a resolution that "Thursday, the twentieth of July next, be observed throughout the Twelve United Colonies as a day of humiliation, fasting and prayer." Shortly after, a petition by the Congress to George III was dispatched, being the first official announcement to the King of the Colonies' union. The King, of course, could not consistently receive a document from a "Congress" whose legality he denied. For this reason John Dickenson, who authored the petition, disliked the use of the word *Congress.*

"It is the only word I wish altered," he told a group of delegates.

"It is the only word I wish to retain," came the immediate reply of patriot Benjamin Harrison.

The Continental Congress had not met more than a month when one of the most stirring scenes in the dramatic history of what was to become Independence Hall took place. One can imagine the handful of uncertain patriots seated about in high-backed Windsor chairs, the low rumble of their political discussions reverberating against the high paneled walls of the Declaration Chamber. It is late. The room is bathed in candle light from the great chandeliers. The windows have been thrown open on this warm spring night and a light breeze gives movement to the myriad of shadows within the Hall. There is an electric tension in the Hall; the Congress has been in session over three weeks, and the immensity of the task at hand has made itself manifest. Here assembled are the great *idealists* of the eighteenth century, faced with the most *realistic* crisis of a crucial age. No one speaks now of liberty and

230

the rights of man. The great *common cause* is felt so deeply it need not be alluded to. Rather, the talk is of *war*. Eloquence and rhetoric have been cast aside. The talk is practical—of weapons, ammunition, uniforms, food, shelter, and pay; of the unorganized, undisciplined militia voluntarily assembled at Cambridge; of the powerful British and German forces at this moment invading the St. Lawrence River and New York. The talk is of the need for a leader; of the need for a military mystic, as it were, who might miraculously overcome the war force of an empire. The talk is rooted to a single, crushing fact: behind them, beyond the northern green of Independence Square, there is already a war being waged, and they must produce an army to fight in it. Every delegate is mindful of Cage's brash announcement that "thousands of veteran warriors are coming from Russia and German principalities to crush the *unnatural rebellion.*" They now know that there will be no immediate military aid from France, for in a clandestine visit from the French emissary De Bouvoloir, they received only a pessimistic and non-comittal: "Make your proposals, and I will present them."

Out of the talk emerges a desperate financial proposal, and the Congress authorizes an issue of bills of credit to the amount of $2,000,000. A delegate from Massachusetts—John Adams—moves that the Congress designate the band of patriots, which, after the news of Lexington, gathered at Cambridge to resist the British forces, as a *Continental Army*. The resolution is adopted. And now America has an army—a gathering of 20,000 infuriated farmers drawn together by a single cause.

A delegate from Maryland —Thomas Johnson — takes the floor and with an economy of words nominates a member of the Virginia Assembly to lead this newly created army. The vote is a mere formality, for the quiet Virginian is the unanimous choice of every one present. President John Hancock, seated at his desk on a raised platform at the head of the Hall, now stands, announcing to Congress that George Washington has just been elected Commander-in-Chief of the

231

Continental Army. There is no cheering, no clapping of hands. These men have just placed the fate of American freedom in this single pair of hands, realizing that the odds against George Washington are staggering.

Here, within the unostentatious sanctum of Liberty, Washington stood before his countrymen and, in the true humility of greatness, replied:

Mr. President, though I am truly sensible of the high honor done me in this appointment, yet I feel great distress from a consciousness that my abilities and military experience may not be equal to the extensive and important trust. However, as the Congress desires it, I will enter upon the momentous duty, and exert every power I possess in their service and for the support of the glorious cause. I beg they will accept my most cordial thanks for this distinguished testimony of their approbation. But, lest some unlucky event should happen, unfavorable to my reputation, I beg it may be remembered by every gentleman in the room that I this day declare, with the utmost sincerity, I do not think myself equal to the command I am honored with. As to pay, sir, I beg leave to assure Congress that, as no pecuniary consideration could have tempted me to accept the arduous employment, at the expense of domestic ease and happiness, I do not wish to make any profit from it. I will keep an exact account of my expenses. These, I doubt not, they will discharge, and that is all I desire.

Dr. Franklin, whose wisdom was ever in demand by the Congress, returned home that night and wrote tersely to his acquaintances in England, "Americans will fight; England has lost her colonies forever." Such was his faith in the ability of young General Washington!

The movement toward independence spread rapidly throughout the colonies. King George continued to ignore the petitions of "those wicked men." The clash of British and American arms had intensified during the winter months. Tom Paine's passionate arguments for independence, on sale in almost every village and hamlet ("*Common Sense* for Eighteen Pence!"), heated the blood of hesitant patriots. Into this atmosphere, the stalwarts of Independence Hall sent a resolution recommending to all colonies a radical change of government, so that they might be better prepared to meet the serious emergencies of the Revolution.

The first response came from North Carolina, on April 12, 1776, which accepted the recommendation and also unanimously "empowered their delegates in the Continental Congress to concur with the delegates of the other colonies in declaring independence and forming foreign alliances." During the months of May and June other colonies became, *de facto* or *de jure,* in favor of independent government and a national severance from the British Crown. Men and women were swept up in the tide of patriotic fervor, and children could be heard singing the popular lyrics published in Bickerstaff's Almanac:

> *In Freedom we're born, and, like sons of the brave*
> *Will never surrender,*
> *But swear to defend her,*
> *And scorn to survive if unable to save.*

On May 15, the Virginia Assembly instructed its delegates to formally propose to Congress a declaration of the colonies as free and independent states. And as these instructions were reiterated in the form of rumor, the eyes of the world turned as one to the mysterious, but as yet silent, edifice on Chestnut Street in the metropolitan hub of the New World.

Within the Hall there was tension and drama, but hardly glamour. As the members of Congress filed into the East Room on the morning of June 7, flies buzzed ignominiously about. Each member nodded politely to door-keeper Andrew McNeare and stepped into the sun-baked room for another "closed-door" session. The Declaration Chamber was almost stark in its furnishings. Straight-backed chairs, arranged in no special formation, were provided for the delegates. The "rising-sun" chair and modest desk were reserved for the presiding officer. The lone show of elegance emanated from the silver ink well, pen-holder and sanding box (purchased from Syng, the celebrated silversmith in 1752 for twenty-five pounds), which

233

gleamed from atop Hancock's desk. Each delegate would eventually use that priceless quill.

Here was assembled the most distinguished group of Americans in the history of our country. Their hour of decision was iminent, for the colonies could no longer continue to profess allegiance to the Crown while refusing to obey its Parliament. On this day, Richard Henry Lee, speaking on behalf of Virginia and in the interest of all who were here represented (including you and me) rose in Congress and moved, "That these United Colonies are, and of right ought to be, Free and Independent States." A wave of emotion swept through the Hall! There were cheers, shouts, warnings, rejections, grumblings, and silent contemplation.

"Let this happy day," urged the patriotic Lee, "give birth to an American republic! The eyes of Europe are fixed upon us; she demands of us a living example of freedom . . . If we are not this day wanting in our duty to our country, the names of the American Legislators of '76 will be placed by posterity at the side of those . . . whose memory . . . forever will be dear."

Delegates needed time to consult their respective assemblies on a course of action, and the explosive proposal was referred to a "Committee of the Whole" for debate and re-consideration on July 2.

In the meantime, Congress appointed a committee membered by Thomas Jefferson, John Adams, Benjamin Franklin, Roger Sherman and Robert Livingston to prepare a written "declaration" to speed up action in the event that Lee's motion carried. The committee, in turn, selected Jefferson as a committee of one to author this declaration.

On July 1, the Committee of the Whole reconvened at the Hall to consider both the "Resolution respecting Independency," and the written "declaration" itself. John Adams, who had seconded Lee's motion, delivered "an unprepared, sudden, and impetuous speech in favor of the resolution." John Dickinson then spoke in elaborate terms of "the arguments against independence." Others voiced their opinions, almost

234

all of them in favor of the resolution. Then they retired with prayer and anxiety in their hearts.

The following day twelve colonies (New York was ready to make the vote unanimous but her delegates had to wait until July 9 for positive instructions):

RESOLVED, That these United Colonies are, and of right ought to be, Free and Independent States; that they are absolved from all allegiance to the British Crown, and that all political connection between them and the State of Great Britain is and ought to be totally dissolved.

Of this fortuitous day in history, John Adams predicted—inaccurately but beautifully—"The greatest question which ever was debated in America was decided; and a greater, perhaps, never was nor ever will be decided among men . . . The 2nd day of July, 1776, will be the most memorable epoch in the history of America—to be celebrated by succeeding generations as the great anniversary festival, commemorated as the day of deliverence by solemn acts of devotion to God Almighty from one end of the continent to the other from this time forward forevermore." With the *formal* adoption yet to come, the slight anachronism of Adams is understandable and of little importance when weighed against the great faith and confidence to be found in his words.

Two days later the "Monumental Event" took place. Congress officially adopted the Declaration of Independence on behalf of the people of the United States of America. The old State House of Pennsylvania became "Independence Hall" in name and in spirit, from that day forward. The East Room, in which the official signatures of President Hancock and Secretary Thomson were placed on that priceless document, was from that moment immortalized as the "Declaration Chamber." The *spirit* of Independence Hall wrote its message across the face of the earth, that all might learn of its precious legacy, that all the oppressed of the world might take on new hope under the long shadow of its strength:

This *is the Sacred Fane wherein assembled*
The fearless champions on the side of right—

235

Men at whose Declaration *empires trembled,*
Moved by the Truth's clear and eternal light.

This *is the hallowed spot where first, unfurling,*
Fair Freedom *spread her blazing scroll of light—*
Here *from Oppression's throne the tyrant hurling,*
She stood supreme in majesty and might.

In 1769, the American Philosophical Society (founded by Ben Franklin) had erected a temporary observation tower in State House Square to observe the transit of Venus across the sun. It was from this tower, "the awful platform," as John Adams later described it, that the Declaration of Independence was publicly read for the first time, on July 8, 1776. Philadelphia historian Agnes Repplier tells of an "unseen auditor who has left us an account of that day. Deborah Norris, then a girl of fifteen, had climbed her garden wall to catch a glimpse of what was going on. The reader was hidden from her by the side of the observatory, but she heard distinctly from her high perch every word he uttered, and was awed into a childish terror as the grave voice—Charles Thomson's voice, she fancied, but it was really that of Captain John Nixon—repeated slowly those memorable words, the full significance of which she was too young to understand. 'It was,' she wrote years afterwards, 'a time of fearful doubt and great anxiety with the people'."

But the citizens (as they could be truly called for the first time in their lives) who had assembled in the Square to hear that first reading responded with thunderous applause. The Liberty Bell—whose inscription to "Proclaim Liberty" had been ironically etched on the original bell in the country from which *liberty* had been won—rang throughout the day in honor of the great event. And later that night bonfires and torches were lit in celebration of independence.

The Declaration was immediately printed and distributed throughout the states, bearing only the names of Hancock and Thomson. The Declaration of Independence was, however, signed on the day of its adoption by every member who

236

voted for it to show that a majority of the colonies approved the measure. The Declaration was later engrossed on parchment and signed again on August Second. The original signatures, attached to a copy on paper, were withheld from the public for fear of British reprisal, and it wasn't until January of the next year that broadsides with names of all the signers were finally issued.

Another of the significant events which have endeared Independence Hall to the people of America occurred less than a year later. The necessity for a national flag was felt by the Congress. And once again assembled in that "Sacred Fane," the founding fathers adopted the following resolution on June 14, 1777:

RESOLVED, That the flag of the United States be thirteen stripes, alternate red and white; that the union be thirteen stars, white, on a blue field, representing a new constellation.

The Congress defined the symbolic meaning of the colors used in the Flag: "White signifies Purity and Innocence; Red, Hardiness and Valor; Blue signifies Vigilance, Perseverance and Justice."

And thus it came to be that the three greatest symbols of Americanism were united to form the shrine of shrines:

Independence Hall, symbol of our national origin; the American Flag waving above its roof, symbol of our Land; the Liberty Bell ensconced in its tower, symbol of individual freedom. Together they reign, expressing in the thunder of their silence that which mere words cannot possibly say.

A few months after the adoption of the new Flag, in the autumn of 1777, the Continental Congress learned that British forces were marching toward Independence Hall! After the heart-breaking defeat at Brandywine, General Washington had gathered his troops and begun a march toward Philadelphia, encamping at Germantown along the way. On September Sixteenth, he crossed the Schuylkill at that point to stave off an advancing British force. Two days later he sent an urgent message to Independence Hall, advising that the Congress adjourn as quickly as possible and evacuate the city. Even as the message was read, the opposing forces were engaged in battle less than twenty miles away. But on the banks of the Schuylkill, a violent storm intervened and cut short the skirmish. Washington re-crossed the river and, while maneuvering to keep General Howe's forces from crossing above him, the enemy crossed the Schuykill below him—and was thus placed between the American army and the city of Philadelphia. Nothing but a battle and victory could save Independence Hall from British conquest. But Washington's handful of ill-equipped patriots was no match for the British force.

The Congress adjourned on September twenty-seventh and moved from the city only a few hours before the enemy arrived. They reconvened at York three days later, while British artillery gathered in Independence Square. Wagon-loads of wounded British soldiers were moved into a temporary hospital set up in the Banquet Chamber of Independece Hall. The forty-second Highlanders moved into nearby private homes.

The public papers of Independence Hall had been safely moved to Lancaster. The Liberty Bell, too, had been moved for the first time. Guarded by two-hundred North Carolina and Virginia cavalrymen, it had been secretly carted to Allentown, and there hidden under the floor of the Zion Reformed Church, where it was destined to remain for nearly a year. (Years later, a trolley line, known as "the Liberty Bell Route" was established, following the actual route taken by the Bell from Chestnut Hill to Allentown.)

A young Lieutenant Colonel named Telghman entered the city of Philadelphia around midnight of a rainy autumn Thursday. He went directly to the home of Thomas McKean, then President, of the Congress. So violently did Telghman knock on the door of McKean, that a watchman was "disposed to avert him." The two stood outside the door, ignoring the rain, conversing in low tones, the watchman patiently, the officer with obvious irritation. Presently, the watchman

238

went on his way, proclaiming the hour and giving the usual cry, "All's well," but this time he joyfully added, *"and Cornwallis is taken!"*

The date was October 23, 1781.

Lt. Col. Telghman had been a personal emissary of General George Washington, sent to inform the Congress that General Cornwallis had surrendered at Yorktown. Congress assembled at dawn and with great emotion listened to Charles Thomson read the dispatch from the Commander-in-Chief. At the conclusion it was resolved to attend services in a body and "return thanks to Almighty God for crowning the allied armies of the United States and France with success." Outside, a throng of happy Americans sent a roar of acclaim through the Hall, and the faithful Liberty Bell, that honored herald of Independence, was back in its tower once again to "proclaim liberty through all the land to all the inhabitants thereof." The following month, in a formal ceremony at Independence Hall, Congress was presented with twenty-four battle flags taken from the defeated Cornwallis.

The victorious end of the War for Independence hardly concluded the incredible epoch of Independence Hall. Even before the Revolution had ended there were forces at work which would soon effect the destiny of Andrew Hamilton's sturdy creation.

The Articles of Confederation and Perpetual Union had been hastily drawn up and ratified by the Continental Congress of 1776. It was soon after learned how utterly ineffective they were, and young statesmen like Alexander Hamilton, James Madison and John Jay were thoroughly convinced that something had to be done. As early as 1780, (Hamilton then only twenty-three years old) outlined a sketch of a national constitution and suggested the calling of a convention to frame such a system of government.

Several years later the same youth almost single-handedly induced the New York Senate to recommend to Congress a national convention. Secretary of the Treasury Robert Morris, who recognized, perhaps better than any other statesman of

239

that day, the need for a constitutional convention, welcomed young Hamilton to the national legislature with these sparse words:

"A firm, wise, manly system of federal Government is what I once wished, what I now hope, what I dare not expect, but what I will not despair of."

And so it was, that a mere decade after the historic Declaration of Independence, the Declaration Chamber of Independence Hall once again was filled with the great founders of our Republic. Throughout the summer of 1787 that famous hall trembled as the fifty-five Constitution-makers hammered out clause after clause, debating every issue, analyzing every phrase. Madison and Jay fought tirelessly for ratification, writing many of the anonymous, highly effective *Federalist Papers* and speaking with clarity from the convention floor. Hamilton constantly urged the delegates to sign the Constitution. "No man's ideas are more remote from the plan than my own," he once cried, "but is it possible to deliberate between anarchy and confusion on the one hand and the chance of good on the other?"

Word by word the Constitution was framed, as conflicting opinions gradually resolved themselves. One can almost hear the exhausted sighs of September 17, 1787, when the Constitution was finally ratified. One can picture the torpid faces, flushed and perspiring in the crowded hall, giving way to satisfied smiles; the formally attired gentlemen of law, rising at last from the littered delegation tables of Independence Hall, gathering in their notebooks and ledgers, going home finally after long battle, profound statesmanship, and hard-won victory. Independence Hall witnessed many stirring and historic events during the birth of America's Republic, but if Independence Hall had been only the place wherein the Constitution of the United States was drawn, there would be more than enough reason for its certain immortality. For truly were assembled within these hallowed walls "the fearless champions on the side of right."

240

THE SHRINE

History's Hallowed Hall

As each successive generation of those who have benefitted by the great Declaration made within it shall make their pilgrimage to that shrine, may they not think it unseemly to call its walls Salvation and its gates Praise. EDWARD EVERETT

EDWARD EVERETT, STATESMAN AND PATRIOT of the Civil War era, is remembered for many notable orations, but few of his fine speeches surpassed the eloquent little panegyric delivered July 4, 1858, in honor of Independence Hall. "Let the rain of heaven distill gently on its roof," declaimed Everett, "and the storms of winter beat softly on its door. As each successive generation of those who have benefitted by the great Declaration made within it shall make their pilgrimage to that shrine, may they not think it unseemly to call its walls Salvation and its gates Praise."

Speaking to his countrymen more than one hundred years ago, Edward Everett predicted, or rather he took for granted, that the sacred historical significance of Independence Hall would live on. And, of course, he was right. The "Cradle of Democracy" has retained all of its original eminence as one of the world's great shrines of human freedoms fought for and triumphantly secured.

There are two aspects of the story of Independence Hall. First and foremost, there is the historic role it played in the founding of our Constitutional Republic. But there is also the resultant spiritual position it has ever since maintained as our national "shrine of shrines." The later story of Independence

Hall is to a large extent, therefore, the record of a rare and priceless relic: an account of tender care, occasional neglect, and a spiritual tradition that will continue to outlive the generations which sustain it.

The first formal display of respect for Independence Hall as an historical shrine occured in 1783 when steps were taken to improve the Square. At that time elm trees were planted, walks were laid out, and here and there a wooden bench was placed. However, it was in 1799 that it actually became a national monument. Philadelphia had already given up its role as the seat of national government, but it wasn't until this time that Independence Hall was abandoned, in favor of Harrisburg, as the Pennsylvania State House.

The "Birthplace of our Country," like the Father of our Country, was born in 1732 and led an active, noble life which ended in 1799. What a superb coincidence that both man and building secured in that identical span of epic years the well-deserved honor of immortality. The day that George Washington died, the Liberty Bell tolled from dawn to dusk, proclaiming the grief of a nation and the liberty of his valiant soul.

Three years after Independence Hall "retired," its Banquet Chamber became what was probably the first museum in America. Charles Wilson Peale, the famous artist and patriot who rendered portraits of almost all the leading statesmen, established a modest gallery to exhibit his work.

Philadelphia became by purchase the owner of Independence Hall in 1816, and measures were soon taken to restore the building and grounds. The two arcades and outside stairways were removed about this time and architect Robert Mills replaced them with neat, two-story structures. The present replicas of the original bell tower and steeple were built by William Strickland in 1828. The work of Mills didn't fare as well as that of Strickland. His buildings were later torn down in favor of new wings with interior stairs, joined as before to the main building by arcades.

As the result of patriotic contributions by school children, the Square is adorned by a handsome marble statue of George Washington (on the Chestnut Street side) sculptured by J. A. Bailey. In the center of the Square stands a bronze statue of Commodore Barry, a fine piece of work by Samuel Murray. (In a rare instance of vandalism, the iron chain which surrounded this $10,000 work of art was stolen one night in 1910 and it has never been returned or replaced.) Even though the Square is located in the heart of a large city, it possesses a great deal of rustic charm. William Pitt, who aspired to a "greene country towne" would be proud of this four-acre tract.

The Square was entirely refurbished in 1875 in anticipation of the National Centennial, and again in 1915 it was restored. Fifty-six ornate gas lamps—one for each signer of the Declaration—were installed, and among the trees are 13 red oaks, one for each of the original colonies. The oaks were planted by the National Association of Gardeners and it is interesting to note that the roots of each tree are nurtured in soil brought from the state which the tree represents.

As for the Liberty Bell, its historic voice continued to serve America for many years after the death of Washington. It rang out a warm welcome to Lafayette when he paid a visit to the Shrine in 1824. Lafayette, who endeared himself to this nation as few foreign friends have before or since his time, used Independence Hall as his levee room during his triumphal tour of America.

The great Bell tolled again in sorrow when Thomas Jefferson and John Adams both died on the fiftieth anniversary of the Independence they were so instrumental in achieving.

After yeoman service for almost a century, the Liberty Bell acquired its world famous *crack* in 1835, once more tolling for the death of a great American, this time Chief Justice Marshall.

Years of neglect followed. It seemed now that the great voice of Liberty had ceased its lucid conversations with the people—now that it no longer could vent its anger, welcome its friends, mourn its beloved dead—it was generally forgotten. However, contrary to several inaccurate accounts, the Liberty Bell is not known ever to have been treated with outright dis-

243

respect. There is one particularly grotesque example of historical "gossip" that is still popular today although it has no basis in fact. According to this myth, the priceless relic was once offered as a down-payment, or "trade-in," on a new bell. A Germantown bell maker was supposed to have delivered the new and then refused to haul the old bell away from Independence Hall. He complained (the debunking story goes) that "Drayage costs more than the bell's worth." We are expected to believe that the city fathers of Philadelphia (who spent large sums of money to preserve Independence Hall) became incensed and had the bell maker brought into court for refusing to remove the Liberty Bell as a piece of junk. The *same* bell, mind you, that had in its triumphant life-time felt the tears of grown men touch the surface of its hard metal shell; that had felt the innocent gaze of children against its cold scars. Well, the Liberty Bell was not removed. The story is not true and contains none of the merits which justify the many fine folk-legends that have come down to us from the past.

Today the Liberty Bell is valued beyond estimation by every American worthy of the name. It has been mute for well over a century, having last rung in 1843, but it has not lost its fascinating charm. It has traveled to San Francisco, New Orleans, Chicago, Atlanta, Charleston, Boston, St. Louis. But its journeys opened a narrow crack above the old one. Since 1917, when the Bell was used in a street parade to help sell Liberty Bonds, it has remained in its place at Independence Hall, where every precaution is taken to preserve its condition. Two bolts have been inserted into the original crack, which has been bored out in an unsuccessful attempt to prevent further cracking. Within its cone, a mechanical spider has been installed to lighten the pressure. The Bell itself is attached to a platform with wheels and can be removed in a matter of moments in case of emergency.

The most recent manifestation of public esteem for the Independence Hall shrine, and perhaps the most farseeing for preservation of our noble shrines was expressed by the federal

244

government's intense effort to preserve it for all times, so our posterity can draw inspiration and strength from it.

The fact that liberty was in jeopardy seemed to make millions of people more conscious of it than ever before. The sudden threat made by totalitarian powers caused America to become acutely aware of her form of government, her personal freedom, and her epic history. During this rare period of national introspection, attention was subsequently turned to Independence Hall. For the first time, city, state, and federal governments joined forces to ensure the shrine of complete restoration and perpetual care.

In 1943, Independence Square was designated a national historic site by the United States Department of Interior, whereby custody of the buildings and grounds was assumed by the National Park Service. An extensive program of rehabilitation was begun. Facilities for visitors were provided, and an important project of historical research was undertaken. Two years later, the Commonwealth of Pennsylvania authorized expenditure of funds to acquire three city blocks between Fifth and Sixth streets from the Delaware River bridgehead at Race Street to Independence Square. The area was officially christened "Independence Mall," and removal of structures within the area was begun in order that a grand concourse could be formed and thus provide a dignified approach to the nation's foremost shrine.

The following year the site became the subject of study by a federal commission, the result of which was an act of Congress (Public Law 795, 80th Congress) defining the federal area. The city of Philadelphia which carried the burden of preserving the shrine for many years, readily accepted state and federal assistance. In a fine show of civic cooperation, the city fathers transferred the operative rights of Independence Hall to the National Park Service on January 1, 1951. The title to the property remains, as it should, with the city.

As mentioned earlier, this display of public concern for Independence Hall commenced with the beginning of World War II. The work itself, the overall project of transforming

245

the Independence Hall group into an historic park, is still in process. The demolition of buildings and the landscaping required by operation "Independence Mall," for instance, was only at the half-way mark (in late 1953) eight years after it was started. One could say, in fact, that the task of sustaining the birthplace of our nation, in substance as well as in Spirit, has been going on continuously for about eighteen decades, and in all likelihood it will continue to go on for countless more.

Now, we are not exactly considered to be an overly sentimental nation. There are many European and Latin countries that erect national shrines for each of their accomplished artists, scholars, musicians, authors, humanitarians. Generally speaking, we do not. In a country whose cities can grow from 5,000 to 40,000 in one man's lifetime (as Philadelphia did in Benjamin Franklin's time) there is little room for trophies of antiquity. How, then, is the costly and elaborate survival of Independence Hall to be explained? Why have men, whom we never hear of, poured thousands of dollars and hours into the preservation of this singular building? There can only be one answer. Patriots of every generation have desired to perpetuate a unique, vivid, and vital reminder of America's spiritual meaning.

All who set foot in that noble repository of liberty are instantly reminded of their heritage, of the finest American ideals. They are reminded of the lofty, non-utilitarian values on which American life has really rested from the beginning; and of their God-intended rights to act, to speak, to worship, to dissent, to dream, to build, to fail and to succeed. Surely, every citizen who has visited Independence Hall became a better American because of it. It is this kind of gratifying return that makes the investment of money and effort and time so very worthwhile.

Can you imagine what it would mean to the American character if instead of one there were hundreds of Independence Halls scattered across the United States — if every city (or even every county) had its own Independence Hall to

246

serve as a beacon of patriotism for the community? It would undoubtedly amount to a moral revolution, a conscious return to the Spirit of '76. After all, it is this spirit of loyalty and love — alive, stirring, enriching — that constantly flows through that immortal shrine. Year in, year out, the people come. The spirit flows on with ceaseless human tides. Tourist, traveler, student, statesman, people of every age, every walk of life, converge upon Independence Hall every day. Those enthralled by this many-phantomed place, who inwardly relive that aggrandizing epoch of America's history, take home a fierce new love of country. And as the restless spirit of Liberty continues to move with the ebb and flow of daily visitors, none of us will ever know how many seeds of patriotism are swept into the living stream for future dispersion among the towns and cities of our land.

Each year more than one and a half million people make the pilgrimage to Independence Hall, and the neighboring Supreme Court and Congress Hall buildings situated at either corner of Independence Square. And these people, walking along the broad flag-stone walks passing the eighteenth century hitching posts, staring at the living history directly ahead, cannot as Americans help but feel a lump of patriotic pride swell in their throats. Entering the same Independence Hall that Thomas Jefferson so often entered, standing within arms' length of the very desk at which George Washington sat during those tense months of the Constitutional Convention, viewing the fine portraits of these great men with the knowledge that they were painted from life—the men and their great deeds come vividly to life. Indeed, there are countless reminders of the precious legacy that was left us in this awesome Temple of Liberty. This shrine is American history. Knowledge of Independence Hall is knowledge of America.

From within this $16,000 structure issued a nation of multi-billion-dollar wealth.

From within this building of two floors has sprung a nation which now contemplates the mile-high structures of Frank Lloyd Wright.

From within this candle-lit hall has emerged a nation of nuclear magic and electronic genius.

From within this special antique surrounded by horse-and-buggies there emerged an age of jet travel and space flights.

From within Independence Hal—built by a people of free men.

These are things that we should know, and that our children should know. The birthplace of our nation is a symbol of all that we stand for as free Americans. It stands as testimony of your right to own your own "Independence Hall." Its very existence is concrete proof that the Declaration of Independence was written for you, that the Constitution was created to protect your rights, that *you* are the posterity for which men fought and died.

The *spirit* of a great heritage is not easily woven into words. There is really not much one can say about truly worthwhile things. But this much can be said — Independence Hall is more than mortar and brick.

It is. *least of all* a building.

Footnotes

PART ONE

Chapter One

1. Heritage by Ralph Bradford, Judd & Detweiler, 1952, p. 125.   2

Chapter Two

1. Why Did Many GI Captives Cave In? from a copyrighted interview by Major William E. Mayer, U. S. News & World Report, Feb. 24, 1956.   37

Chapter Four

1. America in Perspective, edited by Henry Steele Commager, Random House, New York, 1947.   69

PART TWO

Introduction

1. A History of Education by F.V.N. Painter, D. Appleton & Co., N.Y., 1897.   78

Chapter Five

1. Independence Hall Association Survey, 1959 (See Appendix).   86

2. SPX—Area V—Cause & Cure by E. Merrill Root, Educational News Service, Vol. 5, No. 10, April, 1959.   87

3. The Dodd Report to the Reese Committee on Tax Exempt Foundations by Norman Dodd, Director of Research, The Long House, Inc., N.Y., 1954.   91

4. Religion in American Life by Ben Moreell, Ideas on Liberty, May, 1955.   92

5. The Fixation of Belief by Charles Sanders Peirce, Popular Science Monthly, 1877.   93

6. Pragmatism by William James, Longmans, Green & Co., Inc. N. Y., 1907, 1928.   94

7. The Shaping of the Modern Mind (concluding half of Ideas and Man) by Crane Brinton, Prentice Hall, Inc., 1950, 1953.   95

Chapter Six

1. The Study of History in the Schools, Report to the American Historical Association by the Committee of Seven, The Macmillan Co., N. Y., 1899. Members of the Committee were: Andrew C. McLaughlin, Herbert B. Adams, George L. Fox, Albert Bushnell Hart, Charles H. Haskins, Lucy M. Salmon, and H. Morse Stephens.   99

2. The School and Society by John Dewey, University of Chicago Press, 1900, p. 155 (for additional comment see page 32 of Education or Indoctrination by Mary L. Allen, The Caxton Printers, Ltd., Caldwell, Idaho, 1955).   101

3. The Teaching of History by Paul Klapper, Ph.D., D. Appleton and Co., N. Y., 1926. (Dr. Klapper was Dean of

the School of Education, City College, N.Y. at this time.) 108

Chapter Seven

1. Children's Thinking—A Study of the Thinking Done By a Group of Grade Children When Encouraged to Ask Questions about United States History by Inga Olla Helseth, Series No. 209 of Columbia Univ. Contributions to Education, 1926. 117

2. The Teaching of History by Paul Klapper, D. Appleton & Co., N. Y., 1926. 117

3. A Preface to the Reconstruction of the American School Curriculum by Harold Rugg, Teachers College Record, 27:600-616, March, 1926. 119

4. Changing Civilizations in the Modern World by Harold Rugg, Ginn & Co., Boston, 1930. p. vii. 120

5. That Men May Understand by Harold Rugg, Doubleday-Doran & Co., Inc., N. Y., 1941, p. 44. 120

6. An Introduction to American Civilization by Harold Rugg, Ginn & Co., Boston, 1929, p. iii. 120

7. *Ibid.* p. 33. 123

8. See General Bibliography. 124

9. America's Crisis in Education by Hon. B. Carroll Reece, Congressional Record, Proceedings and Debates of the 85th Congress, Second Session, June 11, 1958. 124

10. Bending the Twig by Augustin G. Rudd, New York Chapter, Sons of the American Revolution, 1957, p. 80. For complete treatment of the Rugg System see Chapter VI, Rugg—Frontier Thinker of this excellent documentary. 125

11. The Great Technology by Harold Rugg, John Day Co., N. Y., 1933, p. 271. 125

12. Dare the School Build a New Social Order by George S. Counts, published as a John Day pamphlet, April, 1932. 125

13. Conclusions and Recommendations, Charles Scribner's Sons, N. Y.,

1934, p. 16. Among the masterminds of this AHA Commission on Social Studies were: Charles A. Beard, William H. Kilpatrick, Harold O. Rugg and George S. Counts. 126

14. Collaborators of The Educational Frontier, D. Appleton-Century Co., Inc., N. Y., 1933. Contributor and editor William H. Kilpatrick p. 266. 127

15. The Social-Economic Situation and Educaion, by John Dewey, John L. Childs, The Educational Frontier, pp. 36, 37. 128

16. Character Education, Department of Superintendent, Tenth Yearbook, NEA, 1932, p. 23. The material here relating to Character Education is adapted from Prelude to Darkness by Mary Helen Brengel, published in the Oct., 1958 issue of Educational News Service, Vol. 5, No. 4. 130

17. The Social-Economic Situation and Education, by John Dewey, John L. Childs, The Educational Frontier, 69. 133

18. Professional Education from the Social Point of View by William H. Kilpatrick, The Educational Frontier, p. 268. 132

19. *Ibid.* p. 270. 133

20. The Social-Economic Situation and Education by John Dewey, John L. Childs, The Educational Frontier, p. 69. 132

21. *Ibid.* 133

22. *Ibid.* p. 72. 134

23. The New Conception of the Profession of Education by R. B. Raup, The Educational Frontier, p. 78. 133

24. *Ibid.* pp. 79, 80. 133

25. Professional Education from the Social Point of View by William H. Kilpatrick, The Educational Frontier, p. 271. 134

26. The School: Its Tasks and its Administration—1 by H. Gordon Hullfish. The Educaional Frontier, p. 160. 134

27. The Underlying Philosophy of

Education by John Dewey, John L. Childs, The Educational Frontier, p. 317. 134

PART I

Chapter Eight

1. Prelude to Darkness by Mary Helen Brengel, Educational News Service, Vol. 5, No. 4, Oct. 1958. p. 3. 139
2. Thirteenth Yearbook, Department of Superintendence by John L. Childs, NEA, N. Y., 1935, p. 133. 141
3. 7th Report, Calif. Un-American Activities Committee, 1953, p. 169. 141
4. A Call to the Teachers of the Nation, Committee on Social and Economic Problems (Chairman, George S. Counts), Progressive Education Association, 1933, pp. 24, 25. 141
5. Social Frontier by Harold Rugg, Oct. 1936, p. 12. 141
6. The Social Frontier by James M. Shields, June 1936, p. 281. 142
7. The Social Frontier by John Dewey, Dec. 1938, p. 72. 143
8. Frontiers of Democracy by Harold Rugg, PEA, Oct. 15, 1939, pp. 9, 11. 143
9. Frontiers of Democracy by Theodore Brameld, Jan. 15, 1940, pp. 111, 112. 144
10. Frontiers of Democracy by Harry Elmer Barnes, Jan. 15, 1940, pp. 106, 110. 144
11. New York Herald Tribune, June 29, 1938. 145
12. Frontiers of Democracy by Harold Rugg, Dec. 15, 1942, pp. 75, 81. 147
13. Frontiers of Democracy by Harold Rugg, Jan. 15, 1943, pp. 101, 108. 147
14. Teaching the Social Studies, Second Edition, by Edgar Bruce Wesley, D. C. Heath & Co., Boston, 1942, p. 17. 149
15. The Propositions are quoted from Design for America by Theodore Brameld, 1945, as they appear in the Turning of the Tides by Shafer and Snow, pp. 50, 51. 152
16. *Ibid.* p. 51. 153

PART II

Chapter Eight

17. New York Journal-American, Nov. 30, 1947. 154
18. Progressive Education, Nov. 1947-Jan. 1948. 154
19. The Turning of the Tides by Hon. Paul W. Shafer, John Howland Snow, Long House, New Canaan, Conn. 1953, 1956, pp. 52, 55. 155
20. A Handbook for the Improvement of Textbooks and Teaching Materials as Aids to International Understanding, UNESCO, Paris, 1949, pp. 69, 90. 156
21. Education for a World Society, 11th Yearbook, John Dewey Society, 1951, p. 200. 157
22. Education for International Understanding in American Schools, (Committee on International Relations, the Association for Supervision and Curriculum Development, the National Council for the Social Studies), NEA, 1948, p. 183. 157
23. Eighth Report, Senate Investigating Commitee on Education, Calif. Legislature, 1951. pp. 93, 96 . 162
24. *Ibid* 163
25. Progressive Education by John L. Childs, Feb. 1950, pp. 118, 120. 163
26. Challenge, American Council of Christian Laymen, Madison, Vol. 6, No. 2, Sept. 1958. 164
27. Education and American Civilization by George S. Counts, Columbia Univ. Teachers College, 1952. 164
28. The United Nations—Ten Years of Achievement by William A. DeWitt, Public Affairs Pamphlet No. 226, 1955, p. 7. 167
29. Life Adjustment Education for Every Youth, Bulletin 1951, No. 22, (Reprint 1953), U. S. Dept. Health, Education, and Welfare, Office of Education, 1953, p. 58. 168

30. Time Magazine, July 16, 1956.
169

31. Freedom, Education, and the Fund by Robert M. Hutchins, Essays and Addresses, 1946-1956, Meridian Books, N. Y., 1956, p. 138.
169

32. Is This American Education? by Theodore Guerin, Ladies Home Journal, Feb. 1959, pp. 182, 183.
170

33. A Historian Looks at the American High School by Henry Steele Commager, The High School In a New Era, University of Chicago Press, 1958, pp. 10, 13.
171

34. International Understanding Through the Secondary School Curriculum, Bulletin of the National Association of Secondary School Principals of the NEA, Vol. 40, No. 224, Dec. 1956, pp. 9, 10.
173

Chapter Nine

1. Value Judgments in the Classroom by Patrick M. Boarman, The Freeman, Vol. 8, No. 8, Aug. 1958, p. 7.
179

2. From American Mercury Newsletter, 1959.
180

3. NEA Journal, Vol. 45, No. 8, Nov. 1956.
181

4. Academic Freedom and Responsibility by Herbert Brownell, The Bill of Rights, Dec. 15, 1957.
182

5. Semantic Warfare by Gene Wicks, Educational News Service, Vol. 5, No. 2, Aug. 1958, p. 7.
183

6. The Deeper Problem in Education (Editorial) Life, Vol. 5, No. 32, March 31, 1958.
185

7. What Went Wrong with U. S. Schools by Arthur Bestor, U. S. News & World Report, Jan. 24, 1958, Copyright 1958, United States News Publishing Corp.
185

8. Need for a High School Textbook on Democracy and Communism Extension of Remarks of Hon. B. Carroll Reece, Congressional Record, July 29, 1955.
187

9. Communist-Socialist Propaganda in American Schools by Verne P. Kaub, Meador Publishing Co., Boston, 1958, p. 115.
189

10. Educating Children in Grades, Four, Five and Six, U. S. Office of Education, Bulletin 1958, No. 3, Washington, 1958, p. 4.
190

11. Semantic Warfare, Gene Wicks.
191

12. Brainwashing in the High Schools by E. Merill Root, The Devin-Adair Co., N. Y., 1958, pp. 159, 160.
193

Chapter Ten

CHAPTER MOTTO BY CARL SANDBURG

1. Education and School Committee, Kern County Grand Jury, 1956-1957 Report, Calif.
203

2. A Foreign Policy for Americans by Robert A. Taft, Doubleday, 1951, pp. 44, 45.
205

3. Why Did Many GI Captives Cave In? by Major William E. Mayer, U. S. News & World Report, Feb. 24, 1956, from a copyrighted interview.
206

PRINTER'S NOTE

It takes many hands to make a book....Pioneer Composition set the Baskerville type by photo composition, the latest method of typesetting. All the display type is Bulmer and set by hand, etch-proofed and stripped into position for the making of offset plates....Printed on Snowline offset paper by Litho Craftsmen....Jacket designed by Omega Art Service and printed by letterpress at the Norman Press.... Bound by Brock & Rankin and completed at Chicago, Illinois during the month of April, 1960.

DESIGN, TYPOGRAPHY & PRODUCTION
Norman W. Forgue